Microsoft XNA 4.0 Game Development Cookbook

Over 35 intermediate-advanced recipes for taking your XNA development arsenal further

Luke Drumm

PUBLISHING

BIRMINGHAM - MUMBAI

Microsoft XNA 4.0 Game Development Cookbook

First published: June 2012

Production Reference: 1130612

Published by Packt Publishing Ltd.
Livery Place
35 Livery Street
Birmingham B3 2PB, UK.

ISBN 978-1-84969-198-7

www.packtpub.com

Cover Image by Sandeep Babu (sandyjb@gmail.com)

Credits

Author
Luke Drumm

Reviewers
Jason Mitchell

Kenneth Dahl Pedersen

Acquisition Editor
Stephanie Moss

Lead Technical Editor
Kedar Bhat

Technical Editors
Rati Pillai

Ankita Shashi

Copy Editor
Insiya Morbiwala

Project Coordinator
Michelle Quadros

Proofreader
Joel T. Johnson

Indexer
Rekha Nair

Production Coordinator
Melwyn Dsa

Cover Work
Melwyn Dsa

About the Author

Luke Drumm is an experienced software developer and consultant who wrote his first computer game at age 10, and has been enthusiastically exploring the world of game development ever since. With the first public release of XNA in 2006, Luke quickly latched onto the technology and began creating and talking about how to create games within XNA at every possible opportunity. This culminated in his regular presence at conferences, game camps, and user groups, and in his becoming a recipient of the Microsoft MVP Award, for XNA and DirectX, for at least four successive years. Luke lives in Sydney, Australia, with his amazing, patient, and supportive wife Cheryl, and two dogs, who may or may not rule the roost.

About the Reviewers

Jason Mitchell is a passionate .NET developer and an independent game development enthusiast. He has worked with Microsoft's XNA Game Studio since its initial release and has experience using it to create games on Windows, Xbox 360, and Windows Phone.

Kenneth Dahl Pedersen, now aged 35, has been programming basically since he got his first computer at age 6, starting on the Commodore 64, with small programs that could do next to nothing. This quickly evolved when he migrated to the much more powerful Amiga 500 with some demos and light applications, and finally culminated when he got his first PC.

Since then, game development has held his interest in a vice grip, and Kenneth has studied numerous programming languages and APIs for this purpose. His repertoire includes C/C++, OpenGL, DirectX, C#, WPF, WCF, MDX, and XNA.

With the appearance of readily-available, high-end engines, such as Unreal Development Kit, Kenneth found another interest to keep him well-sated in his thirst for game development knowledge, UnrealScript, providing another mountain top to climb.

Kenneth is a Systems Analyst and Developer. Originally from Denmark, where he still works, he now lives in Sweden with his wife and baby daughter.

Other than being with his wife and daughter, he uses his spare time for game development, seeking new knowledge and dabbling in 3D visual arts in applications, such as 3D Studio Max and ZBrush. And of course, Kenneth is an avid gamer. After all, you cannot make games if you don't enjoy playing them!

First of all, I would like to thank my wife, Nina, for the patience she's shown me while I was doing this review. I have probably not been as helpful around the house as I should have been, while this was going on.

My beautiful daughter, Nadia, for always giving me a reason to smile and laugh.

And last, but certainly not least, Michelle Quadros, for believing in me and giving me this incredible experience and opportunity to do a tech review of this awesome book on XNA.

My advice to you, the Reader: Read it, cover-to-cover. You will not regret it, as it contains some absolute treasures of tips and techniques for your own game projects.

www.PacktPub.com

Support files, eBooks, discount offers, and more

You might want to visit www.PacktPub.com for support files and downloads related to your book.

Did you know that Packt offers eBook versions of every book published, with PDF and ePub files available? You can upgrade to the eBook version at www.PacktPub.com and as a print book customer, you are entitled to a discount on the eBook copy. Get in touch with us at service@packtpub.com for more details.

At www.PacktPub.com, you can also read a collection of free technical articles, sign up for a range of free newsletters and receive exclusive discounts and offers on Packt books and eBooks.

http://PacktLib.PacktPub.com

Do you need instant solutions to your IT questions? PacktLib is Packt's online digital book library. Here, you can access, read and search across Packt's entire library of books.

Why Subscribe?

- Fully searchable across every book published by Packt
- Copy and paste, print and bookmark content
- On demand and accessible via web browser

Free Access for Packt account holders

If you have an account with Packt at www.PacktPub.com, you can use this to access PacktLib today and view nine entirely free books. Simply use your login credentials for immediate access.

Table of Contents

Preface

The Microsoft XNA 4.0 Game Development Cookbook is all about what happens once you've completed the various introductory tutorials, and want to create something with a little more substance.

In this book, you'll find examples of how to flesh out some of the more complex, or initially less intuitive, pieces of what goes into a full-blown game.

Not sure what it takes to add water to your Xbox 360 Indie game? Confused about maps for your Windows Phone game? Curious over what it takes to get started using Kinect with XNA? Then this book may just be for you.

What this book covers

Chapter 1, Applying Special Effects: Discover the principles behind some common special effects used in big budget titles, and add them to your own games.

Chapter 2, Building 2D and 3D Terrain: Learn some of the tricks behind creating landscapes in both two and three dimensions.

Chapter 3, Procedural Modeling: Explore what's involved in creating models in code, instead of using an external 3D modeling package.

Chapter 4, Creating Water and Sky: Add depth to your worlds with some virtual atmosphere.

Chapter 5, Non-Player Characters: Inhabit your virtual worlds with characters that can move and interact in intelligent and interesting ways.

Chapter 6, Playing with Animation: Have a peek into some of the ways that animation can be both produced and displayed.

Chapter 7, Creating Vehicles: Launch your players onto the roads or into the skies with the addition of vehicles.

Chapter 8, Receiving Player Input: Discover how your players can drag, drop, point, and type their way through your games.

Chapter 9, Networking: Expand your virtual world across to the real one by adding the ability to communicate.

What you need for this book

To write games using the examples presented in this book, you'll need:

▸ Windows Vista (SP2) or later

▸ XNA Game Studio 4.0 (usually bundled as part of the Windows Phone SDK) or later

For the Kinect-based recipe, a Kinect or Kinect for Windows unit is required along with the Kinect for Windows SDK.

Who this book is for

If you are an XNA developer who has already successfully dabbled in some of the simple 2D and 3D functionality provided by XNA, and are eager to find out how to achieve some of the more advanced features presented in popular games, dive into the *Microsoft XNA 4.0 Game Development Cookbook* for an example-based approach that should have you safely on your way towards the next level of game creation. You should be comfortable with the basics of the XNA framework and have experience with C#.

Conventions

In this book, you will find a number of styles of text that distinguish between different kinds of information. Here are some examples of these styles, and an explanation of their meaning.

Code words in text are shown as follows: "We will be using the `BasicEffect` class in this example, but any effect that implements the `IEffectMatrices` interface and has some way to darken the rendered model should be adequate."

A block of code is set as follows:

```
Vector3 lightDirection;
BasicEffect reachShadowEffect;
Matrix flattenShadow;
```

New terms and **important words** are shown in bold. Words that you see on the screen, in menus or dialog boxes, for example, appear in the text like this: "Start by adding a new **Content Pipeline Extension** project to the solution."

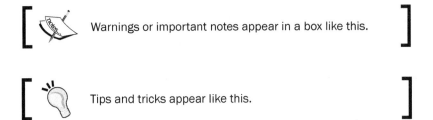

Warnings or important notes appear in a box like this.

Tips and tricks appear like this.

Reader feedback

Feedback from our readers is always welcome. Let us know what you think about this book—what you liked or may have disliked. Reader feedback is important for us to develop titles that you really get the most out of.

To send us general feedback, simply send an e-mail to feedback@packtpub.com, and mention the book title through the subject of your message.

If there is a topic that you have expertise in and you are interested in either writing or contributing to a book, see our author guide on www.packtpub.com/authors.

Customer support

Now that you are the proud owner of a Packt book, we have a number of things to help you to get the most from your purchase.

Downloading the example code

You can download the example code files for all Packt books you have purchased from your account at http://www.packtpub.com. If you purchased this book elsewhere, you can visit http://www.packtpub.com/support and register to have the files e-mailed directly to you.

Errata

Although we have taken every care to ensure the accuracy of our content, mistakes do happen. If you find a mistake in one of our books—maybe a mistake in the text or the code—we would be grateful if you would report this to us. By doing so, you can save other readers from frustration and help us improve subsequent versions of this book. If you find any errata, please report them by visiting http://www.packtpub.com/support, selecting your book, clicking on the **errata submission form** link, and entering the details of your errata. Once your errata are verified, your submission will be accepted and the errata will be uploaded to our website, or added to any list of existing errata, under the Errata section of that title.

Piracy

Piracy of copyright material on the Internet is an ongoing problem across all media. At Packt, we take the protection of our copyright and licenses very seriously. If you come across any illegal copies of our works, in any form, on the Internet, please provide us with the location address or website name immediately so that we can pursue a remedy.

Please contact us at `copyright@packtpub.com` with a link to the suspected pirated material.

We appreciate your help in protecting our authors, and our ability to bring you valuable content.

Questions

You can contact us at `questions@packtpub.com` if you are having a problem with any aspect of the book, and we will do our best to address it.

1

Applying Special Effects

In this chapter we will cover:

- ▶ Creating shadows within the Reach profile
- ▶ Creating shadows within the HiDef profile
- ▶ Implementing lens flare within the Reach profile
- ▶ Implementing lens flare within the HiDef profile
- ▶ Implementing smoke within the Reach profile
- ▶ Creating explosions within the Reach profile
- ▶ Creating explosions within the HiDef profile

Introduction

In this chapter, we will be creating some of the common special effects used in 3D games to help increase the level of realism, and thereby help the player to immerse themselves in the virtual world.

The examples in this chapter assume that at least the bare bones of a 3D scene are already present, with one or more 3D objects being rendered successfully to the screen. If inspiration for how to achieve this is in short supply, *Chapter 2, Building 2D and 3D Terrain* and *Chapter 3, Procedural Modeling*, provide some examples on possible ways to get started.

Creating shadows within the Reach profile

Shadows are one of the most common ways to make something appear like it is part of the surrounding environment, and for a lot of games written within the **Reach profile**, a simple static image of a dark patch beneath the character's feet is sufficient, as seen in the following illustration:

There are, however, times where a non-descript blur isn't going to cut it, and a more realistic looking shadow is required.

This recipe will teach you how to create a detailed shadow of an in-game element, as seen in the following illustration, using one of the matrix transformation helper methods supplied in the XNA framework.

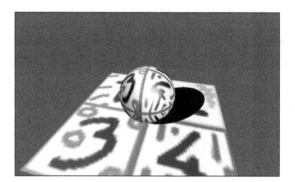

Getting ready

We will be using the `BasicEffect` class in this example, but any effect that implements the `IEffectMatrices` interface and has some way to darken the rendered model should be adequate.

Prior to adding the code presented in this example, ensure that a model is being loaded and rendered onto the screen.

How to do it...

To create a disc programmatically:

1. Define an instance-level variable to hold the direction of the virtual light source, another to hold the effect that's going to render the shadow, and a third to hold the transformation to give the shadow its shape:

```
Vector3 lightDirection;
BasicEffect reachShadowEffect;
Matrix flattenShadow;
```

2. In the `LoadContent()` method, define the direction of the light source:

```
lightDirection = Vector3.Normalize((Vector3.Backward * 2) +
                 (Vector3.Up * 2) +
                 (Vector3.Left * 2));
```

3. Next, define the matrix that will be used to transform objects into their flattened shadow form:

```
var flattenShadow = Matrix.CreateShadow(
                    lightDirection,
                    new Plane(Vector3.Up, 0.95f));
```

4. Now use a calculation that takes the `world` matrix used to transform the regular object, and alters it into a transformation to project a shadow onto a flat surface:

```
var shadowWorld = world * flattenShadow;
```

5. Next, implement the effect that will be used to render the shadow:

```
reachShadowEffect = new BasicEffect(GraphicsDevice)
{
    View = view,
    Projection = projection,
    World = shadowWorld,
    AmbientLightColor = Vector3.Zero,
    DiffuseColor = Vector3.Zero,
    SpecularColor = Vector3.Zero,
    Alpha = 0.5f
};
```

6. After drawing the game scene's floor, but prior to drawing the object to be shadowed, insert the following code to give the shadow transparency:

```
graphicsDevice.BlendState = BlendState.AlphaBlend;
graphicsDevice.DepthStencilState = DepthStencilState.DepthRead;
```

7. Drawing the object with the shadow effect will then render a shadow:

```
gameObject.Draw(reachShadowEffect);
```

8. Setting the `BlendState` and `DepthStencilState` back to their defaults will allow you to draw the object normally. For example:

```
graphicsDevice.BlendState = BlendState.Opaque;
graphicsDevice.DepthStencilState = DepthStencilState.Default;

gameObject.Draw(regularEffect);
```

Downloading the example code

You can download the example code files for all Packt books you have purchased from your account at `http://www.packtpub.com`. If you purchased this book elsewhere, you can visit `http://www.packtpub.com/support` and register to have the files e-mailed directly to you.

How it works...

Utilizing one of the built-in transformations of the XNA framework, we are squashing a blackened copy of the mesh onto a given plane.

It's a simple technique, but it does come at the cost of having to render your shadow casting meshes at least one more time than normal. These particular shadows are as stiff as a board too and won't bend if they happen to fall upon a wall or other vertical surface.

If you're after a shadow with a softer edge within the Reach profile, you may want to render the shadow to a separate render target and blur in a similar fashion to the technique demonstrated in the *Implementing lens flare within the Reach profile* section of this chapter.

There's more...

In the example, a simplified call to a game object's `Draw()` method was made, passing in the effect to be used in rendering.

If you're interested in how such a method might be constructed, sneak a peek at the `Draw()` method of the `GeometricBuffer` class covered in the *Modeling triangles* recipe in *Chapter 3, Procedural Modeling* .

► *Implementing lens flare within the Reach profile* recipe of this chapter.

Creating shadows within the HiDef profile

Creating realistic-looking shadows without sacrificing a huge amount of memory or processing power remains one of the great challenges in computer graphics. While I may not be able to offer a perfect solution for every shadow-related problem you have in your games, I can at least get you started in the world of shadow creation through the demonstration of one of the more well-known techniques, **shadow mapping**, seen in the following illustration.

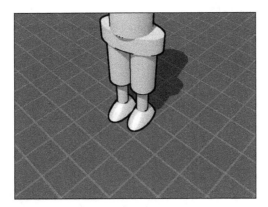

Getting ready

For this recipe, it's best to start with a simple existing scene containing a floor and at least one mesh floating or standing above it, as shown in the previous illustration.

How to do it...

To create a disc programmatically:

1. Add a new effect file to your game content project named Shadows.fx.

2. Define the input parameters of the new shader:

```
float4x4 World;
float4x4 View;
float4x4 Projection;
float4x4 LightViewProj;

float3 LightDirection;
float4 AmbientColor = float4(0.15, 0.15, 0.15, 0);
```

```
float DepthBias = 0.001f;

texture Texture;
sampler TextureSampler = sampler_state
{
    Texture = (Texture);
};

texture ShadowMap;
sampler ShadowMapSampler = sampler_state
{
    Texture = <ShadowMap>;
};
```

3. Define the structures used to pass data between the pixel and vertex shaders:

```
struct DrawWithShadowMap_VSIn
{
    float4 Position : POSITION0;
    float3 Normal   : NORMAL0;
    float2 TexCoord : TEXCOORD0;
};

struct DrawWithShadowMap_VSOut
{
    float4 Position : POSITION0;
    float3 Normal   : TEXCOORD0;
    float2 TexCoord : TEXCOORD1;
    float4 WorldPos : TEXCOORD2;
};

struct CreateShadowMap_VSOut
{
    float4 Position : POSITION;
    float Depth     : TEXCOORD0;
};
```

4. Next, create a vertex shader for rendering a depth map:

```
CreateShadowMap_VSOut CreateShadowMap_VertexShader(
  float4 Position: POSITION)
{
    CreateShadowMap_VSOut Out;
    Out.Position = mul(Position, mul(World, LightViewProj));
    Out.Depth = Out.Position.z / Out.Position.w;
    return Out;
}
```

5. Create the vertex shader's partner-in-crime, the pixel shader, to render a depth map:

```
float4 CreateShadowMap_PixelShader(
  CreateShadowMap_VSOut input) : COLOR
{
    return float4(input.Depth, 0, 0, 0);
}
```

6. Next, make the vertex shader render the shadows:

```
DrawWithShadowMap_VSOut DrawWithShadowMap_
VertexShader(DrawWithShadowMap_VSIn input)
{

    float4x4 WorldViewProj = mul(mul(World, View), Projection);

    DrawWithShadowMap_VSOut Output;

    Output.Position = mul(input.Position, WorldViewProj);
    Output.Normal =  normalize(mul(input.Normal, World));
    Output.TexCoord = input.TexCoord;
    Output.WorldPos = mul(input.Position, World);

    return Output;
}
```

7. Create the matching pixel shader, which will, for every pixel, compare the depth of the scene from the player's perspective to that of the previously captured shadow depth map:

```
float4 DrawWithShadowMap_PixelShader(
        DrawWithShadowMap_VSOut input) : COLOR
{
   float4 diffuseColor = tex2D(
      TextureSampler, input.TexCoord);

   float diffuseIntensity = saturate(
     dot(LightDirection, input.Normal));

   float4 diffuse = diffuseIntensity *
                    diffuseColor + AmbientColor;


   float4 lightingPosition = mul(
           input.WorldPos, LightViewProj);

   float2 ShadowTexCoord = 0.5 * lightingPosition.xy /
```

```
                                  lightingPosition.w +
                                  float2( 0.5, 0.5 );
        ShadowTexCoord.y = 1.0f - ShadowTexCoord.y;


        float shadowdepth = tex2D(ShadowMapSampler,
                                  ShadowTexCoord).r;

        float ourdepth = (lightingPosition.z / lightingPosition.w) -
    DepthBias;

        if (shadowdepth < ourdepth)
        {
            diffuse *= float4(0.5,0.5,0.5,0);
        };

        return diffuse;
    }
```

8. Add some technique definitions to specify which shader to use in which circumstance:

```
technique CreateShadowMap
{
    pass Pass1
    {
        VertexShader = compile vs_2_0
                            CreateShadowMap_VertexShader();
        PixelShader = compile ps_2_0
                            CreateShadowMap_PixelShader();
    }
}


technique DrawWithShadowMap
{
    pass Pass1
    {
        VertexShader = compile vs_2_0
                            DrawWithShadowMap_VertexShader();
        PixelShader = compile ps_2_0
                            DrawWithShadowMap_PixelShader();
    }
}
```

9. In your game class, add some instance variables to hold details about the
   virtual camera:

```
Matrix view;
Matrix projection;
Matrix world;
BoundingFrustum cameraFrustum = new BoundingFrustum(Matrix.
Identity);
```

10. Then, add some details about the lighting:

```
Vector3 lightDirection;
Matrix lightViewProjection = Matrix.Identity;
```

11. Now, add some variables to hold the various effects that are going to be used
    to render the scene:

```
BasicEffect basicEffect;
Effect hiDefShadowEffect;
RenderTarget2D shadowRenderTarget;
```

12. In the `LoadContent()` method, start by setting up the lighting and
    camera positions:

```
lightDirection = Vector3.Normalize(
                    (Vector3.Backward * 2) +
                    (Vector3.Up * 2) +
                    (Vector3.Left * 2));

view = Matrix.CreateLookAt(
        (Vector3.Backward * 4) +
          (Vector3.Up * 3) +
          (Vector3.Right),
        Vector3.Zero,
        Vector3.Up);
projection = Matrix.CreatePerspectiveFieldOfView(
        MathHelper.ToRadians(60f),
        GraphicsDevice.Viewport.AspectRatio,
        0.002f,
        100f);
world = Matrix.CreateTranslation(Vector3.Zero);
cameraFrustum.Matrix = view * projection;
```

13. Continue by creating a render target to hold the shadow map:

```
var shadowMapWidthHeight = 2048;
var pp = GraphicsDevice.PresentationParameters;
shadowRenderTarget = new
    RenderTarget2D(graphics.GraphicsDevice,
```

```
            shadowMapWidthHeight,
            shadowMapWidthHeight,
            false,
            pp.BackBufferFormat,
            DepthFormat.Depth24);
```

14. Then, set up the effects used to render the objects within the scene, and the shadows cast by them:

```
basicEffect = new BasicEffect(GraphicsDevice)
{
    View = view,
    Projection = projection,
    World = world,

};


basicEffect.EnableDefaultLighting();


hiDefShadowEffect = Content.Load<Effect>("Shadows");
```

15. Add a new method to calculate the position and size of the virtual camera used to record a depth map from the point of view of the light source:

```
Matrix CreateLightViewProjectionMatrix()
{
```

16. Insert a matrix into the new method to rotate things towards the direction of the light:

```
Matrix lightRotation = Matrix.CreateLookAt(
        Vector3.Zero,
        -lightDirection,
        Vector3.Up);
```

17. Calculate the corners of the visible area for the "light" camera:

```
Vector3[] frustumCorners = cameraFrustum.GetCorners();
for (int i = 0; i < frustumCorners.Length; i++)
    {
        frustumCorners[i] = Vector3.Transform(frustumCorners[i],
lightRotation);
    }
```

18. Work out the smallest box that could fit the corners of the visible area:

```
BoundingBox lightBox = BoundingBox.CreateFromPoints(frustumCorne
rs);

    Vector3 boxSize = lightBox.Max - lightBox.Min;
    Vector3 halfBoxSize = boxSize * 0.5f;
```

19. From the previously calculated box dimensions, derive the position of the light camera:

```
Vector3 lightPosition = lightBox.Min + halfBoxSize;
    lightPosition.Z = lightBox.Min.Z;
lightPosition = Vector3.Transform(
                  lightPosition,
Matrix.Invert(lightRotation));
```

20. Calculate the associated view projection matrix:

```
Matrix lightView = Matrix.CreateLookAt(
                  lightPosition,
                  lightPosition - lightDirection,
                  Vector3.Up);
Matrix lightProjection = Matrix.CreateOrthographic(
                  boxSize.X, boxSize.Y,
                   -boxSize.Z, boxSize.Z);


return lightView * lightProjection;
```

21. Create a new method to set up the shadow effect:

```
private void PopulateShadowEffect(bool createShadowMap)
{
    string techniqueName = createShadowMap ?
              "CreateShadowMap" : "DrawWithShadowMap";

    hiDefShadowEffect.CurrentTechnique = hiDefShadowEffect.
Techniques[techniqueName];
    hiDefShadowEffect.Parameters["World"].SetValue(world);
    hiDefShadowEffect.Parameters["View"].SetValue(view);
    hiDefShadowEffect.Parameters["Projection"].SetValue(
      projection);
    hiDefShadowEffect.Parameters["LightDirection"].SetValue(
      lightDirection);
    hiDefShadowEffect.Parameters["LightViewProj"].SetValue(
      CreateLightViewProjectionMatrix());

    if (!createShadowMap)
        hiDefShadowEffect.Parameters["ShadowMap"].SetValue(
        shadowRenderTarget);
}
```

22. In your game's `Draw()` method, start by setting the `GraphicsDevice` to render to the `shadowRenderTarget`:

```
GraphicsDevice.SetRenderTarget(shadowRenderTarget);
    GraphicsDevice.Clear(Color.White);
    PopulateShadowEffect(true);
```

23. Next, render any shadow casting objects using the `hiDefShadowEffect`:

```
sphere.Draw(hiDefShadowEffect);
```

24. Switch the rendering from the `shadowRenderTarget`, back to the screen:

```
GraphicsDevice.SetRenderTarget(null);
GraphicsDevice.BlendState = BlendState.Opaque;
GraphicsDevice.DepthStencilState = DepthStencilState.Default;
PopulateShadowEffect(false);
```

25. Set the texture of the `hiDefShadowEffect` to the corresponding scene object, and render it in a similar fashion to this (where `floorTexture` has already been loaded with the texture for the floor):

```
hiDefShadowEffect.Parameters["Texture"].SetValue(floorTexture);
floor.Draw(hiDefShadowEffect);
```

26. For any scene objects you don't want shadows to be cast upon, use a shader such as the `BasicEffect` shader you created earlier which will do the job nicely:

```
basicEffect.Texture = texture;
    basicEffect.TextureEnabled = true;
    sphere.Draw(basicEffect);
```

How it works...

Shadow mapping, for all the code and math involved, really comes down to the relatively simple idea of identifying all the spots in a scene where a player can see something but a light cannot, due to an obstruction blocking the light's view.

A depth map is generated from the light's view of the scene, and another from the player's perspective. The shader darkens any pixels that correspond to the player's view being "deeper" than the light's.

There's more...

In the example given in this recipe, we've set up a 2048 x 2048 24-bit texture to hold our shadow map. Depending on the scene, you may find this is either a waste, or not nearly enough.

In the cases where it's an overkill, don't be afraid to drop the resolution to reclaim some memory for better use elsewhere.

On the other hand, if you find yourself unable to create a large enough shadow map to produce a sufficiently detailed shadow, the addition of blur to a shadow can be a useful tool to diminish or completely eliminate such issues.

See also

▶ _Creating shadows within the Reach profile_ recipe of this chapter.

Implementing lens flare within the Reach profile

A realistic lens flare can be achieved within the Reach profile by being "physically correct" and performing a check of each frame to confirm that the source of light is, at least partially, visible from the camera's point of view. (Tests involving whether something is in line of sight from something else are commonly referred to as **occlusion tests**.)

The bad news is, that without the benefit of hardware accelerated occlusion testing like the HiDef profile's OcclusionQuery class can offer, this test can be beyond the processing resources available to a game (especially one running on either mobile or older hardware).

The good news is that we do have a relatively cheap alternative that may just provide enough approximation for a game, and no one need be the wiser that the "proper" technique wasn't used, as the following illustration of the approximation in use demonstrates:

Getting ready

For this special effect, we're going to need an image that will form the basis of our glow. The image can be a simple white circle that fades out to complete transparency, as shown in the following illustration, but don't be afraid to make things even more visually interesting and swap it out for a more complex image later.

How to do it...

To create a lens flare within the Reach profile:

1. Start by creating a new class to hold the lens flare behavior:

```
class ReachLensFlare
    {
```

2. Inside the new class, define some instance variables to hold details concerning the appearance of the glow:

```
Texture2D glow;
Vector2 glowOrigin;
float glowScale = 0.25f;
Vector2 lightPosition;

public Vector3 LightDirection = Vector3.Normalize(new
Vector3(0.5f, -0.1f, 0.5f));
```

3. Next, define some instance variables to hold details concerning the rendering of the glow:

```
SpriteBatch spriteBatch;
GraphicsDevice graphicsDevice;

RenderTarget2D flareTarget;
List<RenderTarget2D> blurTargets;
Viewport flareViewport;

public BasicEffect ShadowCaptureEffect;
```

4. Then, add a constructor:

```
public ReachLensFlare(GraphicsDevice graphicsDevice,
ContentManager content)
        {
```

5. Next, load the glow image details:

```
glow = content.Load<Texture2D>(@"lensflare/glow");
glowOrigin = new Vector2(glow.Width, glow.Height) / 2;
```

6. We now need to pre-calculate the size of the screen onto which the glow is going to be displayed:

```
flareViewport = new Viewport(0,0,
        graphicsDevice.Viewport.Bounds.Width / 8,
        graphicsDevice.Viewport.Height /8);
```

7. Define the render targets, which will aid in the final composition of the overall effect:

```
this.graphicsDevice = graphicsDevice;
spriteBatch = new SpriteBatch(graphicsDevice);

var pp = graphicsDevice.PresentationParameters;

flareTarget = new RenderTarget2D(graphicsDevice,
                flareViewport.Width,
                flareViewport.Height,
                false,
                pp.BackBufferFormat,
                pp.DepthStencilFormat);
blurTargets = new List<RenderTarget2D>()
            {
                new RenderTarget2D(graphicsDevice,
                    3, 5,
                    false,
                    pp.BackBufferFormat,
                    pp.DepthStencilFormat),

                new RenderTarget2D(graphicsDevice,
                    7 ,4,
                    false,
                    pp.BackBufferFormat,
                    pp.DepthStencilFormat),

                new RenderTarget2D(graphicsDevice,
                    5, 9,
                    false,
```

```
                        pp.BackBufferFormat,
                        pp.DepthStencilFormat),

                new RenderTarget2D(graphicsDevice,
                        15, 10,
                        false,
                        pp.BackBufferFormat,
                        pp.DepthStencilFormat),

                new RenderTarget2D(graphicsDevice,
                        33, 43,
                        false,
                        pp.BackBufferFormat,
                        pp.DepthStencilFormat),
                new RenderTarget2D(graphicsDevice,
                        90, 90,
                        false,
                        pp.BackBufferFormat,
                        pp.DepthStencilFormat)
            };
```

8. Complete the constructor with the effect that will be used to mask out any portions of the lens flare that are blocked by scenery:

```
ShadowCaptureEffect = new BasicEffect(graphicsDevice)
{
    DiffuseColor = Vector3.Zero,
};
```

9. Next, add an `Update()` method to the class:

```
public void Update(GameTime gameTime, Matrix view, Matrix
projection)
{
```

10. Add in a check to determine if the lens flare is visible at all where the player is currently looking:

```
view.Translation = Vector3.Zero;

var projectedPosition = flareViewport.Project(
        -LightDirection, projection,
        view, Matrix.Identity);

if ((projectedPosition.Z < 0) || (projectedPosition.Z > 1))
{
    return;
}
```

11. If the lens flare is visible from the player's point of view, complete the `Update()` method by storing the light's screen space position:

```
lightPosition = new Vector2(projectedPosition.X,
projectedPosition.Y);
```

12. Create a method to begin the process of capturing the silhouette of the scene:

```
public void BeginShadowCapture()
{
```

13. Set the render target, clear the silhouette to black, and place the glow image in the background; ready to be possibly covered by scene elements:

```
graphicsDevice.SetRenderTarget(flareTarget);
graphicsDevice.Clear(Color.Black);

spriteBatch.Begin();

spriteBatch.Draw(
    glow, lightPosition, null, Color.White, 0,
    glowOrigin, glowScale, SpriteEffects.None, 0);

spriteBatch.End();
```

14. Create the method to complete the silhouette capture and apply some blur:

```
public void EndShadowCapture()
{
```

15. Paint the captured silhouette scene onto each of the blur targets:

```
foreach (var blurTarget in blurTargets)
{
    graphicsDevice.SetRenderTarget(blurTarget);
    spriteBatch.Begin(
        SpriteSortMode.Deferred,
        BlendState.Opaque,
        SamplerState.AnisotropicClamp, null, null);

    spriteBatch.Draw(
        flareTarget,
        blurTarget.Bounds,
        Color.LightBlue);
    spriteBatch.End();
}
```

16. Paint the blur targets onto the final target:

```
graphicsDevice.SetRenderTarget(flareTarget);
graphicsDevice.Clear(Color.Black);
spriteBatch.Begin(
    SpriteSortMode.Deferred,
    BlendState.Additive,
    SamplerState.AnisotropicClamp,
    null, null);

foreach (var blurTarget in blurTargets)
{
    spriteBatch.Draw(
        blurTarget,
        flareTarget.Bounds,
        Color.White);
}
spriteBatch.End();

graphicsDevice.SetRenderTarget(null);
```

17. Add a `Draw()` method to render the final target on screen:

```
public void Draw()
{
    spriteBatch.Begin(
        SpriteSortMode.Deferred,
        BlendState.Additive,
        SamplerState.AnisotropicClamp,
        null, null);
    spriteBatch.Draw(
        flareTarget,
        graphicsDevice.Viewport.Bounds,
        Color.White);
    spriteBatch.End();
}
```

18. Next in our game code, we add an instance variable for the new lens flare:

```
ReachLensFlare reachLensFlare;
```

19. Initialize an instance of the lens flare in the `LoadContent()` method:

```
reachLensFlare = new ReachLensFlare(GraphicsDevice, Content);
```

20. Inside the `Draw()` method, there are two parts. The first part is where we draw the elements of the game scene which are likely to block out the lens flare as the player moves through the scene. Here's an example of the required call to the lens flare, followed by a rendering of the scene with the silhouette effect:

```
reachLensFlare.BeginShadowCapture();

// draw scene here.
// e.g. here's some building and ground objects
// being rendered via their own custom Draw methods


foreach (var building in buildings)
{
   building.Draw(camera, reachLensFlare.ShadowCaptureEffect);
}

ground.Draw(camera, reachLensFlare.ShadowCaptureEffect);

reachLensFlare.EndShadowCapture();
```

21. The second part of the rendering process is drawing the scene normally, followed by a call to render the now fully formed lens flare:

```
GraphicsDevice.Clear(Color.CornflowerBlue);

foreach (var building in buildings)
{
   building.Draw(camera);
}
ground.Draw(camera);

reachLensFlare.Draw();
```

How it works...

The lens flare class works by drawing a silhouette of the scene in front of the light source, our glow image, and then applying various levels of blurring until we achieve a "flare" appearance.

In the constructor of the lens flare class, we can see the elements of this strategy being set up with the loading of the glow image and the creation of some render targets, which will be used later to facilitate blurring.

Also note the creation of the shadow effect, which when used in the drawing of game objects, will make them appear as solid black shapes, perfect for our silhouette needs.

Moving down to the `Update()` method, the calculation of the glow position in screen space can be spotted. In this case, we're taking advantage of the `Project()` method on the `ViewPort` class, which is conveniently designed to do that very calculation for us.

 To simulate the sun's distance and size, the view has been altered so that the glow is always just in front of the camera. This step is not required if the lens flare being displayed is in place of something a lot closer, such as a lamp or headlight.

Finally, we have the three methods that form the working heart of the lens flare.

> ▸ The `BeginShadowCapture()` method sets the render target, so that any rendering performed from this point onwards will be diverted into the `flareTarget`. It clears the contents of the render target to black, and draws the glow image.

> ▸ Next is the `EndShadowCapture()` method, which is called by the game after the scene has finished being drawn onto the render target. This is where the blurring process takes place.

> The captured image in the render target is drawn onto each of the blur render targets, and then all of the blur render targets are combined back into one image.

> A combination of the low resolution of each one of the blur render targets, along with the smoothed sampling method used in their combination, gives us our desired blurred effect.

> ▸ The `Draw()` method performs the important act of actually drawing the newly created blurred glow on the screen.

 `SpriteBatch` alters a few `GraphicsDevice` settings when it renders to the screen, and this can cause strange side effects in the appearance of any 3D graphics rendered afterwards. If your 3D world stops rendering correctly, be sure to reset the `GraphicsDevice.BlendState` and `GraphicsDevice.DepthStencilState` properties upon completing any `SpriteBatch` operations.

There's more...

This technique for producing lens flares will probably need to be fine-tuned in your game on a case-by-case basis, to achieve the best result and avoid any distracting artifacts produced during its construction.

Altering the resolutions and tints of the blur render targets can make a significant difference to how convincing the effect is.

Implementing lens flare within the HiDef profile

Modern GPUs are very good at determining whether one set of polygons is obscured by another set. We can use this to our advantage when creating lens flares within a HiDef profile.

Getting ready

This recipe assumes that you've already got a scene, rendering correctly, albeit without a lens flare.

How to do it...

To create a lens flare within the HiDef profile:

1. Create a new class to hold the lens flare behavior:

    ```
    class HiDefLensFlare
    {
    ```

2. Add some instance-level variables to hold the details of the occlusion test, the lighting, and the glow image:

    ```
    SpriteBatch spriteBatch;
    GraphicsDevice graphicsDevice;
    public BasicEffect ShadowCaptureEffect;

    OcclusionQuery occlusionQuery;
    bool occlusionQueryActive;
    float occlusionAlpha;
    const float querySize = 50;
    VertexPositionColor[] queryVertices;

    public Vector3 LightDirection = Vector3.Normalize(new
    Vector3(0.5f, -0.1f, 0.5f));
    Vector2 lightPosition;
    bool lightBehindCamera;

    Texture2D glow;
    Vector2 glowOrigin;
    float glowScale = 400f;
    ```

3. Next, add a constructor to set up the occlusion test prerequisites and load the glow texture:

```
public HiDefLensFlare(GraphicsDevice graphicsDevice,
ContentManager content)
{
    this.graphicsDevice = graphicsDevice;
    spriteBatch = new SpriteBatch(graphicsDevice);

    ShadowCaptureEffect = new BasicEffect(graphicsDevice)
    {
        View = Matrix.Identity,
        VertexColorEnabled = true
    };

    occlusionQuery = new OcclusionQuery(graphicsDevice);
    queryVertices = new VertexPositionColor[4];

    queryVertices[0].Position = new Vector3(-querySize / 2,
-querySize / 2, -1);
    queryVertices[1].Position = new Vector3(querySize / 2,
-querySize / 2, -1);
    queryVertices[2].Position = new Vector3(-querySize / 2,
querySize / 2, -1);
    queryVertices[3].Position = new Vector3(querySize / 2,
querySize / 2, -1);

    glow = content.Load<Texture2D>(@"lensflare/glow");
    glowOrigin = new Vector2(glow.Width, glow.Height) / 2;
}
```

4. Create a new `BlendState` instance-level variable so the ocular test can proceed without changing the visible image:

```
static readonly BlendState ColorWriteDisable = new BlendState
{
    ColorWriteChannels = ColorWriteChannels.None
};
```

5. Add a new method to perform the ocular test:

```
public void Measure(Matrix view, Matrix projection)
{
```

6. Calculate the position of the lens flare on screen, and exit early if it's behind the player's viewpoint:

```
var infiniteView = view;
infiniteView.Translation = Vector3.Zero;
```

```
var viewport = graphicsDevice.Viewport;
var projectedPosition = viewport.Project(
        -LightDirection, projection,
        infiniteView, Matrix.Identity);

if ((projectedPosition.Z < 0) ||
    (projectedPosition.Z > 1))
{
    lightBehindCamera = true;
    return;
}

lightPosition = new Vector2(projectedPosition.X,
projectedPosition.Y);
lightBehindCamera = false;
```

7. Add the calculation for how much of the lens flare test area is occluded by the scene once the previous occlusion test has completed:

```
if (occlusionQueryActive)
{
    if (!occlusionQuery.IsComplete)
    {
        return;
    }
    const float queryArea = querySize * querySize;
    occlusionAlpha = Math.Min(
        occlusionQuery.PixelCount / queryArea, 1);
}
```

8. Set up for the next occlusion query:

```
graphicsDevice.BlendState = ColorWriteDisable;
graphicsDevice.DepthStencilState = DepthStencilState.DepthRead;
ShadowCaptureEffect.World = Matrix.CreateTranslation(
    lightPosition.X,
    lightPosition.Y, 0);
ShadowCaptureEffect.Projection = Matrix.
CreateOrthographicOffCenter(0,
    viewport.Width,
    viewport.Height,
    0, 0, 1);
ShadowCaptureEffect.CurrentTechnique.Passes[0].Apply();
```

9. Render the lens flare test vertices inside the occlusion test to determine how many pixels were rendered:

```
occlusionQuery.Begin();
graphicsDevice.DrawUserPrimitives(PrimitiveType.TriangleStrip,
queryVertices, 0, 2);
occlusionQuery.End();
occlusionQueryActive = true;
```

10. Complete the class by adding a `Draw()` method to render the glow:

```
public void Draw()
{
    if (lightBehindCamera || occlusionAlpha <= 0)
        return;

    Color color = Color.White * occlusionAlpha;
    Vector2 origin = new Vector2(glow.Width, glow.Height) / 2;
    float scale = glowScale * 2 / glow.Width;

    spriteBatch.Begin();

    spriteBatch.Draw(glow, lightPosition, null, color, 0,
                     origin, scale, SpriteEffects.None, 0);

    spriteBatch.End();
}
```

How it works...

XNA and the underlying DirectX infrastructure contain a rather handy little diagnostic tool in the form of the **occlusion test**. With this test, you can count how many pixels were filled when trying to render a particular portion of a scene.

We utilize this in the lens flare example by attempting to render a small rectangle across the opposite side of the scene from the player's viewpoint, and measuring how much of it is obscured by the scene's meshes. With this number, we adjust the opacity of the lens flare's glow texture up or down to simulate the sun disappearing either partially or completely behind an object.

Implementing smoke within the Reach profile

If implemented in a naive fashion, rendering smoke could place a significant burden on the hardware of a device running a game under the Reach profile.

In this recipe, you'll learn a method for improving the distribution of work and data between the CPU and GPU, to hopefully get as close as possible to the unachievable goal of hardware instancing in an environment that doesn't allow for custom shaders.

In the following illustration, you can see this recipe in use within a stylized city scene:

Getting ready

An image of a smoke "particle" is required for this special effect, but don't feel pressured to spend too much time or effort creating anything too elaborate. Although it forms the heart of the display, the technique's repetition and distortion of even the most basic smoke pattern can result in some quite intricate and realistic results.

How to do it...

To create smoke within the Reach Profile:

1. Start by creating a new smoke particle class:

```
class ReachSmokeParticle
{
```

2. Insert instance variables for the position and age of the particle:

```
public Vector3 Position;
public float PositionDelta;
public float Scale;
public float Rotation;
public float RotationDelta;
public float Age;
public float AgeDelta;
public bool Visible;
public Texture2D Texture;
public Vector2 TextureOrigin;
```

3. Add an `Update()` method to calculate a particle's details:

```
public void Update(
    GameTime gameTime,
    Vector3 wind,
    Vector3 spawnPoint,
    float spawnRadius,
    Random random)
{
    var timeScale = (float)gameTime.ElapsedGameTime.TotalSeconds;
    Position += ((Vector3.Up * PositionDelta) + wind) *
        timeScale;
    Rotation += RotationDelta * timeScale;
    Age += AgeDelta * timeScale;

    if (Age > 1)
    {
        var offset = ((.5f - (float)random.NextDouble()) *
                        (Vector3.Right * spawnRadius)) +
                      ((.5f - (float)random.NextDouble()) *
                        (Vector3.Forward * spawnRadius));
        Position = spawnPoint + offset;
        Age = 0;
        Visible = true;
    }
}
```

4. Continue by adding a `Draw()` method:

```
public void Draw(
    SpriteBatch spriteBatch,
    Viewport viewport,
    Matrix view,
    Matrix projection,
    float projectedScale)
{
    if (!Visible)
    {
        return;
    }
    var projectedPosition = viewport.Project(
        Position,
        projection,
        view,
        Matrix.Identity);

    var screenPosition = new Vector2(
        projectedPosition.X, projectedPosition.Y);

    var tint = Color.FromNonPremultiplied(
                255, 255, 255, 255 - (int)(255f * Age));

    var displayScale = Scale * projectedScale;

    spriteBatch.Draw(
        Texture, screenPosition,
        null, tint, Rotation, TextureOrigin,
        displayScale,
        SpriteEffects.None, projectedPosition.Z);
}
```

5. Now, add the class that will be emitting the freshly defined particles:

```
class ReachSmoke
{
```

6. Insert some instance variables to the new class to hold the details of the particles:

```
SpriteBatch spriteBatch;
Texture2D smoke;
Vector2 halfSmokeSize;
List<ReachSmokeParticle> particles;
Vector3 spawnPoint = Vector3.Zero;
float spawnRadius = 0.2f;
```

```
Random random = new Random();
Vector3 wind = Vector3.Right * 0.3f;
```

7. Add a constructor to create instances of all the particles:

```
public ReachSmoke(
    GraphicsDevice graphicsDevice,
    ContentManager content)
{
    spriteBatch = new SpriteBatch(graphicsDevice);
    smoke = content.Load<Texture2D>("smoke/smoke");
    halfSmokeSize = new Vector2(
        smoke.Width / 2, smoke.Height / 2);
    var particleCount = 300;

    particles = new List<ReachSmokeParticle>();

    for (var index = 0; index < particleCount; index++)
    {
        var particle = new ReachSmokeParticle()
        {
            Texture = smoke,
            TextureOrigin = halfSmokeSize,
            Position = spawnPoint,
            PositionDelta =
                (0.8f * (float)random.NextDouble()) + .2f,
            Scale =
                (0.8f * (float)random.NextDouble()) + .2f,
            Rotation = (float)random.NextDouble(),
            RotationDelta = 0.5f - (float)random.NextDouble(),
            Age = (float)random.NextDouble(),
            AgeDelta =
                (0.8f * (float)random.NextDouble()) + .2f,
            Visible = false
        };
        particles.Add(particle);
    }
}
```

8. Add an `Update()` method to update all the particles to their latest positions:

```
public void Update(GameTime gameTime)
{
    foreach (var particle in particles)
    {
        particle.Update(
```

```
        gameTime,
        wind,
        spawnPoint, spawnRadius,
        random);
    }
}
```

9. Finish the class with the addition of the `Draw()` method to render the particles onto the screen:

```
public void Draw(
    Matrix view, Matrix projection, Matrix world,
    Viewport viewport)
{
    var scaleTestPositionOne = viewport.Project(
            Vector3.Zero,
            projection, view, Matrix.Identity);
    if (scaleTestPositionOne.Z < 0)
    {
        return;
    }
    var scaleTestPositionTwo = viewport.Project(
            Vector3.Up + Vector3.Right,
            projection, view, Matrix.Identity);
    var projectedScale = Vector3.Distance(
            scaleTestPositionOne, scaleTestPositionTwo) /
            (smoke.Height * 2);
    if (projectedScale > 5f)
    {
        return;
    }

    spriteBatch.Begin(
            SpriteSortMode.Deferred,
            BlendState.AlphaBlend, null,
            DepthStencilState.DepthRead, null);

    foreach (var particle in particles)
    {
        particle.Draw(spriteBatch,
            viewport, view, projection, projectedScale);
    }
    spriteBatch.End();
}
```

How it works...

Inspecting the constructor of the `ReachSmoke` class, we can see the creation of the smoke particles.

A diverse selection of random sizes, speeds, and states throughout the particles lessens the chance of players being able to spot any obvious signs of repetition, despite the use of only one texture across all of the particles.

In order to lessen the chance of unwanted pressure on the garbage collector, we create a set number of particles at the beginning and recycle them as required.

Within the `Update()` method of the `ReachSmokeParticle` class, the code to move and rotate each particle can be seen along the recycling process that re-spawns a particle once it has reached the end of its life.

Eagle-eyed readers may notice that a given particle's visibility isn't enabled until it has re-spawned at least once. This delay in visibility is done to give the particles the best chance of appearing in a reasonably even manner, and avoid one large, unrealistic clump at the beginning.

To enjoy the best chance of maximum performance, the `Draw()` methods of both the `ReachSmoke` and `ReachSmokeParticle` classes are designed with the idea of harnessing the optimizations present in the `SpriteBatch` class.

With this in mind, the transformation from 3D world space into 2D screen space is performed on the CPU via .NET code. This allows the GPU to receive and display the particles in one unified update, without the need to recalculate or reload.

Handling the 3D calculations ourselves presents two issues:

▶ The first is that of perspective and the need to scale, which is dependent on how far away the viewer is from the smoke.

   A measurement of the distance between screen positions of two known points in 3D space is made at the start of the `Draw()` method of `ReachSmoke`, to help approximate the scaling of perspective.

▶ The second problem is of depth, where the `SpriteBatch` class is more commonly called upon to draw images over the top of a 3D scene rather than within it.

   Thankfully, the `Draw()` method of the `SpriteBatch` class has an override that allows us to specify the depth of a given texture, and use this to ensure that particles appear correctly in front of, and behind other elements in a 3D scene.

There's more...

With some tweaking of the numbers and the texture, a variety of effects from flame, to steam, and even bubbles, can be achieved with a similar approach.

One addition that can really improve the realism of particle-based effects such as smoke, is animating the texture of each particle as it moves through the scene.

Examples of this can be found in games such as Naughty Dog's Uncharted 3, where they utilized an additional texture as a "movement map", where the color of each pixel in the movement map dictated the direction and intensity of the translation/distortion applied to the corresponding pixel in the texture map.

Creating explosions within the Reach profile

If there's one thing I really appreciate, it's explosions that have a visceral and almost palpable presence in a game.

Much of the presence of an explosion tends to come from the more subtle in-game artifacts, such as a deep, complex, sound design and shaking of the camera, and for a lot of games this is more than enough. But sometimes, something that is a little more satisfying is required visually, such as the rolling fireball covered in this recipe and pictured in the following illustration:

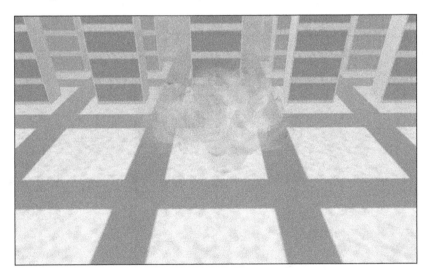

Getting ready

In this special effect, you'll need a textured sphere with a flame or lava appearance.

In the following code, there are references to a `GeometricBuffer` class that can be substituted with any other sort of mesh container. You can find the details of how to construct this kind of mesh programmatically in *Chapter 3, Procedural Modeling*.

A textured sphere mesh from a modeling package would work equally well.

How to do it...

To create an explosion within the Reach profile:

1. As with other particle-based effects, we begin with a new particle class:

    ```
    class ReachExplosionParticle
        {
    ```

2. Start the new class by adding some instance variables to hold its position, age, and other details:

    ```
    public Microsoft.Xna.Framework.Matrix World;
    public float Size;
    public float HorizontalAngle;
    public float HorizontalOffset;
    public float VerticleOffset;
    public float Roll;
    public float Age;
    public float AgeDelta;
    ```

3. Next, define the class that will render each particle:

    ```
    class ReachExplosionParticleDisplay
    {
    ```

4. Add some instance-level variables to hold the mesh, effect, and lifetime details of the particle displayed:

    ```
    GeometricBuffer<VertexPositionNormalTexture> sphereBuffer;
    BasicEffect sphereEffect;
    Curve alphaCurve;
    Curve lightCurve;
    ```

5. Create a constructor to initialize everything:

    ```
    public ReachExplosionParticleDisplay(
        GeometricBuffer<VertexPositionNormalTexture> sphereBuffer,
        BasicEffect sphereEffect)
    {
    ```

```
        this.sphereBuffer = sphereBuffer;
        this.sphereEffect = sphereEffect;

        alphaCurve = new Curve();
        alphaCurve.Keys.Add(new CurveKey(0, 0.75f));
        alphaCurve.Keys.Add(new CurveKey(0.125f, 0.5f));
        alphaCurve.Keys.Add(new CurveKey(0.35f, 0.125f));
        alphaCurve.Keys.Add(new CurveKey(1f, 0f));

        lightCurve = new Curve();
        lightCurve.Keys.Add(new CurveKey(0, 1f));
        lightCurve.Keys.Add(new CurveKey(0.2f, 1f));
        lightCurve.Keys.Add(new CurveKey(1f, 0.25f));
    }
```

6. Add the `Draw()` method to render the particles and finish the class:

```
internal void Draw(
    Matrix view,
    Matrix projection,
    Matrix world,
    float age)
{
    sphereEffect.View = view;
    sphereEffect.Projection = projection;
    sphereEffect.World = world;
    sphereEffect.Alpha = alphaCurve.Evaluate(age);
    sphereEffect.DiffuseColor =
        Vector3.One * lightCurve.Evaluate(age);

    sphereBuffer.Draw(sphereEffect);
}
```

7. Create a new class to orchestrate all the particles and their displays:

```
class ReachExplosion
{
```

8. Add the instance-level variables to hold the display renderer, the particles, and some animation settings:

```
ReachExplosionParticleDisplay particleDisplay;
List<ReachExplosionParticle> particles;

Random random = new Random();

Curve horizontalRateCurve;
```

```
Curve verticleRateCurve;
private bool exploding;
```

9. Initialize everything in a constructor:

```
public ReachExplosion(
    GraphicsDevice graphicsDevice,
    ContentManager content)
{
    particleDisplay =    ReachExplosionParticleDisplayFactory.
Create(
    graphicsDevice, content);
    particles = new List<ReachExplosionParticle>();
    for (var index = 0; index < 100; index++)
    {
        particles.Add(new ReachExplosionParticle());
    }

    horizontalRateCurve = new Curve();
    horizontalRateCurve.Keys.Add(new CurveKey(0, 0f));
    horizontalRateCurve.Keys.Add(new CurveKey(0.025f, 0.8f));
    horizontalRateCurve.Keys.Add(new CurveKey(0.25f, 1f));

    verticleRateCurve = new Curve();
    verticleRateCurve.Keys.Add(new CurveKey(0.2f, 0.1f));
    verticleRateCurve.Keys.Add(new CurveKey(0.3f, 0.25f));
}
```

10. Create a variable and a method to indicate when things should start exploding:

```
public void Explode()
{
    foreach (var particle in particles)
    {
        Reset(particle);
    }
    exploding = true;
}
```

11. Add the ability to reset particles back to an initial position ready to explode:

```
private void Reset(ReachExplosionParticle particle)
{
    particle.Size = (float)random.NextDouble() * 0.2f;
    particle.HorizontalAngle = (float)random.NextDouble() *
        MathHelper.TwoPi;
    particle.HorizontalOffset = (float)random.NextDouble() *
```

```
                    0.5f;
        particle.Roll = ((0.4f *
                             (float)random.NextDouble()) +
                             0.6f) * 2f * MathHelper.TwoPi;
        particle.VerticleOffset = (0.2f *
                             (float)random.NextDouble());
        particle.Age = 0f;
        particle.AgeDelta = ((0.6f *
                             (float)random.NextDouble()) + 0.4f);
    }
```

12. Update the state of all the particles through the addition of an `Update()` method:

```
public void Update(GameTime gameTime)
{
    if (!exploding)
    {
        return;
    }

    var liveParticleCount = 0;

    foreach (var particle in particles)
    {
        if (particle.Age > 1)
        {
            continue;
        }

        particle.Age += particle.AgeDelta *
            (float)gameTime.ElapsedGameTime.TotalSeconds;

        particle.VerticleOffset +=
            verticleRateCurve.Evaluate(particle.Age) *

            (float)gameTime.ElapsedGameTime.TotalSeconds *
                5f;

        particle.Roll +=
            (float)gameTime.ElapsedGameTime.TotalSeconds;

        var horizontalOffset =
                horizontalRateCurve.Evaluate(particle.Age) *
                        particle.HorizontalOffset *
                        Vector3.Backward;
```

```
                    var verticleOffset = Vector3.Up *
                                    particle.VerticleOffset;

            particle.World = Matrix.CreateScale(particle.Size) *
                    Matrix.CreateRotationX(particle.Roll) *
                    Matrix.CreateTranslation(horizontalOffset) *

                Matrix.CreateRotationY(particle.HorizontalAngle) *
                        Matrix.CreateTranslation(verticleOffset);

            liveParticleCount++;
        }

        exploding = liveParticleCount > 0;
    }
```

13. And completing the class, we come to rendering the particles onscreen:

```
public void Draw(
    Matrix view,
    Matrix projection,
    GameTime gameTime)
{
    if (!exploding)
    {
        return;
    }

    foreach (var particle in particles)
    {
        if (particle.Age > 1)
        {
            continue;
        }
        particleDisplay.Draw(
            view,
            projection,
            particle.World,
            particle.Age);
    }
}
```

14. To complete the example, add a factory class to create a new instance of the particle mesh. Here's an example using the GeometricBuffer classes from *Chapter 3, Procedural Modeling*:

```
class ReachExplosionParticleDisplayFactory
{

    public static ReachExplosionParticleDisplay
Create(GraphicsDevice graphicsDevice, ContentManager content)
    {
        var sphereEffect = new BasicEffect(graphicsDevice)
        {
            SpecularColor = Color.Black.ToVector3(),
            DiffuseColor = Color.White.ToVector3(),
            Texture = content.Load<Texture2D>("lava"),
            TextureEnabled = true
        };

        var factory = new
VertexPositionNormalTextureGeometricBufferFactory();

        var radius = 1f;
        var vStep = -MathHelper.Pi / 8f;
        var uStep = -MathHelper.TwoPi / 8f;

        for (var v = MathHelper.PiOver2;
            v > -MathHelper.PiOver2;
            v += vStep)
        {
            var nextV = v + vStep;
            var vY = radius * (float)Math.Sin(v);
            var nextVY = (float)Math.Sin(nextV);

            var bandRadius = radius * (float)Math.Cos(v);
            var nextBandRadius = radius *
                    (float)Math.Cos(nextV);

            var top = new Vector3(
                        bandRadius,
                        vY,
                        bandRadius);
            var bottom = new Vector3(
                        nextBandRadius,
                        nextVY,
                        nextBandRadius);

            for (var u = MathHelper.Pi;
                u > -MathHelper.Pi;
```

```
                u += uStep)
      {
            var nextU = u + uStep;

            var uX = (float)Math.Sin(u);
            var nextUX = (float)Math.Sin(nextU);

            var uZ = (float)Math.Cos(u);
            var nextUZ = (float)Math.Cos(nextU);

            var right = new Vector3(uX, 1f, uZ);
            var left = new Vector3(nextUX, 1f, nextUZ);

            var topLeft = top * left;
            var topRight = top * right;
            var bottomRight = bottom * right;
            var bottomLeft = bottom * left;

            var textureLeft = (float)(
                    (nextU + MathHelper.Pi) /
                    MathHelper.TwoPi);
            var textureRight = (float)(
                    (u + MathHelper.Pi) /
                    MathHelper.TwoPi);
            var textureTop = 1f - (float)(
                    (v + MathHelper.PiOver2) /
                    Math.PI);
            var textureBottom = 1f - (float)(
                    (nextV + MathHelper.PiOver2) /
                    Math.PI);

            var topLeftNormal =
                    Vector3.Normalize(topLeft);
            var topRightNormal =
                    Vector3.Normalize(topRight);
            var bottomRightNormal =
                    Vector3.Normalize(bottomRight);
            var bottomLeftNormal =
                    Vector3.Normalize(bottomLeft);

        factory.AddPane(
            topLeft,
            new Vector2(textureLeft, textureTop),
            topLeftNormal,
```

```
                    topRight,
                    new Vector2(textureRight, textureTop),
                    topRightNormal,
                    bottomRight,
                new Vector2(textureRight, textureBottom),
                    bottomRightNormal,
                    bottomLeft,
                new Vector2(textureLeft, textureBottom),
                    bottomLeftNormal);
            }

        }

        var sphereBuffer = factory.Create(graphicsDevice);
        sphereBuffer.IsTextureTransparent = true;

        return new ReachExplosionParticleDisplay(
                    sphereBuffer, sphereEffect);
    }
}
```

How it works...

The heart of the `ReachExplosion` class lies with the use of the XNA `Curve` class.

Via the `Curve` class, we can take the relatively random nature of the particle stream and mold it into the visually satisfying shape of a gaseous explosion.

Two instances of the `Curve` class are created within the constructor of the `ReachExplosion` class.

The first curve determines the shape of the explosion by expanding or contracting the distance between each particle and the center of the explosion. The second curve determines how quickly the particles rise.

Another two instances of the `Curve` class can be observed in the `ReachExplosionParticleDisplay` class controlling the luminescence and transparency of each particle, thereby simulating the particle's transition from flame, to smoke, to thin air.

There's more...

Just like in film, the difference between a convincing explosion and one less so can usually be found not in the explosion itself, but in the impact it has on the world around it.

A deep bass explosion sound along with a small shake of the virtual camera, possibly also achieved via the `Curve` class, would go a long way towards enhancing the realism of this effect.

Creating explosions within the HiDef profile

One of the more visceral elements of a good explosion is the shockwave that races ahead of the flames. Extracting and modifying one of the standard Microsoft examples of distortion mapping can let us enjoy the rather gratifying joy of shockwave-laden explosions in our own games.

Getting ready

This recipe assumes you have access to a spherical mesh and some sort of flame texture. It was originally written with the sphere generator presented in the *Modeling spheres* recipe of *Chapter 3*, *Procedural Modeling*, but should work equally well with any other method of creating spheres. Where you find the call to a `CreateSphere()` method in the following example code, feel free to replace that with your own.

Likewise, any references to `GeometricBuffer` classes of *Chapter 3*, *Procedural Modeling* can be substituted for any other mesh container style classes.

How to do it...

To create an explosion within the HiDef profile:

1. Add a new effect file to your game's content project, named `DistortionGenerator.fx`.

2. Inside the new file, clear any existing content and add the input parameters:

    ```
    float4x4 WorldViewProjection;
    float4x4 WorldView;
    float DistortionScale;
    ```

3. Define the structure of the data that passes between the vertex and pixel shaders:

    ```
    struct PositionNormal
    {
        float4 Position : POSITION;
        float3 Normal : NORMAL;
    };

    struct PositionDisplacement
    {
        float4 Position : POSITION;
    ```

```
    float2 Displacement : TEXCOORD;
};
```

4. Add a vertex shader that calculates the distortion on behalf of the pixel shader based upon a vertex's normal:

```
PositionDisplacement PullIn_VertexShader(PositionNormal input)
{
    PositionDisplacement output;

    output.Position = mul(input.Position, WorldViewProjection);
    float3 normalWV = mul(input.Normal, WorldView);
    normalWV.y = -normalWV.y;

    float amount = dot(normalWV, float3(0,0,1)) * DistortionScale;
    output.Displacement = float2(.5,.5) + float2(amount * normalWV.
xy);

    return output;
}
```

5. Next, add the corresponding pixel shader that emits the distorted normal as a color:

```
float4 DisplacementPassthrough_PixelShader(float2 displacement :
TEXCOORD) : COLOR
{
    return float4(displacement, 0, 1);
}
```

6. Complete the file by tying the vertex and pixel shader together into a technique:

```
technique PullIn
{
    pass
    {
        VertexShader = compile vs_2_0 PullIn_VertexShader();
        PixelShader = compile ps_2_0 DisplacementPassthrough_
PixelShader();
    }
}
```

7. Create a new effect file named `DistortionApplicator.fx` and add it to your content project.

8. Specify the effect's inputs to receive two textures and the weighting arrays for a Gaussian blur:

```
sampler SceneTexture : register(s0);
sampler DistortionMap : register(s1);
```

```
#define SAMPLE_COUNT 15

float2 SampleOffsets[SAMPLE_COUNT];
float SampleWeights[SAMPLE_COUNT];
```

9. Add a constant to help in the translation of a zero amount when moving between 0-1 and 0-255 ranges:

```
const float ZeroOffset = 0.5f / 255.0f;
```

10. Include a pixel shader that renders a distorted and possibly blurred version of the scene texture if the distortion map texture is any color other than black:

```
float4 Distort_PixelShader(float2 TexCoord : TEXCOORD0,
    uniform bool distortionBlur) : COLOR0
{
    float2 displacement = tex2D(DistortionMap, TexCoord).rg;

    float4 finalColor = 0;
    if ((displacement.x == 0) && (displacement.y == 0))
    {
        finalColor = tex2D(SceneTexture, TexCoord);
    }
    else
    {
        displacement -= .5 + ZeroOffset;

        if (distortionBlur)
        {
            for (int i = 0; i < SAMPLE_COUNT; i++)
            {
                finalColor += tex2D(
                    SceneTexture,
                    TexCoord.xy +
                    displacement +
                    SampleOffsets[i]) *
                    SampleWeights[i];
            }
        }
        else
        {
            finalColor = tex2D(SceneTexture, TexCoord.xy +
displacement);
        }
    }
```

```
        return finalColor;
    }
```

11. Add two techniques to allow the pixel shader to be used with or without blurring:

```
technique Distort
{
    pass
    {
        PixelShader = compile ps_2_0 Distort_PixelShader(false);
    }
}

technique DistortBlur
{
    pass
    {
        PixelShader = compile ps_2_0 Distort_PixelShader(true);
    }
}
```

12. In your game project, create a new factory class to produce explosions:

```
class HiDefExplosionFactory
{
```

13. Add a static method to create new explosions:

```
public static HiDefExplosion Create(
  GraphicsDevice graphicsDevice,
  ContentManager content)
{
    var buffer = CreateSphere(graphicsDevice);

    var occlusionEffect = new BasicEffect(graphicsDevice)
    {
        DiffuseColor = Color.Black.ToVector3()
    };

    var flameEffect = new BasicEffect(graphicsDevice)
    {
        DiffuseColor = Color.White.ToVector3(),
        Texture = content.Load<Texture2D>("explosion/lava"),
        TextureEnabled = true,
        Alpha = 0.5f
    };
```

```
        var distortionGeneratorEffect = content.
    Load<Effect>("explosion/DistortionGenerator");
        var distortionApplicatorEffect = content.
    Load<Effect>("explosion/DistortionApplicator");
        return new HiDefExplosion(
            graphicsDevice,
            buffer,
            occlusionEffect ,
            flameEffect,
            distortionGeneratorEffect,
            distortionApplicatorEffect);
    }
```

14. Create a new Explosion class:

```
class HiDefExplosion
{
```

15. Add the instance-level variables that will be used to render the flames:

```
GeometricBuffer<VertexPositionNormalTexture> buffer;
BasicEffect flameEffect;
RenderTarget2D sceneRenderTarget;
```

16. Declare the instance-level variables that will be used to render the shockwave:

```
RenderTarget2D distortionRenderTarget;
public BasicEffect OcclusionEffect;
Effect distortionGeneratorEffect;
Effect distortApplicatorEffect;
```

17. Append the instance-level variables used to display the completed animation:

```
SpriteBatch spriteBatch;

float explosionLifeSpanSeconds;
Curve sizeCurve;
Curve flameAlphaCurve;

public Matrix World;

private bool exploding;
private double explosionStartTime;
private double explosionEndTime;
private float flameAlpha;
private const float blurAmount = 1.25f;
```

18. Add a constructor:

```
public HiDefExplosion(
    GraphicsDevice graphicsDevice,
    GeometricBuffer<VertexPositionNormalTexture> buffer,
    BasicEffect occlusionEffect,
    BasicEffect flameEffect,
    Effect distortersEffect,
    Effect distortEffect)
{
```

19. Inside the constructor, populate the instance- level variables:

```
this.buffer = buffer;
OcclusionEffect = occlusionEffect;
this.flameEffect = flameEffect;
this.distortionGeneratorEffect = distortersEffect;
this.distortApplicatorEffect = distortEffect;
```

20. Set up the pieces required to capture and display the various elements of the explosion:

```
spriteBatch = new SpriteBatch(graphicsDevice);

var pp = graphicsDevice.PresentationParameters;
sceneRenderTarget = new RenderTarget2D(graphicsDevice,
    pp.BackBufferWidth, pp.BackBufferHeight,
    false, pp.BackBufferFormat, pp.DepthStencilFormat);
distortionRenderTarget = new RenderTarget2D(graphicsDevice,
    pp.BackBufferWidth, pp.BackBufferHeight,
    false, pp.BackBufferFormat, pp.DepthStencilFormat);
```

21. Populate the Gaussian blur weight arrays of the distortion effect:

```
SetBlurEffectParameters(
    1f / (float)pp.BackBufferWidth,
    1f / (float)pp.BackBufferHeight);
```

22. Create the timings for the explosion animation:

```
explosionLifeSpanSeconds = 5f;
sizeCurve = new Curve();
sizeCurve.Keys.Add(new CurveKey(0, 0.1f));
sizeCurve.Keys.Add(new CurveKey(0.75f, 5f));

flameAlphaCurve = new Curve();
flameAlphaCurve.Keys.Add(new CurveKey(0, 0f));
flameAlphaCurve.Keys.Add(new CurveKey(0.05f, 1f));
flameAlphaCurve.Keys.Add(new CurveKey(0.15f, 0f));
```

23. Add a method to begin capturing a scene into the sceneRenderTarget:

```
public void BeginSceneCapture(GraphicsDevice graphicsDevice)
{
    graphicsDevice.SetRenderTarget(sceneRenderTarget);
}
```

24. Create a method to render the flame as a final element onto the scene, before switching the rendering from the sceneRenderTarget back to the screen:

```
public void EndSceneCapture(
        GraphicsDevice graphicsDevice,
    Matrix view,
    Matrix projection)
{
    if (exploding)
    {
        flameEffect.View = view;
        flameEffect.Projection = projection;
        flameEffect.World = World;
        flameEffect.Alpha = flameAlpha;

        // draw explosion particle.
        // e.g. here's how it would be done using
        // Chapter 3's GeometricBuffer classes
        buffer.IsTextureTransparent = true;
        buffer.Draw(flameEffect);
    }

    graphicsDevice.SetRenderTarget(null);
}
```

25. Next up is the method to begin capturing any objects within a scene that may be occluding the explosion from the player:

```
public void BeginOcclusionCapture(
    GraphicsDevice graphicsDevice)
{
    if (!exploding)
    {
        return;
    }

    graphicsDevice.SetRenderTarget(distortionRenderTarget);
    graphicsDevice.Clear(Color.Black);

}
```

26. Add the method to render the distortion effect into a render target, and shift the rendering to the screen once more:

```
public void EndOcclusionCapture(
    GraphicsDevice graphicsDevice,
    Matrix view,
    Matrix projection)
{
    if (!exploding)
    {
        return;
    }

    Matrix meshWorldView = Matrix.CreateScale(1.5f) * World *
view;

    distortionGeneratorEffect.CurrentTechnique =
        distortionGeneratorEffect.Techniques["PullIn"];
    distortionGeneratorEffect.Parameters["WorldView"].
SetValue(meshWorldView);
    distortionGeneratorEffect.Parameters["WorldViewProjection"].
SetValue(
        meshWorldView * projection);
    distortionGeneratorEffect.Parameters["DistortionScale"].
SetValue(
        0.0125f);

    buffer.Draw(distortionGeneratorEffect);
    graphicsDevice.SetRenderTarget(null);
}
```

27. Specify the method and the associated variables to start the animation:

```
public void Explode(GameTime gameTime)
{
    exploding = true;
    explosionStartTime = gameTime.TotalGameTime.TotalSeconds;
    explosionEndTime = explosionStartTime +
    explosionLifeSpanSeconds;
}
```

28. Insert an `Update()` method to play the animation once it has begun:

```
public void Update(GameTime gameTime)
{
    if (!exploding)
    {
```

```
                return;
            }

            if (gameTime.TotalGameTime.TotalSeconds >= explosionEndTime)
            {
                exploding = false;
                return;
            }

            var explosionTimeOffset = gameTime.TotalGameTime.TotalSeconds
        - explosionStartTime;

            World = Matrix.CreateScale(sizeCurve.Evaluate((float)
        explosionTimeOffset)) *
                Matrix.CreateTranslation(Vector3.Zero);
            flameAlpha = flameAlphaCurve.Evaluate((float)
        explosionTimeOffset);
        }
```

29. Add the `Draw()` method to render the scene along with any explosion that may be in progress:

```
public void Draw(GraphicsDevice graphicsDevice)
{
    if (exploding)
    {
        spriteBatch.Begin(0, BlendState.Opaque, null, null, null,
distortApplicatorEffect);
        distortApplicatorEffect.CurrentTechnique =
distortApplicatorEffect.Techniques["DistortBlur"];
        graphicsDevice.Textures[1] = distortionRenderTarget;
        graphicsDevice.SamplerStates[1] = SamplerState.PointClamp;
    }
    else
    {
        spriteBatch.Begin();
    }

    var viewport = graphicsDevice.Viewport;
    spriteBatch.Draw(
        sceneRenderTarget,
        new Rectangle(0, 0, viewport.Width, viewport.Height),
        Color.White);
    spriteBatch.End();
}
```

30. Finish the class with methods to calculate Gaussian blur weightings:

```
void SetBlurEffectParameters(float dx, float dy)
{
    EffectParameter weightsParameter, offsetsParameter;
    weightsParameter = distortApplicatorEffect.
                Parameters["SampleWeights"];
    offsetsParameter = distortApplicatorEffect.
                Parameters["SampleOffsets"];

    int sampleCount = weightsParameter.Elements.Count;

    float[] sampleWeights = new float[sampleCount];
    Vector2[] sampleOffsets = new
                        Vector2[sampleCount];

    sampleWeights[0] = ComputeGaussian(0);
    sampleOffsets[0] = new Vector2(0);

    float totalWeights = sampleWeights[0];

    for (int i = 0; i < sampleCount / 2; i++)
    {
        float weight = ComputeGaussian(i + 1);
        sampleWeights[i * 2 + 1] = weight;
        sampleWeights[i * 2 + 2] = weight;
        totalWeights += weight * 2;
        float sampleOffset = i * 2 + 1.5f;
        var delta = new Vector2(dx, dy) *
                sampleOffset;
        sampleOffsets[i * 2 + 1] = delta;
        sampleOffsets[i * 2 + 2] = -delta;
    }

    for (int i = 0; i < sampleWeights.Length; i++)
    {
        sampleWeights[i] /= totalWeights;
    }

    weightsParameter.SetValue(sampleWeights);
    offsetsParameter.SetValue(sampleOffsets);
}

static float ComputeGaussian(float n)
{
```

```
            return (float)((1.0 /
                    Math.Sqrt(2 * Math.PI * blurAmount)) *
                            Math.Exp(-(n * n) /
                    (2 * blurAmount * blurAmount)));
    }
```

How it works...

I find it easiest to imagine how this recipe works in terms of how I might try to achieve a similar effect using more traditional real-world artistic techniques.

For example, if this was an airbrushed artwork, I might paint the surrounding scene first, apply masking tape to any area where I didn't want the explosion to appear, spray a fiery design over the top, remove the tape, and voila! A scene with an explosion is produced.

Between the `BeginSceneCapture()` and `EndSceneCapture()` methods is where we draw the surrounding scene.

Next, we create a mask by painting the shape of the explosion amongst a completely blackened version of our scene, through calling the `BeginOcclusionCapture()` and `EndOcclusionCapture()` methods, and the `DistortionGenerator` effect.

Rendering this "heat map" amongst a blackened version of the scene means that any elements of the scene that would normally obscure the explosion are rendered as black, over the top of the explosion shape, thereby masking those portions out.

The color we fill the explosion shape in with is not the final color of the rendered explosion though. Instead, it is a sort of a "heat map", indicating the direction and amount of distorted explosive effect that will be applied to each pixel in the final image.

Inside the `Draw()` method is where we bring all the elements together with the help of the `DistortionApplicator` effect.

Taking note of which pixels are black and which are not within the masked image, the `DistortionApplicator` effect renders the original scene image with the appropriate amount of distortion in each area, thereby achieving the final result: a scene with an explosive bubble of distortion flooding across the landscape.

There's more...

The draw, mask, and combine technique demonstrated in this recipe is the foundation of a vast array of effects found in games.

Apply the distortions to a flattened pane and you're half way towards producing a patch of water. Change the intensity of the distortion based upon the depth of the original scene, and you're very close to a passable focal blur effect.

See also...

▸ _Rendering water within the HiDef profile_ recipe in _Chapter 4, Creating Water and Sky._

2
Building 2D and 3D Terrain

In this chapter we will cover:

- ▶ Displaying hexagonal maps
- ▶ Displaying 2D isometric maps
- ▶ Importing and displaying 3D isometric maps
- ▶ Generating 3D height maps
- ▶ Creating block worlds within the Reach profile
- ▶ Creating block worlds within the HiDef profile

Introduction

Some of my all time favorite moments in a game have involved staring out across the vista and marveling at the world before me. Catching sight of some interesting looking places to explore, the appreciation of the subtle artistry to distinguish one area from the next, and the sheer joy of seemingly having an entire virtual world to experience all add a tremendous amount of emotional impact and that's even before acknowledging the primary purpose of the surrounding landscape: to keep stuff from falling off into space.

In this chapter, we will explore creating and displaying terrains utilizing a variety of methods ranging from the retro board game style of hexagonal tiles up to the popular block world style reminiscent of games such as Minecraft.

Displaying hexagonal maps

Hexagons have formed the basis of a number of strategic board games over the last three decades, both physical and virtual, and thus the ability to deal with them in one's own games can be advantageous.

In reality, drawing a hexagonal map usually doesn't present the greatest challenge. On the other hand, it's not unusual for a lot of hexagonal-based computer games to rely upon either mouse or touch input as the selection mechanism for hexagons and the challenge of how to correlate a mouse click with a particular hexagon can be a surprisingly unintuitive problem to solve.

With this in mind, we will be covering not only the drawing of the hexagons onto the screen, but also the thorny issue of how to map screen coordinates into their corresponding hexagon as the following image illustrates:

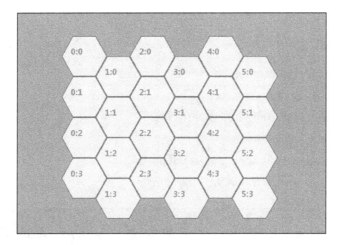

Getting ready

In order to draw a hexagonal map, we're going to need an image of a hexagon.

The code demonstrated here was written with an image of 100x87 pixels in mind, but it can be easily tweaked to accommodate other sizes should the game graphics require more space or if the intended screen resolution is significantly different.

 A mouse pointer is assumed in the code provided, but this can be easily substituted with any form of input that can be expressed in terms of a set of screen coordinates.

How to do it...

1. First, define some variables to hold the details of the hexagons you'll be drawing:

```
Texture2D hexagon;
int leftHexagonWidth = 76;
int topHexagonHeight = 44;
int hexagonHeight = 88;
int hexagonSlopeHeight = 25;
float hexagonSlope;

Vector2 scrollOffset;
```

2. In the `LoadContent()` method load the image, calculate the hexagon's slope, make the mouse visible, and set where on the screen the map is going to be positioned:

```
hexagon = Content.Load<Texture2D>("Hexagon");
hexagonSlope = (float)topHexagonHeight / (float)
hexagonSlopeHeight;

scrollOffset = new Vector2(100, 50);

IsMouseVisible = true;
```

3. Using the `Draw()` method, draw a 6x4 grid of hexagons:

```
spriteBatch.Begin();

for (var u = 0; u < 6; u++)
{
    for (var v = 0; v < 4; v++)
    {
        var positionX = (leftHexagonWidth * u) +
                        scrollOffset.X;
        var alternate = u % 2;
        var positionY = (hexagonHeight * v) +
                        (alternate * topHexagonHeight) +
                        scrollOffset.Y;
        var position = new Vector2(positionX, positionY);
        spriteBatch.Draw(hexagon, position, Color.White);

    }
}
spriteBatch.End();
```

4. Next, define the start of the method that will translate screen coordinates into the corresponding hexagonal grid location:

```
private static Point CalculateTile(Point pointer, Vector2 offset,
int halfWidth, int height, int halfHeight, float slope)
{
```

5. Calculate the x axis relative to the map:

```
var offsetAdjustedX = (int)(pointer.X - offset.X);
```

6. Work out if this is a column that is "shifted down" half a tile:

```
var tileX = offsetAdjustedX / halfWidth;
var alternate = tileX % 2;
var offsetAjdustedY = (int)(pointer.Y - offset.Y) -
                             (alternate * halfHeight);
var tileY = (offsetAjdustedY / height);
```

7. Calculate the x and y coordinates in terms of whole rectangular-shaped tiles:

```
var tileXOffset = (offsetAdjustedX -
                          (tileX * halfWidth)) %
                      halfWidth;
var tileYOffset = (offsetAjdustedY -
                          (tileY * height)) %
                      height;
```

8. Complete the method by adjusting the coordinates if the pointer is over the diagonally-sloped area of a neighboring tile:

```
        if (tileXOffset * slope < (-tileYOffset + halfHeight))
        {
            tileX -= 1;
        }

        if (tileXOffset * slope < (tileYOffset - halfHeight))
        {
            tileX -= 1;
            tileY += 1;
        }
        var tile = new Point(tileX, tileY);
        return tile;

}
```

9. Finally, within the `Update()` method, we can take the screen coordinates of mouse pointer and calculate which hexagon it's currently over:

```
var mouse = Mouse.GetState();
var pointer = new Point(mouse.X, mouse.Y);
```

```
var tile = CalculateTile(pointer, scrollOffset, leftHexagonWidth,
hexagonHeight, topHexagonHeight, hexagonSlope);
```

How it works...

The placement of hexagons on screen can be thought of as being somewhat like a brickwork pattern turned onto its side, where each alternate column is offset by approximately half of a hexagon.

The reason why the values that determine the position and overlap were hardcoded at the beginning, as opposed to being calculated from the dimensions of the texture directly, is that there's usually some minor tweaking of values required to account for any anti-aliasing artifacts within the image.

Translating screen coordinates to hexagonal grid coordinates can be thought of in terms of two smaller problems that are as follows:

▶ The first issue is dealing with the brickwork layout of the hexagons. For this, the calculations appear similar to how we might deal with a regular grid, but with an additional vertical displacement applied to each alternate column.

▶ The second issue is how to deal with the sloped edges. What we need to do is determine whether the screen coordinate corresponds with a point over the current hexagon or one of its neighbors.

To do this we calculated the position relative to the top-left corner of the texture and then determined whether it was located to the left of one of the two slopes as highlighted in red in the following image:

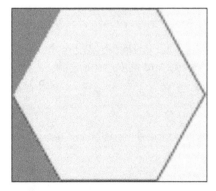

If the position is to the left of either slope, then we can adjust our original hexagonal grid calculation, either "left and up" or "left and down" as required.

There's more...

It turns out that the silhouette of a cube viewed from an isometric perspective is pretty close to that of a hexagon, so next time you're constructing an isometric game and wondering how to determine which cube was clicked, the technique demonstrated here might be a good place to start.

Displaying 2D isometric maps

Despite the advent of modern graphics hardware that can support full-blown 3D imagery quite easily, isometric displays continue to be a popular choice for many games as it can speed up the production of both code and artwork considerably when you only need to deal with two-dimensional images instead of three-dimensional models. If there's one thing that game designers at all levels appreciate, it's the ability to get things done even faster.

Getting ready

An image of an isometric element such as the following cube is required for this recipe:

It can be something as simple as a flat isometric square, but a cube may prove to be an easier subject to deal with for initial testing and alignment.

How to do it...

1. First, define the texture and the dimensions of both the cubes and the visible world as follows:

   ```
   Vector2 scrollOffset;

   Texture2D cube;
   int halfCubeWidth = 50;
   int halfCubeHeight = 25;
   float depthVolume = 5f * 5f * 5f;
   ```

2. Using the `LoadContent()` method, load the texture:

```
cube = Content.Load<Texture2D>("Cube");
```

3. With the `Draw()` method, display a collection of cubes measuring 5x5x2:

```
spriteBatch.Begin();

for (var z = 0; z < 5; z++)
{
    for (var x = 5; x > 0; x--)
    {
        for (var y = 0; y < 2; y++)
        {
            var u = (x * halfCubeWidth) +
                    (z * halfCubeWidth) +
                    (int)scrollOffset.X;
            var v = (-x * halfCubeHeight) +
                    (z * halfCubeHeight) +
                    (-y * halfCubeHeight * 2) +
                    (int)scrollOffset.Y;
            var position = new Vector2(u, v);

            var depth = (x + y + z) / depthVolume;
            spriteBatch.Draw(cube, position, null, Color.White,
0f, new Vector2(halfCubeWidth, halfCubeHeight), 1f, SpriteEffects.
None, depth);
        }
    }
}
spriteBatch.End();
```

How it works...

The transformation from isometric to screen coordinates is relatively simple with each one of the three axes contributing a linear amount of horizontal or vertical screen offset.

A possibly more interesting facet lies in the calculation and inclusion of a depth variable in the `SpriteBatch.Draw()` call.

This depth variable represents the intended draw order of the cubes.

What this means is that we no longer need to explicitly manage the draw order ourselves. We are free to call the `Draw()` method of `SpriteBatch` in whatever order makes most sense in terms of our wider game architecture, instead of the specific rendering order.

It should be noted that we calculate the depth by totaling the offset along each one of the axes and dividing it by the maximum possible total. This should result in the depth being expressed in terms of a figure between 0 and 1.

In this example, the maximum total of all axes has been called `depthVolume` and was initialized to be the same size as the rendered collection of cubes.

There's more...

Blizzard's Diablo 2 amazed audiences with a 'trick' that converted the normally isometric view of the playing field into something closer to a perspective view.

They've never revealed the specifics as far as I know but my guess is that it was achieved through the subtle use of scaling, with objects progressively down vertically the 'further away' they were from the camera in a manner not entirely dissimilar to the scaling demonstrated in the *Implementing smoke within the Reach profile* section of *Chapter 1, Applying Special Effects*:

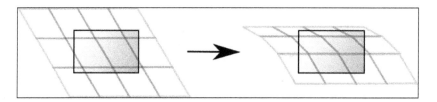

If one imagines the landscape extending beyond the edges of the screen, and the vertical scaling being less dramatic than the example pictured, quite a subtle but believable perspective should be achievable.

See also

Implementing smoke within the Reach profile section of *Chapter 1, Applying Special Effects*.

Importing and displaying 3D isometric maps

One of the key components of the XNA framework is the content pipeline and the ability to easily extend it.

In this section, we're going to extend the content pipeline so that we can include a height map image file in the content and have it automatically converted to a more easily accessible format as part of the build process.

Getting ready

An image to be used as the height map for terrain generation is required for this example. Any image will do, although it's probably best to initially keep it relatively small in size initially to limit the amount of data to wade through during debugging, and to keep the individual polygons big enough to spot any issues more easily. An image like the following, for example, will work:

The model display and construction `GeometricBuffer` classes from *Chapter 3, Procedural Modeling*, are utilized in the construction of the landscape. The method of mesh construction is not important to the demonstration since the focus is on the import process instead, and can be substituted with any mesh building techniques of your choosing.

How to do it...

1. Name the data container class `HeightMap` for convenience and define it as follows:

```
public class HeightMap
{
    public int Width;
    public int Depth;
    public Dictionary<Point, float> depthByPosition = new
Dictionary<Point,float>();

    public float this[int x, int y]
    {
        get
        {
            return depthByPosition[new Point(x, y)];
        }
        set
        {
            depthByPosition[new Point(x, y)] = value;
        }
    }
}
```

2. Add a second project of type **Content Pipeline Extension** to the solution.

3. Within the new pipeline project, add a reference to the previously added project containing the `HeightMap` class.

4. Next, add the `HeightMapProcessor` to the pipeline project as follows:

```
[ContentProcessor(DisplayName = "HeightMap Processor")]
public class HeightMapProcessor : ContentProcessor<Texture2DConte
nt, HeightMap>
{
    public override HeightMap Process(Texture2DContent input,
ContentProcessorContext context)
    {
        var bitmap = (PixelBitmapContent<Color>)input.Mipmaps[0];

        var heightMap = new HeightMap()
        {
            Width = bitmap.Width,
            Depth = bitmap.Height
        };

        for (var y = 0; y < bitmap.Height; y++)
        {
            for (var x = 0; x < bitmap.Width; x++)
            {
                var color = bitmap.GetPixel(x,y);
                heightMap[x,y] = (float)(color.R +
                            color.G +
                            color.B) / (256f * 3f);
            }
        }

        return heightMap;
    }
}
```

5. In the content project, add the height map image along with a reference to the previously constructed content pipeline extension project.

6. After a compile, it should be possible to inspect the properties of the image within the content project, and then select **HeightMap Processor** as the **Content Processor** for the image as shown in the following screenshot:

7. In the `game.cs` file, add the method to translate the imported terrain data into a mesh:

```
GeometricBuffer<VertexPositionNormalTexture> buffer;


private void CreateLand()
{
    var heightMap = Content.Load<HeightMap>("heightmap");

    var factory = new
VertexPositionNormalTextureGeometricBufferFactory();

    var terrainWidth = 10f;
    var terrainDepth = 10f;
    var halfTerrainWidth = terrainWidth / 2f;
    var halfTerrainDepth = terrainDepth / 2f;
    var terrainHeightScalar = 3f;
    var zStep = 0.5f;
    var xStep = 0.5f;

    for (var z = -halfTerrainDepth;
        z < (halfTerrainDepth - zStep);
        z += zStep)
    {
        var nextZ = z + zStep;

        for (var x = -halfTerrainWidth;
            x < (halfTerrainWidth - xStep);
```

```
      x += xStep)
{
    var nextX = x + xStep;

    var u = (int)(
                ((x + halfTerrainWidth) /
                    terrainWidth) *
                heightMap.Width);
    var v = (int)(
                ((z + halfTerrainDepth) /
                    terrainDepth) *
                heightMap.Depth);

    var nextU = (int)(
                ((nextX + halfTerrainWidth) /
                    terrainWidth) *
                heightMap.Width);
    var nextV = (int)(
                ((nextZ + halfTerrainDepth) /
                    terrainDepth) *
                heightMap.Depth);

    var forwardLeft = new Vector3(
        x,
        heightMap[u, v] * terrainHeightScalar,
        z);
    var forwardRight = new Vector3(
        nextX,
        heightMap[nextU, v] * terrainHeightScalar,
        z);
    var backwardRight = new Vector3(
        nextX,
        heightMap[nextU, nextV] * terrainHeightScalar,
        nextZ);
    var backwardLeft = new Vector3(
        x,
        heightMap[u, nextV] * terrainHeightScalar,
        nextZ);
```

```
        factory.AddPane(
            forwardLeft, new Vector2(0, 0),
            forwardRight, new Vector2(1, 0),
            backwardRight, new Vector2(1, 1),
            backwardLeft, new Vector2(0, 1));
    }
}


    buffer = factory.Create(GraphicsDevice);
}
```

8. Add the method to create an instance of the effect used to display the terrain as follows:

```
BasicEffect effect;

private void CreateEffect()
{
    effect = new BasicEffect(GraphicsDevice)
    {
        DiffuseColor = Color.Green.ToVector3(),
        SpecularColor = Color.Orange.ToVector3() / 2f,
        PreferPerPixelLighting = true,
        View = Matrix.CreateLookAt(
            new Vector3(0, 5f, 3f),
            new Vector3(0, 1f, 0),
            Vector3.Up),
        Projection = Matrix.CreateOrthographic(10f, 10f, 0.01f,
1000f),
        World = Matrix.CreateRotationY(MathHelper.ToRadians(45))
    };
    effect.EnableDefaultLighting();
}
```

9. Modify the `LoadContent()` method so that the land and effect are loaded:

```
protected override void LoadContent()
{
    CreateLand();
    CreateEffect();
}
```

10. Complete the process by drawing the land using the effect in the `Draw()` method:

```
protected override void Draw(GameTime gameTime)
{
    GraphicsDevice.Clear(Color.CornflowerBlue);

    buffer.Draw(effect);

    base.Draw(gameTime);
}
```

How it works...

The `HeightMapProcessor` class is instantiated and called as part of the content build process. It has the single responsibility of taking the image content feed to it from the inbuilt XNA texture content importer, and converting it into a collection of height values stored in an instance of the `HeightMap` class.

Inside the `CreateLand()` method of the game, a terrain mesh is created using the data contained in the `HeightMap` instance.

An example of creating an orthographic projection can be seen in the call to `Matrix.CreateOrthographic()` with the `CreateEffect()` method.

The width and depth parameters that make up the first two arguments of the `CreateOrthographic()` method specify the area visible with the projection, and can be thought of as a **zoom mechanism**. To increase the zoom, decrease the width and depth. To decrease it, increase the width and depth.

Generating 3D height maps

Sometimes it makes sense to stop trying to handcraft each and every portion of a game and get a computer onto the job. For some games, such as **SimCity**, it can be a core gameplay mechanic, and for others, such as a number of the modern open world RPGs, it's a handy way to fill out those bits of the world that lie between more action-packed parts of the story.

In this recipe, we'll be exploring the basis for a lot of these world generation schemes with an approach to landscape generation that borrows heavily from the same family of algorithms used to produce plasma textures. This can be extended to any occasion where a map of random but natural looking values are needed.

Getting ready

This example is focused purely on the generation of height map data, and as such does not cover any display-related code. It is also written with the HeightMap class described in the *Importing and displaying 3D isometric maps* recipe of this chapter, but should work equally well with any 2D array of floating point values.

How to do it...

1. Extend the existing HeightMap class to include a method to test and retrieve a height for a given position in a single call:

```
public bool TryGetHeight(int x, int y, out float height)
{
    return heightByPosition.TryGetValue(
new Point(x, y),
out height);
}
```

2. Add a new `GenerateHeightMap` method to your game class as follows:

```
private HeightMap GenerateHeightMap()
{
```

3. Define the dimensions and a new instance of the terrain data container:

```
var width = 100;
var depth = 100;
var heightMap = new HeightMap() {
  Width = width, Depth = depth };
```

4. Create a new instance of a random number generator for later use:

```
var random = new Random();
```

5. Add a new queue to hold an area of the landscape pending generation:

```
var queue = new Queue<Rectangle>();
queue.Enqueue(new Rectangle(0, 0, width, depth));
```

6. Iterate through each pending area of landscape generation as follows:

```
while (queue.Count > 0)
{
    var area = queue.Dequeue();
```

7. Retrieve the height at each one of the area's corners and keep a count of any corners that don't have a height generated yet:

```
float existingHeightTally = 0;
var existingHeightCount = 0;

float leftTopHeight = RetrieveOrTally(
    heightMap, area.Left, area.Top,
    ref existingHeightTally, ref existingHeightCount);

float rightTopHeight = RetrieveOrTally(
    heightMap, area.Right, area.Top,
    ref existingHeightTally, ref existingHeightCount);

float rightBottomHeight = RetrieveOrTally(
    heightMap, area.Right, area.Bottom,
    ref existingHeightTally, ref existingHeightCount);

float leftBottomHeight = RetrieveOrTally(
    heightMap, area.Left, area.Bottom,
    ref existingHeightTally, ref existingHeightCount);
```

8. Calculate the average height of the corners as a basis for determining the height of any new points on the map:

```
float averageExistingHeight = 0;
if (existingHeightCount != 0)
{
    averageExistingHeight = existingHeightTally / (float)
existingHeightCount;
}
```

9. For any area corners that aren't known, populate the map with new heights:

```
if (!heightMap.TryGetHeight(area.Left, area.Top, out
leftTopHeight))
{
    leftTopHeight = averageExistingHeight;
    heightMap[area.Left, area.Top] = leftTopHeight;
}

if (!heightMap.TryGetHeight(area.Right, area.Top, out
rightTopHeight))
{
    rightTopHeight = averageExistingHeight;
    heightMap[area.Right, area.Top] = rightTopHeight;
}

if (!heightMap.TryGetHeight(area.Right, area.Bottom, out
rightBottomHeight))
{
    rightBottomHeight = averageExistingHeight;
    heightMap[area.Right, area.Bottom] = rightBottomHeight;
}

if (!heightMap.TryGetHeight(area.Left, area.Bottom, out
leftBottomHeight))
{
    leftBottomHeight = averageExistingHeight;
    heightMap[area.Left, area.Bottom] = leftBottomHeight;
}
```

10. If the area being generated isn't actually large enough to have anything but the existing corner elements, then skip immediately to the next pending area:

```
if (area.Width <= 2 && area.Height <= 2)
{
    continue;
}
```

11. Determine the middle of the area and generate a new height that is the average of the corners that surround it, plus a random amount which is in proportion to how far away the corners are:

```
var midpoint = new Point(
    area.X + (area.Width / 2),
    area.Y + (area.Height / 2));

var midPointHeight = (
    (leftTopHeight + rightTopHeight +
        rightBottomHeight + leftBottomHeight) / 4f) +
            +(NewRandomOffset(random) * (float)Math.Sqrt(area.
Width * area.Height) * 0.05f);
heightMap[midpoint.X, midpoint.Y] = midPointHeight;
```

12. Split the area up into four approximately equal quadrants:

```
var topLeftArea = new Rectangle(
    area.Left, area.Top,
    midpoint.X - area.Left + 1, midpoint.Y - area.Top + 1);
var topRightArea = new Rectangle(
    midpoint.X, area.Top,
    area.Right - midpoint.X, midpoint.Y - area.Top + 1);
var bottomRightArea = new Rectangle(
    midpoint.X, midpoint.Y,
    area.Right - midpoint.X, area.Top + area.Height -
    midpoint.Y);
var bottomLeftArea = new Rectangle(
    area.Left, midpoint.Y,
    midpoint.X - area.Left + 1, area.Top + area.Height -
    midpoint.Y);
```

13. Add the quadrants to the processing queue as follows:

```
queue.Enqueue(topLeftArea);
queue.Enqueue(topRightArea);
queue.Enqueue(bottomRightArea);
queue.Enqueue(bottomLeftArea);
```

14. Close the loop and return the results of the generation:

```
}
return heightMap;
```

15. Add a new method to your game class to track the heights (or lack thereof) from the map:

```
private static float RetrieveOrTally(
    HeightMap heightMap, int x, int y,
    ref float existingHeightTally,
    ref int existingHeightCount)
{
    float height;
    if (heightMap.TryGetHeight(x, y, out height))
    {
        existingHeightTally += height;
        existingHeightCount++;
    }
    return height;
}
```

16. Complete the class by adding a helper method to generate new heights between -0.25 and 0.25:

```
private float NewRandomOffset(Random random)
{
    return (0.5f * (float)random.NextDouble()) - 0.25f;
}
```

How it works...

This method of generation is based on the concepts of recursion, and that the likelihood of two pieces of land being of a similar height is directly proportional to how close they are to each other.

We recursively divide up the land-to-be into smaller squares by determining the height of each part by the average of its neighbors plus a random amount which is influenced by how far away the neighboring heights are.

There's more...

To increase the realism of the terrain being generated, you may wish to add some processing steps that replicate the sorts of changes that happen in real-world terrain generation.

For example, to replicate the wearing motion of the sea, you may wish to apply a smoothing function to any areas that are likely to be covered by water.

Likewise, you may find that selecting random areas and rotating them slightly gives an effect not entirely dissimilar to tectonic shifting and collision.

Once you've generated a height map for the terrain, the very same technique can be reused to populate what sits upon the terrain. Imagine generating secondary maps where each value on the map determines the probability of a tree appearing, a virtual villager living there, or how much gold is buried beneath the ground.

Creating block worlds within the Reach profile

With the popularity of the game **Minecraft** a wave of games pursuing a similar type of block-based imagery have followed.

Presented here is a suitable starting point for creating tracts of block-based geometry utilizing the mesh creation classes discussed in *Chapter 3, Procedural Modeling*.

It also highlights one possible method of incorporating sprite sheets into your game.

Getting ready

We're going to need a sprite sheet image containing all of the textures intended for use on the blocks, along with a text file providing the mapping details for each texture.

For example, here is a sprite sheet:

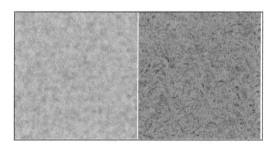

Along with the contents of the associated text file that are as follows:

```
Grass = 0 0 128 128
Ground = 129 0 128 128
```

An online search for *XNA sprite sheet packers* should hopefully reveal a few, including my favorite at the time of writing produced by **Nick Gravelyn** available at http://spritesheetpacker.codeplex.com

This example also makes use of the GeometricBuffer classes listed in the recipes of *Chapter 3, Procedural Modeling*, although any 3D mesh builder process could be substituted.

How to do it...

1. Start by adding a new **Content Pipeline Extension** project to the solution. This is to hold the two classes used to parse the sprite sheet mapping details.

2. Next, add the sprite sheet texture, the sprite sheet map text file, and a project reference to the previously added project.

3. After a compile, set the **Content Importer** and **Content Processor** properties of the sprite sheet map text file to the corresponding pipeline extension classes `SpriteMapImporter` and `SpriteMapProcessor`.

4. Within the game project, add an `enum` to define what sort of blocks you want in the game:

```
enum BlockMaterial
{
    Ground,
    Grass
}
```

5. Add a class to build the blocks as follows:

```
class BlocksDisplayFactory
{
```

6. Begin a new `Create()` method:

```
public static BlocksDisplay Create(
        float size,
        GraphicsDevice graphicsDevice,
        Dictionary<Vector3, BlockMaterial> materialByPosition,
        Dictionary<string, Rectangle> materialsMap,
        int materialTextureWidth, int materialTextureHeight)
    {
```

7. Create a new instance of a Geometric Buffer factory to help with constructing the blocks:

```
var factory = new
VertexPositionNormalTextureGeometricBufferFactory();
        var halfSize = size / 2f;
```

8. Iterate through each block position and the associated material:

```
foreach (var positionMaterialPair in materialByPosition)
{
    var position = positionMaterialPair.Key;
    var scaledPosition = position * size;
    var materialName = positionMaterialPair.Value.ToString();
    var map = materialsMap[materialName];
```

9. Calculate the texture coordinates for the given material on the sprite sheet:

```
var textureTop = ((float)map.Top) /
                    ((float)materialTextureHeight);
var textureBottom = ((float)map.Bottom) /
                    ((float)materialTextureHeight);
var textureLeft = ((float)map.Left) /
                    ((float)materialTextureWidth);
var textureRight = ((float)map.Right) /
                    ((float)materialTextureWidth);

var textureTopLeft = new Vector2(textureLeft, textureTop);
var textureTopRight = new Vector2(textureRight, textureTop);
var textureBottomRight = new Vector2(textureRight,
                            textureBottom);
var textureBottomLeft = new Vector2(textureLeft,
                            textureBottom);
```

10. Calculate the coordinates of the vertices for the block:

```
var leftForwardUp = (Vector3.Left + Vector3.Forward +
                    Vector3.Up) * halfSize;
var leftBackwardUp = (Vector3.Left + Vector3.Backward +
                    Vector3.Up) * halfSize;
var leftForwardDown = (Vector3.Left + Vector3.Forward +
                    Vector3.Down) * halfSize;
var leftBackwardDown = (Vector3.Left + Vector3.Backward +
                    Vector3.Down) * halfSize;
var rightForwardUp = (Vector3.Right + Vector3.Forward +
                    Vector3.Up) * halfSize;
var rightBackwardUp = (Vector3.Right + Vector3.Backward +
                    Vector3.Up) * halfSize;
var rightForwardDown = (Vector3.Right + Vector3.Forward +
                    Vector3.Down) * halfSize;
var rightBackwardDown = (Vector3.Right + Vector3.Backward +
                    Vector3.Down) * halfSize;
```

11. Add a pane to the top of the block only if there's not going to be another block sitting on top of it:

```
var adjacentPositionUp = position + Vector3.Up;
if (!materialByPosition.ContainsKey(adjacentPositionUp))
{
    factory.AddPane(
                    leftForwardUp + scaledPosition,
                    textureTopLeft,
                    rightForwardUp + scaledPosition,
```

```
                    textureTopRight,
                    rightBackwardUp + scaledPosition,
                    textureBottomRight,
                    leftBackwardUp + scaledPosition,
                    textureBottomLeft);
    }
```

12. Add a bottom pane if there's nothing directly underneath:

```
var adjacentPositionDown = position + Vector3.Down;
if (!materialByPosition.ContainsKey(adjacentPositionDown))
{
    factory.AddPane(
                    rightForwardDown + scaledPosition,
                    textureTopLeft,
                    leftForwardDown + scaledPosition,
                    textureTopRight,
                    leftBackwardDown + scaledPosition,
                    textureBottomRight,
                    rightBackwardDown + scaledPosition,
                textureBottomLeft);
}
```

13. Perform adjacency checks in front and behind the cube, only adding panes if nothing is found:

```
var adjacentPositionBackward = position + Vector3.Backward;
if (!materialByPosition.ContainsKey(adjacentPositionBackward))
{
    factory.AddPane(
                    leftBackwardUp + scaledPosition,
                    textureTopLeft,
                    rightBackwardUp + scaledPosition,
                    textureTopRight,
                    rightBackwardDown + scaledPosition,
                    textureBottomRight,
                    leftBackwardDown + scaledPosition,
                    textureBottomLeft);
}

var adjacentPositionForward = position + Vector3.Forward;
if (!materialByPosition.ContainsKey(adjacentPositionForward))
{
    factory.AddPane(
                    rightForwardUp + scaledPosition,
                    textureTopLeft,
```

```
                    leftForwardUp + scaledPosition,
                    textureTopRight,
                    leftForwardDown + scaledPosition,
                    textureBottomRight,
                    rightForwardDown + scaledPosition,
                    textureBottomLeft);
}
```

14. Complete the cube by performing adjacency checks and an optional pane addition for the left and right sides of the cube:

```
var adjacentPositionLeft = position + Vector3.Left;
if (!materialByPosition.ContainsKey(adjacentPositionLeft))
{
    factory.AddPane(
                    leftForwardUp + scaledPosition,
                    textureTopLeft,
                    leftBackwardUp + scaledPosition,
                    textureTopRight,
                    leftBackwardDown + scaledPosition,
                    textureBottomRight,
                    leftForwardDown + scaledPosition,
                    textureBottomLeft);
}

var adjacentPositionRight = position + Vector3.Right;
if (!materialByPosition.ContainsKey(adjacentPositionRight))
{
    factory.AddPane(
                    rightBackwardUp + scaledPosition,
                    textureTopLeft,
                    rightForwardUp + scaledPosition,
                    textureTopRight,
                    rightForwardDown + scaledPosition,
                    textureBottomLeft,
                    rightBackwardDown + scaledPosition,
                    textureBottomRight);
}
```

15. End the loop, generate the buffer, and return a brand new blocks mesh:

```
        }

        var buffer = factory.Create(graphicsDevice, false);
        return new BlocksDisplay(buffer);
    }
}
```

16. Add another class to display the blocks:

```
class BlocksDisplay
{
    private GeometricBuffer<VertexPositionNormalTexture> buffer;

    public BlocksDisplay(GeometricBuffer<VertexPositionNormalTextu
re> buffer)
    {
        this.buffer = buffer;
    }

    public void Draw(BasicEffect blockEffect)
    {
        buffer.Draw(blockEffect);
    }
}
```

17. Within our game class, we can now construct and draw a series of blocks:

```
BlocksDisplay blocksDisplay;
BasicEffect blockEffect;
Texture2D materials;

protected override void LoadContent()
{
    materials = Content.Load<Texture2D>("Materials");
    var materialsMap = Content.Load<Dictionary<string,
Rectangle>>("MaterialsMap");

    blockEffect = new BasicEffect(GraphicsDevice)
    {
        View = Matrix.CreateLookAt(
            (Vector3.Forward * 2) + Vector3.Up,
            Vector3.Zero,
            Vector3.Up),
        Projection = Matrix.CreatePerspectiveFieldOfView(
            MathHelper.ToRadians(60f),
            GraphicsDevice.Viewport.AspectRatio,
            0.01f, 2000f),
        Texture = materials,
        TextureEnabled = true
    };
    blockEffect.EnableDefaultLighting();

    var materialByPosition = new Dictionary<Vector3,
```

```
                                          BlockMaterial>();
            materialByPosition.Add(new Vector3(0, 0, 0),
                              BlockMaterial.Ground);
            materialByPosition.Add(new Vector3(1, 0, 0),
                              BlockMaterial.Grass);
            materialByPosition.Add(new Vector3(0, 1, 0),
                              BlockMaterial.Grass);

            blocksDisplay = BlocksDisplayFactory.Create(
                0.5f,
                GraphicsDevice,
                materialByPosition,
                materialsMap,
                materials.Width, materials.Height);
        }

        protected override void Draw(GameTime gameTime)
        {
            GraphicsDevice.Clear(Color.CornflowerBlue);

            blockEffect.World = Matrix.CreateRotationY(35);
            blocksDisplay.Draw(blockEffect);

            base.Draw(gameTime);
        }
```

How it works...

The heart of the example in this recipe lies in the `Create()` method of the `BlockDisplayFactory` class. This is where we set about the task of creating each block, face by face, beginning with the selection of the appropriate texture for a block of the given material.

Taking the name of the material, a look-up is made into the sprite sheet map dictionary for the coordinates of the corresponding texture, and a conversion is made from the absolute pixel coordinates supplied by the sprite sheet map file into the float values from 0 to 1 that the graphics infrastructure prefers.

Next, we calculated the eight vertices that form the edges of each block, and start building each face of the cube depending on whether it's likely to be obscured by a neighboring cube or not.

Performance is achieved through bundling the vertex, index, and transformation information into one large package so the GPU has all of the information it requires to draw all of the blocks without needing to engage in a series of communications with the CPU for the details of each block.

There's more...

The example provided is fine for a small to medium sized portion of virtual landscape, but will quickly overrun the vertex buffer size limits of any but the most expensive graphics cards in use by gamers.

To overcome this limitation, and allow for larger game worlds, consider splitting the landscape up into smaller chunks, rendering each chunk into its own set of vertex/index buffers, and only loading and rendering them when required.

Textures

Another opportunity to expand this example is use of textures.

We kept it simple and repeated the same texture across all faces of a given cube, but there's nothing stopping us from applying a different texture to each face and thereby allowing for blocks to have a distinct top and bottom.

Despite the fact that block worlds are unlikely to be confused with photorealism, it can be useful to apply techniques such as ambient occlusion to significantly increase the aesthetic qualities of a game.

Ambient occlusion, within the world of computer graphics, refers to the act of manipulation of lighting and shadows to approximate the way non-reflective surfaces radiate light. For example, if a red ball is placed on a white surface in a brightly-lit room, the surface closest to the ball will commonly appear pink.

For games running under the HiDef profile, a technique such as **Screen Space Ambient Occlusion (SSAO)** can be a relatively cheap way to achieve such effects.

Taking advantage of the inbuilt `DualTexture` effect and applying a secondary layer of shadow textures can be an effective way to simulate ambient occlusion in games running within the Reach profile.

Creating block worlds within the HiDef profile

Block worlds tend to consist of a small number of unique elements repeated heavily.

The ability to use custom shaders within the HiDef profile means we're able to harness the dedicated support of the underlying hardware for this sort of scenario and enjoy the possibility of dramatically improved rendering performance.

Microsoft has very nicely provided a working example of how to achieve hardware instancing via a custom shader. There's a fair amount of code included that's not directly applicable to our needs so we'll be utilizing the custom shader from their sample as a starter and then focusing in on just the C# code required for a game.

Getting ready

This example relies on the same sprite sheet files as the *Creating block worlds within the Reach Profile* example in this chapter, so it's assumed that the sprite sheet texture, texture map, and pipeline extension files have already been included in our game by this point.

How to do it...

1. Start by adding a new effect file called `InstancedModel.fx` to the content project.

2. Into the new effect file, add the input parameters which will dictate where objects and the light source will be situated:

```
float4x4 World;
float4x4 View;
float4x4 Projection;


float3 LightDirection = normalize(float3(-1, -1, -1));
float3 DiffuseLight = 1.25;
float3 AmbientLight = 0.25;


texture Texture;

sampler Sampler = sampler_state
{
    Texture = (Texture);
};
```

3. Add the definitions of the data structures used to pass information between the vertex and pixel shader within the effect as follows:

```
struct VertexShaderInput
{
    float4 Position : POSITION0;
    float3 Normal : NORMAL0;
    float2 TextureCoordinate : TEXCOORD0;
};


struct VertexShaderOutput
{
    float4 Position : POSITION0;
    float4 Color : COLOR0;
    float2 TextureCoordinate : TEXCOORD0;
};
```

4. Define the vertex shader:

```
VertexShaderOutput VertexShaderCommon(VertexShaderInput input,
float4x4 instanceTransform)
{
    VertexShaderOutput output;

    float4 worldPosition = mul(input.Position, instanceTransform);
    float4 viewPosition = mul(worldPosition, View);
    output.Position = mul(viewPosition, Projection);

    float3 worldNormal = mul(input.Normal, instanceTransform);

    float diffuseAmount = max(-dot(worldNormal, LightDirection),
0);

    float3 lightingResult = saturate(diffuseAmount * DiffuseLight
+ AmbientLight);

    output.Color = float4(lightingResult, 1);

    output.TextureCoordinate = input.TextureCoordinate;

    return output;
}

VertexShaderOutput HardwareInstancingVertexShader(VertexShaderInp
ut input,
```

```
                                                          float4x4
instanceTransform : BLENDWEIGHT)
{
    return VertexShaderCommon(input, mul(World,
transpose(instanceTransform)));
}
```

5. Define the pixel shader:

```
float4 PixelShaderFunction(VertexShaderOutput input) : COLOR0
{
    return tex2D(Sampler, input.TextureCoordinate) * input.Color;
}
```

6. To complete the shader definition file add the technique definition that will describe which vertex and pixel shader should be used in the effect:

```
technique HardwareInstancing
{
    pass Pass1
    {
        VertexShader = compile vs_3_0
                             HardwareInstancingVertexShader();
        PixelShader = compile ps_3_0 PixelShaderFunction();
    }
}
```

7. Now add a helper class to our game project to help organize the rendering calls correctly:

```
class InstanceDisplay<VertexType> where VertexType : struct
{
    public List<Matrix> Instances = new List<Matrix>();
    private static VertexDeclaration instanceVertexDeclaration =
new VertexDeclaration
    (
        new VertexElement(0, VertexElementFormat.Vector4,
                    VertexElementUsage.BlendWeight, 0),
        new VertexElement(16, VertexElementFormat.Vector4,
                    VertexElementUsage.BlendWeight, 1),
        new VertexElement(32, VertexElementFormat.Vector4,
                    VertexElementUsage.BlendWeight, 2),
        new VertexElement(48, VertexElementFormat.Vector4,
                    VertexElementUsage.BlendWeight, 3)
    );

    private DynamicVertexBuffer instanceVertexBuffer;
```

```csharp
private Matrix[] instanceTransforms;


public void Draw(Effect effect,
                GeometricBuffer<VertexType> buffer)
{
    var graphicsDevice = effect.GraphicsDevice;
    graphicsDevice.BlendState = BlendState.Opaque;
    graphicsDevice.DepthStencilState =
            DepthStencilState.Default;

    Array.Resize(ref instanceTransforms, Instances.Count);

    for (int i = 0; i < Instances.Count; i++)
    {
        instanceTransforms[i] = Instances[i];
    }

    if ((instanceVertexBuffer == null) ||
        (instanceTransforms.Length >
            instanceVertexBuffer.VertexCount))
    {
        if (instanceVertexBuffer != null)
            instanceVertexBuffer.Dispose();

        instanceVertexBuffer = new DynamicVertexBuffer(
                            graphicsDevice,
                            instanceVertexDeclaration,

                            instanceTransforms.Length,

                            BufferUsage.WriteOnly);
    }

    instanceVertexBuffer.SetData(
            instanceTransforms,
            0,
            instanceTransforms.Length,
            SetDataOptions.Discard);


    graphicsDevice.SetVertexBuffers(
                new VertexBufferBinding(
                        buffer.VertexBuffer, 0, 0),
```

```
                    new VertexBufferBinding(
                            instanceVertexBuffer, 0, 1)
                );
            graphicsDevice.Indices = buffer.IndexBuffer;

            for (int i = 0; i < instanceTransforms.Length; i++)
            {
                foreach (EffectPass pass in
                            effect.CurrentTechnique.Passes)
                {
                    pass.Apply();

                    graphicsDevice.DrawInstancedPrimitives(
                        PrimitiveType.TriangleList, 0, 0,

                        buffer.VerticesCount, 0,

                        buffer.PrimitiveCount,
                        instanceTransforms.Length);
                }
            }
        }
    }
```

8. Then in your game class code, create both a new instance of the instancing effect and the terrain:

```
Effect effect;
BlocksDisplay grassBlocks;
BlocksDisplay groundBlocks;

protected override void LoadContent()
{
    var materials = Content.Load<Texture2D>("Materials");
    var materialsMap = Content.Load
        <Dictionary<string, Rectangle>>("MaterialsMap");

    effect = Content.Load<Effect>("InstancedModel");

    effect.CurrentTechnique = effect.Techniques["HardwareInstanci
ng"];

    effect.Parameters["World"].SetValue(Matrix.
CreateTranslation(Vector3.Zero));
```

```
    effect.Parameters["View"].SetValue(
        Matrix.CreateLookAt(
            (Vector3.Backward * 4) + (Vector3.Left * 2) +
(Vector3.Up * 3),
            Vector3.Zero,
            Vector3.Up));

    effect.Parameters["Projection"].SetValue(
        Matrix.CreatePerspectiveFieldOfView(
            MathHelper.ToRadians(60f),
            GraphicsDevice.Viewport.AspectRatio,
            0.01f, 2000f));


    effect.Parameters["Texture"].SetValue(materials);


    grassBlocks = BlocksDisplayFactory.Create(
        1f,
        GraphicsDevice,
        BlockMaterial.Grass,
        materialsMap,
        materials.Width, materials.Height);

    grassBlocks.Instances.Add(
        Matrix.CreateTranslation(new Vector3(1,0,0)));
    grassBlocks.Instances.Add(
            Matrix.CreateTranslation(new Vector3(0,1,0)));


    groundBlocks = BlocksDisplayFactory.Create(
        1f,
        GraphicsDevice,
        BlockMaterial.Ground,
        materialsMap,
        materials.Width, materials.Height);

    groundBlocks.Instances.Add(
        Matrix.CreateTranslation(new Vector3(0,0,0)));

}
```

9. The first few lines in the constructor of the `BlocksDisplayFactory` need to be altered so that they take the material name as a parameter and calculate the associated texture coordinates correctly:

```
public static BlocksDisplay Create(
        float size,
        GraphicsDevice graphicsDevice,
        BlockMaterial material,
        Dictionary<string, Rectangle> materialsMap,
        int materialTextureWidth, int materialTextureHeight)
    {
        var factory = new
VertexPositionNormalTextureGeometricBufferFactory();
        var halfSize = size / 2f;

        var map = materialsMap[material.ToString()];

        var textureTop = ((float)map.Top) /
            ((float)materialTextureHeight);
        var textureBottom = ((float)map.Bottom) /
            ((float)materialTextureHeight);
        var textureLeft = ((float)map.Left) /
            ((float)materialTextureWidth);
        var textureRight = ((float)map.Right) /
            ((float)materialTextureWidth);
```

10. Finish with drawing the terrain using the following effect:

```
protected override void Draw(GameTime gameTime)
{
    GraphicsDevice.Clear(Color.CornflowerBlue);

    grassBlocks.Draw(effect);
    groundBlocks.Draw(effect);

    base.Draw(gameTime);
}
```

How it works...

Unlike the Reach example where each block was represented by a unique set of vertices and indices, hardware instancing allows us to take one of each type of block as a virtual paintbrush, painting copies of a block quickly and efficiently across the scene.

Peeking into the `Draw()` method of the `InstanceDisplay` class reveals how we achieve this from C# code.

In addition to the normal vertex buffer, we create and manage a second buffer to hold the transformation for each instance of a block we wish to render.

The call to `SetVertexBuffers()` includes both buffers so they can be passed to, and utilized by, the shader.

Inspecting the `HardwareInstancingVertexShader()` method within the shader file shows how the world space transformation is performed against the second buffer on the GPU instead of the CPU, thereby leading to the performance gain.

There's more...

In the example given, we had a different set of vertex, index, and instance streams for each type of block.

This can create less than optimal communications between the CPU and GPU during rendering, so consider merging streams in your games if the number of streams starts to grow significantly.

3
Procedural Modeling

In this chapter we will cover:

- ► Modeling triangles
- ► Modeling discs
- ► Modeling spheres
- ► Modeling tori
- ► Modeling trees

Introduction

It's probably an indicator of how deep the roots of software development run in me, that every time I create a 3D model in a modeling package, my brain almost immediately starts wandering off into the possibilities of wondering what recreating it programmatically would have offered me instead.

Instead of needing to implement some weird rigging or slicing regime to facilitate customization in my models with a 3D modeling package, I can do the customizations "on the fly" within my code, as needed. Need those wheels a little larger on later levels? How about a longer blade on that sword? With code, all of these customizations feel a lot more natural to me as they reside "just next to" the gaming logic that feeds them.

This, of course, is not the most pragmatic view to hold in the time-pressure-sensitive world of game construction. For most projects it tends to be a mix of models created in 3D modeling packages and models created via code. Sometimes the path of least effort (and pain) is one way, and sometimes it's the other.

In this chapter we'll be investigating how to, in situations where doing it programmatically is the pragmatic thing to do, create meshes in code.

Modeling triangles

XNA comes with a number of classes to help deal with the construction and use of vertex arrays, but it can sometimes be beneficial to build our own, so we can customize things according to what we need.

In this recipe, we'll be creating what I've called a **Geometry Buffer**, and a corresponding factory to help with their construction. Geometry Buffers are really just a container for the vertex and index buffers used in communication with the GPU. They can be thought of as a simplified substitute for XNA's `Model` and `Mesh` classes.

Getting ready

In order to draw a Geometric Buffer onscreen, an instance of a `BasicEffect` will be required. Although texture coordinate handling has been included, using `BasicEffect` without textures should work just as well.

How to do it...

To create a disc programmatically:

1. Create a new `GeometricBuffer` class to manage the vertex and index buffers, and add the start of a constructor to populate the various instance-level variables:

```
public class GeometricBuffer<VertexType> : IDisposable where
VertexType : struct
{
    private VertexBuffer vertexBuffer;
    private IndexBuffer indexBuffer;
    private int primitiveCount;
    private int verticesCount;
    public VertexType[] VertexArray;

    public GeometricBuffer(
        VertexBuffer vertexBuffer,
        int verticesCount,
        IndexBuffer indexBuffer,
        int primitiveCount,
        VertexType[] vertexArray)
    {
        this.vertexBuffer = vertexBuffer;
        this.indexBuffer = indexBuffer;
        this.primitiveCount = primitiveCount;
        this.verticesCount = verticesCount;
        this.VertexArray = vertexArray;
```

2. Complete the constructor by adding a condition to detect when the vertex buffers may lose their content and need to be repopulated:

```
if (this.vertexBuffer is DynamicVertexBuffer)
{
    ((DynamicVertexBuffer)this.vertexBuffer).ContentLost
+=
new EventHandler<EventArgs>(GeometricBuffer_ContentLost);
}
}
```

3. Provide the ability to repopulate the vertex buffer with the latest data both "manually" from parent code, or internally in the case of dynamic vertex buffer loss:

```
void GeometricBuffer_ContentLost(
        object sender, EventArgs e)
{
    UpdateVertices();
}

public void UpdateVertices()
{
    vertexBuffer.SetData<VertexType>(VertexArray);
}
```

4. Complete the class with logic to correctly clean up any dependant data that implements the IDisposable pattern upon disposal:

```
~GeometricBuffer()
{
    Dispose(false);
}

public void Dispose()
{
    Dispose(true);
    GC.SuppressFinalize(this);
}

protected virtual void Dispose(bool disposing)
{
    if (disposing)
    {
        if (vertexBuffer != null)
        {
            vertexBuffer.Dispose();
        }
```

```
                    if (indexBuffer != null)
                    {
                        indexBuffer.Dispose();
                    }
                }
            }
        }
```

5. Add some properties to expose some common options such as **culling** and **wireframe display**:

```
public bool IsTextureTransparent = false;
public bool IsAdditive = false;
public bool AntiAliasTexture = true;

bool rasterizerIsDirty = true;

bool wireFrame = false;

public bool Wireframe
{
    get
    {
        return wireFrame;
    }
    set
    {
        if (wireFrame == value)
        {
            return;
        }
        wireFrame = value;
        rasterizerIsDirty = true;
    }
}

bool cull = true;

public bool Cull
{
    get
    {
        return cull;
    }
```

```
    set
    {
        if (cull == value)
        {
            return;
        }
        cull = value;
        rasterizerIsDirty = true;
    }
}
```

6. Create the start of the `Draw()` method to render the buffers to the screen:

```
public void Draw(Effect effect)
{
    var graphicsDevice = effect.GraphicsDevice;
```

7. Set the `BlendState` and `DepthStencilState` of the `GraphicsDevice` to the appropriate settings, depending on whether the model being rendered should lighten the existing scene or contain transparent elements:

```
if (IsAdditive)
{
    graphicsDevice.BlendState = BlendState.Additive;
    graphicsDevice.DepthStencilState =
                        DepthStencilState.DepthRead;
}
else if (IsTextureTransparent)
{
    graphicsDevice.BlendState = BlendState.AlphaBlend;
    graphicsDevice.DepthStencilState =
                        DepthStencilState.DepthRead;
}
else
{
    graphicsDevice.BlendState = BlendState.Opaque;
    graphicsDevice.DepthStencilState =
                        DepthStencilState.Default;
}
```

8. Update the `SamplerState` to indicate whether the textures should be anti-aliased:

```
if (AntiAliasTexture)
{
    graphicsDevice.SamplerStates[0] =
                        SamplerState.LinearWrap;
}
```

```
        else
        {
            graphicsDevice.SamplerStates[0] =
                                SamplerState.PointWrap;
        }
```

9. Create a new `RasterizerState` if the existing one doesn't reflect the current settings:

```
if (rasterizerIsDirty)
{
    graphicsDevice.RasterizerState = new RasterizerState()
    {
        CullMode = cull ?
    CullMode.CullCounterClockwiseFace : CullMode.None,
        FillMode = wireFrame ?
    FillMode.WireFrame : FillMode.Solid
    };
    rasterizerIsDirty = false;
}
```

10. Complete the method by setting the vertex and index buffers of the effect, and send the request to render the mesh via the current technique:

```
graphicsDevice.SetVertexBuffer(vertexBuffer);
graphicsDevice.Indices = indexBuffer;

foreach (EffectPass effectPass in
            effect.CurrentTechnique.Passes)
{
    effectPass.Apply();
    graphicsDevice.DrawIndexedPrimitives(
        PrimitiveType.TriangleList,
        0, 0, verticesCount, 0, primitiveCount);
}
}
```

11. Create a new `GeometricBufferFactory` class to help with the creation of Geometric Buffers:

```
public class GeometricBufferFactory<VertexType> where VertexType :
struct
{
    protected List<VertexType> vertices =
        new List<VertexType>();

}
```

12. Insert the `CalculateGeometry()` method to create an optimized vertex and index buffer from a given set of vertices:

```
private void CalculateGeometry(out List<VertexType>
uniqueVertices, out List<ushort> indices)
{
    uniqueVertices = new List<VertexType>();
    indices = new List<ushort>();
    var indexByVertex = new Dictionary<VertexType, ushort>();
    var indexTally = (ushort)0;
    foreach (var vertex in vertices)
    {
        ushort index;
        if (!indexByVertex.TryGetValue(vertex, out index))
        {
            index = indexTally;
            indexByVertex[vertex] = index;
            uniqueVertices.Add(vertex);
            indexTally++;
        }
        indices.Add(index);
    }
}
```

13. Add the `Create()` method to transform a set of vertices and indices into a `GeometricBuffer`:

```
public GeometricBuffer<VertexType> Create(
        GraphicsDevice device,
        bool dynamicVertexBuffer = false)
{
    List<VertexType> uniqueVertices;
    List<ushort> indices;

    CalculateGeometry(out uniqueVertices, out indices);
    var vertexArray = uniqueVertices.ToArray();
    var indexArray = indices.ToArray();
    VertexBuffer vertexBuffer;

    if (dynamicVertexBuffer)
    {
        vertexBuffer = new DynamicVertexBuffer(device,
                            typeof(VertexType),
                            uniqueVertices.Count,
                            BufferUsage.WriteOnly);
    }
```

```
        else
        {
            vertexBuffer = new VertexBuffer(device,
                                    typeof(VertexType),
                                    uniqueVertices.Count,
                                    BufferUsage.None);
        }

        vertexBuffer.SetData(vertexArray);

        var indexBuffer = new IndexBuffer(
                                device,
                                typeof(ushort),
                                indices.Count,
                                BufferUsage.None);

        indexBuffer.SetData(indexArray);

        return new GeometricBuffer<VertexType>(
            vertexBuffer,
            uniqueVertices.Count,
            indexBuffer,
            indices.Count / 3,
            vertexArray);
    }
```

14. Create a new `VertexPositionNormalTextureGeometricBufferFactory` class, which will contain functionality specifically for helping to create vertex buffers of type `VertexPositionNormalTexture`:

```
public class VertexPositionNormalTextureGeometricBufferFactory :
GeometricBufferFactory<VertexPositionNormalTexture>
{
}
```

15. Add some helper methods to aid in the creation of triangles:

```
public void AddTriangle(
    Vector3 vertex1,
    Vector2 textureCoordinate1,
    Vector3 normal1,
    Vector3 vertex2,
    Vector2 textureCoordinate2,
    Vector3 normal2,
    Vector3 vertex3,
    Vector2 textureCoordinate3,
```

```
        Vector3 normal3)
{

    AddTriangle(
        new VertexPositionNormalTexture(
                vertex1, normal1, textureCoordinate1),
        new VertexPositionNormalTexture(
                vertex2, normal2, textureCoordinate2),
        new VertexPositionNormalTexture(
                vertex3, normal3, textureCoordinate3));
}

public void AddTriangle(
    Vector3 vertex1, Vector2 textureCoordinate1,
    Vector3 vertex2, Vector2 textureCoordinate2,
    Vector3 vertex3, Vector2 textureCoordinate3)
{
    var planar1 = vertex2 - vertex1;
    var planar2 = vertex1 - vertex3;
    var normal = Vector3.Normalize(
                    Vector3.Cross(planar1, planar2));

    AddTriangle(
        new VertexPositionNormalTexture(
                vertex1, normal, textureCoordinate1),
        new VertexPositionNormalTexture(
                vertex2, normal, textureCoordinate2),
        new VertexPositionNormalTexture(
                vertex3, normal, textureCoordinate3));
}

public void AddTriangle(
    VertexPositionNormalTexture vertex1,
    VertexPositionNormalTexture vertex2,
    VertexPositionNormalTexture vertex3)
{
    vertices.Add(vertex1);
    vertices.Add(vertex2);
    vertices.Add(vertex3);
}
```

16. Complete the class by adding some more helper methods for adding two triangles (also known as a **pane**) at a time:

```
public void AddPane(
    Vector3 topLeft,
    Vector2 topLeftTexture,
    Vector3 topLeftNormal,
    Vector3 topRight,
    Vector2 topRightTexture,
    Vector3 topRightNormal,
    Vector3 bottomRight,
    Vector2 bottomRightTexture,
    Vector3 bottomRightNormal,
    Vector3 bottomLeft,
    Vector2 bottomLeftTexture,
    Vector3 bottomLeftNormal
    )
{

    AddTriangle(
        topLeft, topLeftTexture, topLeftNormal,
        topRight, topRightTexture, topRightNormal,
        bottomRight, bottomRightTexture, bottomRightNormal);
    AddTriangle(
        bottomRight, bottomRightTexture, bottomRightNormal,
        bottomLeft, bottomLeftTexture, bottomLeftNormal,
        topLeft, topLeftTexture, topLeftNormal);
}


    public void AddPane(
    Vector3 topLeft, Vector2 topLeftTexture,
    Vector3 topRight, Vector2 topRightTexture,
    Vector3 bottomRight, Vector2 bottomRightTexture,
    Vector3 bottomLeft, Vector2 bottomLeftTexture
    )
{

    AddTriangle(
        topLeft, topLeftTexture,
        topRight, topRightTexture,
        bottomRight, bottomRightTexture);
    AddTriangle(
        bottomRight, bottomRightTexture,
        bottomLeft, bottomLeftTexture,
        topLeft, topLeftTexture);
}
```

17. In your game code, usually within the `LoadContent()` method, you can now create and use a new `GeometricBuffer` in a manner similar to adding triangles and panes to the factory and creating a buffer from them. Here's an example of creating a buffer, and the effect used to render it:

```
var factory = new
VertexPositionNormalTextureGeometricBufferFactory();

factory.AddTriangle(
    new Vector3(-1, 0, 0), new Vector2(0, 0),
    new Vector3(0.5f, 1, 0), new Vector2(0.5f, 0),
    new Vector3(1, 0, 0), new Vector2(1, 1));

buffer = factory.Create(GraphicsDevice);

effect = new BasicEffect(GraphicsDevice)
{
    PreferPerPixelLighting = true,
    DiffuseColor = Color.Red.ToVector3(),
    World = Matrix.CreateTranslation(Vector3.Zero)
};
effect.EnableDefaultLighting();
```

18. Finally, draw the newly created buffer in your game's `Draw()` method as shown here:

```
buffer.Draw(effect);
```

How it works...

The `GeometricBuffer` class is responsible for acting as a container for the vertex and index buffers used in communication with the GPU, and the all-important instructions to request the GPU to render them.

If we examine the `Draw()` method of the `GeometricBuffer` class, we can see how various effects such as transparency, wireframes, and culling can be enabled via the use of classes such as `RasterizerState` and `SamplerState`.

Sitting on top of the `GeometricBuffer` is the `GeometricBufferFactory`. The factory's purpose is to remove most of the low-level pain involved with creating the vertex and index buffers that get fed into a `GeometricBuffer`.

Instead of trying to organize it so that vertices and indices are added in a sequence without repeats by the wider game code, the `GeometricBufferFactory` waits until all the vertices have been collected, scans the vertex collection for duplicates, and generates an optimized vertex and index buffer from there.

There's more...

The vertex array type used in the example is of type `VertexPositionNormalTexture`. Given that the `GeometricBuffer` and `GeometericBufferFactory` classes takes the vertex array type as a generic type parameter, it's relatively easy to create alternatives to the `VertexPositionNormalTextureGeometryBufferFactory` helper class for other vertex types.

Dynamic vertex buffers

One of the parameters of the `GeometricBuffer` class is the optional `dynamicVertexBuffer` flag, which is useful when you need to make adjustments to the vertices once the `GeometryBuffer` has been instantiated.

To update vertices, alter the vertex information found in the `vertexArray` of `GeometryBuffer` and then call `Update()`.

Should you need to tackle some more complex situations involving updating index buffers dynamically a similar option is available for index buffers, but it has not been included here as it's essentially the same style of update as the dynamic vertex buffer.

See also

A large proportion of the examples found throughout this book were written with the `GeometricBuffer` classes in mind, so don't be afraid to grab one of the other examples and see what interesting effects can be achieved.

Modeling discs

Discs don't represent a particularly difficult exercise in terms of modeling programmatically, but if you're anything like me, you'll find yourself using them as a basis for a whole lot of other, more complex modeling tasks such as **cylinders**, **tori**, and **hemispheres**. Therefore, having a reference implementation at hand can be useful.

Getting ready

This example was written with the `GeometricBuffer` class, and related ones demonstrated in the *Modeling triangles* recipe covered earlier in this chapter, but is equally applicable for use with any mesh building framework.

How to do it...

To create a disc programmatically:

1. Create some variables to hold the specifications of the disc:

```
var discRadius = 0.5f;
var segmentCount = 16;
var segmentAngle = MathHelper.TwoPi / (float)segmentCount;
```

2. Create a loop to iterate around the circle in steps equaling one segment:

```
for (var segmentIndex = 0f; segmentIndex < segmentCount;
segmentIndex++)
{
```

3. Calculate the left- and right-hand side vertices of each triangle:

```
var leftAngle = (segmentIndex +1f) * segmentAngle;
var leftPoint = Vector3.Transform(Vector3.Zero,
                Matrix.CreateTranslation(
                    Vector3.Up * discRadius) *
                Matrix.CreateRotationZ(leftAngle));
var leftTexturePoint = Vector2.Transform(Vector2.Zero,
                Matrix.CreateTranslation(
                    Vector3.UnitY * -0.5f) *
                Matrix.CreateRotationZ(-leftAngle));

var rightAngle = segmentIndex * segmentAngle;
var rightPoint = Vector3.Transform(Vector3.Zero,
                Matrix.CreateTranslation(
                    Vector3.Up * discRadius) *
                Matrix.CreateRotationZ(rightAngle));
var rightTexturePoint = Vector2.Transform(Vector2.Zero,
                Matrix.CreateTranslation(
                    Vector3.UnitY * -0.5f) *
                Matrix.CreateRotationZ(-rightAngle));
```

4. Add the triangle to the mesh and complete the loop:

```
factory.AddTriangle(
    leftPoint, leftTexturePoint,
    rightPoint, rightTexturePoint,
    Vector3.Zero, new Vector2(0, 0));
}
```

How it works...

We start by dividing up a hypothetical circle into slices and then iterate through each slice.

The two outer vertices of each slice are calculated along with the respective texture coordinates and fed into the `AddTriangle()` method of the mesh factory.

The *Modeling tori* recipe in this chapter is, at its heart, really just a modification of the disc example. Instead of adding a triangle at each point along the circumference, we calculate the edge of another smaller, perpendicular disc, and connect it up to the other smaller discs with panes.

See also...

> ▸ *Modeling tori* recipe in this chapter.

Modeling spheres

Spheres tend to a be a popular choice for modeling programmatically, as they tend to appear in a lot of places in games where manually modeling them would be an exercise in tedium, such as particle effects and planetary bodies.

The method demonstrated here is a personal favorite as it generates a mesh similar in look to a **geodesic dome**, with its surface being built up from a collection of identical triangles woven together as opposed to other techniques, which can result in squashed and irregular triangles near the poles or equator.

Getting ready

This example was written with the `GeometricBuffer` classes in mind, presented in the *Modeling triangles* recipe, but should be equally applicable with any mesh building framework.

How to do it...

To create a disc programmatically:

1. Add a new `Triangle` class to hold the triangle data during the sphere creation calculations:

```
class Triangle
{
    public Vector3 One;
    public Vector3 Two;
    public Vector3 Three;
```

```
    public Vector2 OneTexture;
    public Vector2 TwoTexture;
    public Vector2 ThreeTexture;

    public Vector3 OneNormal;
    public Vector3 TwoNormal;
    public Vector3 ThreeNormal;
}
```

2. Start a `CreateTriangles()` method to create the initial seeding diamond shaped structure by setting out the significant coordinates:

```
private static List<Triangle> CreateTriangles()
{
    var radius = Vector3.Up;

    var top = radius;

    var middleOne = Vector3.Transform(top,
                    Matrix.CreateRotationX(MathHelper.
ToRadians(90)) *
                                                Matrix.
CreateRotationY(MathHelper.ToRadians(45)));

    var middleTwo = Vector3.Transform(top, Matrix.
CreateRotationX(MathHelper.ToRadians(90)) *
                                                Matrix.
CreateRotationY(MathHelper.ToRadians(45 + 90)));

    var middleThree = Vector3.Transform(top, Matrix.
CreateRotationX(MathHelper.ToRadians(90)) *
                                                Matrix.
CreateRotationY(MathHelper.ToRadians(45 + 180)));

    var middleFour = Vector3.Transform(top, Matrix.
CreateRotationX(MathHelper.ToRadians(90)) *
                                                Matrix.
CreateRotationY(MathHelper.ToRadians(45 + 270)));

    var bottom = Vector3.Transform(top, Matrix.
CreateRotationX(MathHelper.ToRadians(180)));

    var topTexture = new Vector2(0.5f, 0.5f);
    var middleOneTexture = new Vector2(1, 1);
    var middleTwoTexture = new Vector2(1, 0);
    var middleThreeTexture = new Vector2(0, 0);
```

```
        var middleFourTexture = new Vector2(0, 1);
        var bottomTexture = new Vector2(0.5f, 0.5f);
```

3. Add triangles to form the top of the initial diamond shape:

```
        var triangles = new List<Triangle>();

        triangles.Add(new Triangle()
        {
            One = middleOne,
            OneTexture = middleOneTexture,
            OneNormal = middleOne,

            Two = top,
            TwoTexture = topTexture,
            TwoNormal = top,

            Three = middleTwo,
            ThreeTexture = middleTwoTexture,
            ThreeNormal = middleTwo,
        });

        triangles.Add(new Triangle()
        {
            One = middleTwo,
            OneTexture = middleTwoTexture,
            OneNormal = middleTwo,

            Two = top,
            TwoTexture = topTexture,
            TwoNormal = top,

            Three = middleThree,
            ThreeTexture = middleThreeTexture,
            ThreeNormal = middleThree
        });

        triangles.Add(new Triangle()
        {
            One = middleThree,
            OneTexture = middleThreeTexture,
            OneNormal = middleThree,

            Two = top,
            TwoTexture = topTexture,
```

```
    TwoNormal = top,

    Three = middleFour,
    ThreeTexture = middleFourTexure,
    ThreeNormal = middleFour
});

triangles.Add(new Triangle()
{
    One = middleFour,
    OneTexture = middleFourTexture,
    OneNormal = middleFour,

    Two = top,
    TwoTexture = topTexture,
    TwoNormal = top,

    Three = middleOne,
    ThreeTexture = middleOneTexture,
    ThreeNormal = middleOne
});
```

4. Complete the method by adding the triangles for the bottom half of the initial diamond shape:

```
triangles.Add(new Triangle()
{
    One = middleOne,
    OneTexture = middleOneTexture,
    OneNormal = middleOne,

    Two = middleTwo,
    TwoTexture = middleTwoTexture,
    TwoNormal = middleTwo,

    Three = bottom,
    ThreeTexture = bottomTexture,
    ThreeNormal = bottom
});

triangles.Add(new Triangle()
{
    One = middleTwo,
    OneTexture = middleTwoTexture,
    OneNormal = middleTwo,
```

```
        Two = middleThree,
        TwoTexture = middleThreeTexture,
        TwoNormal = middleThree,

        Three = bottom,
        ThreeTexture = bottomTexture,
        ThreeNormal = bottom
    });

    triangles.Add(new Triangle()
    {
        One = middleThree,
        OneTexture = middleThreeTexture,
        OneNormal = middleThree,

        Two = middleFour,
        TwoTexture = middleFourTexure,
        TwoNormal = middleFour,

        Three = bottom,
        ThreeTexture = bottomTexture,
        ThreeNormal = bottom
    });

    triangles.Add(new Triangle()
    {
        One = middleFour,
        OneTexture = middleFourTexure,
        OneNormal = middleFour,

        Two = middleOne,
        TwoTexture = middleOneTexture,
        TwoNormal = middleOne,

        Three = bottom,
        ThreeTexture = bottomTexture,
        ThreeNormal = bottom
    });
    return triangles;
}
```

5. Add a `CreateSphere()` method that will take the seeding diamond shape and proceed to split and re-split it a number of times until the sphere shape is suitably smooth:

```
private void CreateSphere()
{
    var trianglesOne = CreateTriangles();
    var trianglesTwo = new List<Triangle>();

    var radius = Vector3.Distance(Vector3.Zero, trianglesOne[0].
One);

    foreach (var triangle in trianglesOne)
    {
        Split(triangle, trianglesTwo, radius);
    }

    for (var splitCount = 0; splitCount < 2; splitCount++)
    {
        trianglesOne.Clear();
        foreach (var triangle in trianglesTwo)
        {
            Split(triangle, trianglesOne, radius);
        }

        trianglesTwo.Clear();
        foreach (var triangle in trianglesOne)
        {
            Split(triangle, trianglesTwo, radius);
        }
    }


    var factory = new
VertexPositionNormalTextureGeometricBufferFactory();

    foreach (var triangle in trianglesTwo)
    {
        factory.AddTriangle(
            triangle.One,
            triangle.OneTexture,
            triangle.OneNormal,
            triangle.Two,
            triangle.TwoTexture,
            triangle.TwoNormal,
```

```
                    triangle.Three,
                    triangle.ThreeTexture,
                    triangle.ThreeNormal);
        }


        buffer = factory.Create(GraphicsDevice);
    }
```

6. Finish with the addition of the `SplitTriangle()` method, which when provided with a triangle, will split it into a convex collection of four smaller triangles:

```
private static void Split(
    Triangle triangle,
    List<Triangle> triangles,
    float radius)
{
    var midPointOne = (triangle.One + triangle.Two) / 2;
    var midPointOneTexture = (triangle.OneTexture +
                                triangle.TwoTexture) / 2;
    var midPointOneNormal = Vector3.Normalize(midPointOne);
    midPointOne = midPointOneNormal * radius;

    var midPointTwo = (triangle.Two + triangle.Three) / 2;
    var midPointTwoTexture = (triangle.TwoTexture +
                                triangle.ThreeTexture) / 2;
    var midPointTwoNormal = Vector3.Normalize(midPointTwo);
    midPointTwo = midPointTwoNormal * radius;

    var midPointThree = (triangle.Three + triangle.One) / 2;
    var midPointThreeTexture = (triangle.ThreeTexture +
                                triangle.OneTexture) / 2;
    var midPointThreeNormal =
                        Vector3.Normalize(midPointThree);
    midPointThree = midPointThreeNormal * radius;

    triangles.Add(new Triangle()
    {
        One = triangle.One,
        OneTexture = triangle.OneTexture,
        OneNormal = triangle.OneNormal,

        Two = midPointOne,
        TwoTexture = midPointOneTexture,
        TwoNormal = midPointOneNormal,
```

```
        Three = midPointThree,
        ThreeTexture = midPointThreeTexture,
        ThreeNormal = midPointThreeNormal
    });

    triangles.Add(new Triangle()
    {
        One = midPointOne,
        OneTexture = midPointOneTexture,
        OneNormal = midPointOneNormal,

        Two = triangle.Two,
        TwoTexture = triangle.TwoTexture,
        TwoNormal = triangle.TwoNormal,

        Three = midPointTwo,
        ThreeTexture = midPointTwoTexture,
        ThreeNormal = midPointTwoNormal
    });

    triangles.Add(new Triangle()
    {
        One = midPointTwo,
        OneTexture = midPointTwoTexture,
        OneNormal = midPointTwoNormal,

        Two = triangle.Three,
        TwoTexture = triangle.ThreeTexture,
        TwoNormal = triangle.ThreeNormal,

        Three = midPointThree,
        ThreeTexture = midPointThreeTexture,
        ThreeNormal = midPointThreeNormal
    });

    triangles.Add(new Triangle()
    {
        One = midPointOne,
        OneTexture = midPointOneTexture,
        OneNormal = midPointOneNormal,

        Two = midPointTwo,
        TwoTexture = midPointTwoTexture,
```

```
            TwoNormal = midPointTwoNormal,

            Three = midPointThree,
            ThreeTexture = midPointThreeTexture,
            ThreeNormal = midPointThreeNormal
        });
    }
```

How it works...

A 3-dimensional diamond shape is constructed in the `CreateTriangles()` method.

Within the `Split()` method, each face of the diamond shape is subdivided into four smaller triangles, "pushed outwards", and repeated by the `CreateSphere()` method until a spherical shape is achieved.

There's more...

With a different choice of base shape, and an alternate choice of where the subdivided triangles are "pushed" to, it's possible to utilize this technique to generate practically any shape that can be described by parametric equation, including **super-ellipsoids** and **Kline bottles**.

The many ways and uses of dividing and combining of triangles could probably fill a book on its own. If you're looking to create landscapes that can automatically scale their mesh complexity depending on how close they are to the viewer's position (commonly referred to as **Level Of Detail** or **L.O.D.**), then it may also be worth looking at the terrain generation recipes in *Chapter 2, Building 2D and 3D Terrain*.

See also

> ▸ *Importing and displaying 3D isometric maps* recipe in *Chapter 2, Building 2D and 3D Terrain*

Modeling tori

I suspect the world of gaming would be a far poorer place without the wonders of doughnuts, inner tubes and other torus related items, so it seems only right to explore how to construct one programmatically.

Getting ready

As with all the other recipes in this chapter, a mesh building framework, such as the one described in the *Modeling triangles* recipe of this chapter, is required. However, the choice isn't limited to any particular one.

How to do it...

To create a disc programmatically:

1. Create an instance of a `VertexPositionTextureNormalGeometricBufferFactory`:

   ```
   var factory = new
   VertexPositionNormalTextureGeometricBufferFactory();
   ```

2. Define the dimensions of the torus you wish to create:

   ```
   var majorRadius = 2f;
   var majorSegmentCount = 16;
   var majorSegmentAngle = MathHelper.TwoPi /
                           (float)majorSegmentCount;
   var majorTranslation = Matrix.CreateTranslation(
                           Vector3.UnitX * majorRadius);

   var minorRadius = 0.5f;
   var minorSegmentCount = 16;
   var minorSegmentAngle = MathHelper.TwoPi /
                           (float)minorSegmentCount;
   ```

3. Create the start of a loop that will iterate around the point of the circumference of the major radius:

   ```
   for (var majorAngle = 0f;
        majorAngle < MathHelper.TwoPi;
        majorAngle += majorSegmentAngle)
   {
   ```

4. Add the calculations to determine the edges of each major segment:

   ```
   var nextMajorAngle = majorAngle + majorSegmentAngle;

   var left = majorTranslation *
              Matrix.CreateRotationY(majorAngle);
   var leftTexture = Vector2.UnitX *
                     (majorAngle / MathHelper.TwoPi);
   var centreLeft = Vector3.Transform(Vector3.Zero, left);
   ```

```
var right = majorTranslation *
            Matrix.CreateRotationY(nextMajorAngle);
var rightTexture = Vector2.UnitX *
                   (nextMajorAngle / MathHelper.TwoPi);
var centreRight = Vector3.Transform(Vector3.Zero, right);
```

5. Create the start of an inner loop that will iterate around the points of the circumference of the minor radius:

```
for (var minorAngle = 0f;
     minorAngle < MathHelper.TwoPi;
     minorAngle += minorSegmentAngle)
{
```

6. Add the calculations to determine the edges of the minor segment:

```
var nextMinorAngle = minorAngle + minorSegmentAngle;

var top = (Vector3.UnitX * minorRadius *
           (float)Math.Sin(minorAngle)) +
          (Vector3.UnitY * minorRadius *
           (float)Math.Cos(minorAngle));
var topTexture = Vector2.UnitY *
                 (float)(minorAngle / MathHelper.TwoPi);

var bottom = (Vector3.UnitX * minorRadius *
              (float)Math.Sin(nextMinorAngle)) +
             (Vector3.UnitY * minorRadius *
              (float)Math.Cos(nextMinorAngle));
var bottomTexture = Vector2.UnitY *
                    (float)(nextMinorAngle / MathHelper.TwoPi);

var topLeft = Vector3.Transform(top, left);
var topLeftTexture = topTexture + leftTexture;
var topLeftNormal = Vector3.Normalize(topLeft - centreLeft);

var topRight = Vector3.Transform(top, right);
var topRightTexture = topTexture + rightTexture;
var topRightNormal = Vector3.Normalize(
                         topRight - centreRight);

var bottomRight = Vector3.Transform(bottom, right);
var bottomRightTexture = bottomTexture + rightTexture;
var bottomRightNormal = Vector3.Normalize(
                         bottomRight - centreRight);
```

```
    var bottomLeft = Vector3.Transform(bottom, left);
    var bottomLeftTexture = bottomTexture + leftTexture;
    var bottomLeftNormal = Vector3.Normalize(
                        bottomLeft - centreLeft);
```

7. Finally, add the newly calculated pane to the factory, close out the two loops, and create a new `GeometricBuffer` of the shape:

```
            factory.AddPane(
                topLeft, topLeftTexture, topLeftNormal,
                topRight, topRightTexture, topRightNormal,
                bottomRight,
                bottomRightTexture,
                bottomRightNormal,
                bottomLeft,
                bottomLeftTexture,
                bottomLeftNormal);
        }
    }
    buffer = factory.Create(GraphicsDevice);
```

How it works...

I find the trick to modeling tori is not to get overwhelmed by the math of it.

We start with plotting out a series of points on the circumference of the major circle. At each one of these points we plot out the circumference of a perpendicular facing the smaller circle.

All we need to do then is join up the points between each one of the smaller circles with panes and, viola! We have a torus.

See also

▶   *Modeling spheres* recipe in this chapter.

Modeling trees

Generating realistic gaming environments is one of the greatest challenges facing modern gaming. The addition of natural looking foliage can go a long way towards transforming a scene from a sterile, virtual-looking environment, into a lush, natural-looking one. Being able to do it programmatically can mean the difference between a minute's or month's worth of work for game artists.

In this example, we'll be exploring one of the ways that trees and smaller plants can be generated, and hopefully provide a starting point for you to explore some of the many variations on the technique to provide your own unique looking flora.

Getting ready

This example relies upon the `GeometricBuffer` classes described in the *Modeling triangles* recipe within this chapter. It can be substituted with any other mesh building process of your choice though.

How to do it...

To create a disc programmatically:

1. Create a new `TreeLimb` class to hold the logic surrounding the creation of an individual tree limb, along with a constructor, to take some required dimensions:

```
class TreeLimb
{

    public float TipSize { get; private set; }
    public float Length { get; private set; }
    public Matrix Rotation { get; private set; }
    public bool ConnectedToParent { get; private set; }
    public TreeLimb Parent { get; private set; }

    public TreeLimb(
        float tipSize,
        float length,
        Matrix rotation,
        bool connectedToParent = true,
        TreeLimb parent = null,
        float? baseSize = null,
        Vector3? baseLocation = null)
    {
        TipSize = tipSize;
        Length = length;
        Rotation = rotation;
        ConnectedToParent = connectedToParent;
        this.baseSize = baseSize;
        this.baseLocation = baseLocation;
        Parent = parent;
    }

}
```

2. Next, add a calculated property to determine the radius of the base of a limb, which can be specified explicitly or taken to be the tip size of the preceding limb. As `BaseSize` is only valid in limbs that are root branches, it's defined as being `null`:

```
private float? baseSize;
public float BaseSize
{
    get
    {
        if (!baseSize.HasValue)
        {
            if (Parent != null)
            {
                return Parent.TipSize;
            }
            throw new Exception("No base size specified");
        }

        return baseSize.Value;
    }
}
```

3. In a similar fashion as the previously defined property, add two more calculated properties for the location of the limb's base and the translation matrix to move it to that location. As with `BaseSize`, the `BaseLocation` and `BaseTranslation` property backing variables are only valid for root limbs, they're defined as `null`:

```
private Vector3? baseLocation;
public Vector3 BaseLocation
{
    get
    {
        if (Parent != null)
        {
            return Parent.TipLocation;
        }
        if (!baseLocation.HasValue)
        {
            throw new Exception("No base location specified");
        }
        return baseLocation.Value;
    }
}

private Matrix? baseTranslation;
public Matrix BaseTranslation
```

```
{
    get
    {
        if (!baseTranslation.HasValue)
        {
            baseTranslation =
                Matrix.CreateTranslation(BaseLocation);
        }

        return baseTranslation.Value;
    }
}
```

4. Next, add the corresponding calculation to determine where the tip of the limb is:

```
private Vector3? tipLocation;
public Vector3 TipLocation
{
    get
    {
        if (!tipLocation.HasValue)
        {
            tipLocation = Vector3.Transform(
                Vector3.Zero,
                Matrix.CreateTranslation(Vector3.Up * Length) *
                    Rotation *
                    BaseTranslation);
        }
        return tipLocation.Value;
    }
}
```

5. Create a property to calculate the points around the base circumference of the limb that will go on to form the lower vertices of the generated mesh:

```
private const int limbSegmentCount = 6;
private const float limbSegmentAngle =
                        (float)(MathHelper.TwoPi /
                        (float)limbSegmentCount);
private List<Vector3> basePoints;
public bool IsEnd;
public List<Vector3> BasePoints
{
    get
    {
        if (ConnectedToParent &&
```

```
            Parent != null)
        {
            return Parent.TipPoints;
        }

        if (basePoints != null)
        {
            return basePoints;
        }

        basePoints = new List<Vector3>();
        var baseWidthTranslation =
            Matrix.CreateTranslation(Vector3.UnitX * BaseSize);

        for (var angle = 0f;
            angle < MathHelper.TwoPi;
            angle += limbSegmentAngle)
        {

            var pointRotation = Matrix.CreateRotationY(angle);
            var basePoint = Vector3.Transform(Vector3.Zero,
                baseWidthTranslation * pointRotation *
                Rotation * BaseTranslation);

            basePoints.Add(basePoint);
        }

        return basePoints;
    }
}
```

6. Insert a similar point calculation property for the tip of the limb:

```
private List<Vector3> tipPoints;

public List<Vector3> TipPoints
{
    get
    {
        if (tipPoints != null)
        {
            return tipPoints;
        }

        tipPoints = new List<Vector3>();
```

```
        var tipWidthTranslation = Matrix.
CreateTranslation(Vector3.UnitX * TipSize);
        var tipTranslation = Matrix.CreateTranslation(Vector3.Up *
Length);

        for (var angle = 0f; angle < MathHelper.TwoPi; angle +=
limbSegmentAngle)
        {
            var pointRotation = Matrix.CreateRotationY(angle);
            var tipPoint = Vector3.Transform(Vector3.Zero,
                tipWidthTranslation * pointRotation *
                tipTranslation *
                Rotation * BaseTranslation);
            tipPoints.Add(tipPoint);
        }

        return tipPoints;
    }
}
```

7. To complete the class, add the method that will populate a factory with the polygons for the limb:

```
internal void Populate(VertexPositionNormalTextureGeometricBuffer
Factory factory)
{
    var lastPointIndex = TipPoints.Count - 1;

    for (var pointIndex = 0;
        pointIndex < TipPoints.Count;
        pointIndex++)
    {
        var topLeft = TipPoints[lastPointIndex];
        var topLeftNormal = Vector3.Normalize(
                topLeft - TipLocation);

        var topRight = TipPoints[pointIndex];
        var topRightNormal = Vector3.Normalize(
                topRight - TipLocation);

        var bottomRight = BasePoints[pointIndex];
        var bottomRightNormal = Vector3.Normalize(
                bottomRight - BaseLocation);

        var bottomLeft = BasePoints[lastPointIndex];
        var bottomLeftNormal = Vector3.Normalize(
                bottomLeft - BaseLocation);
```

```
factory.AddPane(
    topLeft, new Vector2(0, 0), topLeftNormal,
    topRight, new Vector2(1, 0), topRightNormal,
    bottomRight, new Vector2(1, 1), bottomRightNormal,
    bottomLeft, new Vector2(0, 1), bottomLeftNormal);

    lastPointIndex = pointIndex;
}
}
```

8. With the completion of the `TreeLimb` class comes the need for a class that knows how to put tree limbs together to form a tree. Create a new `TreeLimbFactory` class to hold this knowledge:

```
class TreeLimbFactory
{
```

9. Add some variables that describe how the tree limbs will change as the tree is built from the bottom to the top:

```
const float secondLimbThreshold = MathHelper.Pi / 6f;

const float childMaximumAngle = MathHelper.PiOver4;

const float childMinimumSizeDepreciationRate = 0.5f;
const float childMaximumSizeDepreciationRate = 0.7f;

const float childMinimumLengthDepreciationRate = 0.5f;
const float childMaximumLengthDepreciationRate = 0.9f;


const float disconnectedThreshold = MathHelper.Pi * 0.5f;
const float mainChildGeneratedThreshold =
            MathHelper.Pi * 0.2f;
```

10. Insert the method that, given an existing limb, will append new child limbs to it:

```
private static void AddLimbsTo(TreeLimb limb, List<TreeLimb>
limbs, Random random)
{
```

11. Add the following logic to determine when a given limb doesn't require any child limbs to be added:

```
if (limb.TipSize < 0.01f)
{
    limb.IsEnd = true;
    return;
}
```

12. Next, add the limb creation logic:

```
var mainChildGenerated = false;
var minimumChildCount = random.Next(1,3);
var childCount = 0;
var enoughChildren = false;

do {
    childCount++;
    var childTipSize = limb.TipSize *
        Next(
            random,
            childMinimumSizeDepreciationRate,
            childMaximumSizeDepreciationRate);
    var childLength = limb.Length *
        Next(
            random,
            childMinimumSizeDepreciationRate,
            childMaximumLengthDepreciationRate);

    var yaw = Next(random,
                -childMaximumAngle, childMaximumAngle);
    var pitch = Next(random,
                -childMaximumAngle, childMaximumAngle);
    var roll = Next(random,
                -childMaximumAngle, childMaximumAngle);

    var childRotation = Matrix.CreateFromYawPitchRoll(
                (float)yaw, (float)pitch, (float)roll);

    var connected = (Math.Abs(yaw) < disconnectedThreshold &&
                Math.Abs(pitch) < disconnectedThreshold &&
                Math.Abs(roll) < disconnectedThreshold);

    var childLimb = new TreeLimb(
        childTipSize,
        childLength,
        limb.Rotation * childRotation,
        connected, limb);
    limbs.Add(childLimb);
    AddLimbsTo(childLimb, limbs, random);

    mainChildGenerated = (
        Math.Abs(yaw) < mainChildGeneratedThreshold &&
        Math.Abs(pitch) < mainChildGeneratedThreshold &&
```

```
        Math.Abs(roll) < mainChildGeneratedThreshold);
    enoughChildren = childCount >= minimumChildCount;

} while (!enoughChildren || !mainChildGenerated);
```

13. Add a small helper method to generate a random float value within a given range for the benefit of the `AddLimbsTo()` method:

```
private static float Next(Random random, float minimum, float
maximum)
{
    return (float)((maximum - minimum) *
        random.NextDouble()) + minimum;
}
```

14. Complete the class with the `Create()` method that starts the recursive limb generation process:

```
public static List<TreeLimb> Create()
{
    var limbs = new List<TreeLimb>();
    Random random = new Random();

    var yaw = MathHelper.ToRadians(-5f + random.Next(10));
    var pitch = MathHelper.ToRadians(-5f + random.Next(10));
    var roll = MathHelper.ToRadians(-5f + random.Next(10));
    var trunk = new TreeLimb(
        0.25f,
        1f,
        Matrix.CreateFromYawPitchRoll(yaw, pitch, roll),
        false,
        null,
        0.4f,
        Vector3.Zero);
    limbs.Add(trunk);

    AddLimbsTo(trunk, limbs, random);

    return limbs;
}
```

15. To utilize the class in your game, add the following code to create a tree-shaped buffer:

```
var factory = new
VertexPositionNormalTextureGeometricBufferFactory();

var limbs = TreeLimbFactory.Create();
```

```
foreach (var limb in limbs)
{
    limb.Populate(factory);
}
buffer = factory.Create(GraphicsDevice);
```

How it works...

To construct a tree, we start by defining the bottom most section of the trunk in the `Create()` method. From there, we recursively add limbs until the tips of each child limb are sufficiently small enough to appear twig-shaped.

The `AddLimbsTo()` method is where the overall shape of the tree is determined through the generation of new limbs with aesthetically pleasing, albeit random, dimensions.

Each newly generated limb is measured against a set of criteria for a possible continuation of the existing trunk or branch. If a limb doesn't meet the criteria it is treated as a branch and more limbs are generated and added until at least one does.

There's more...

A tree without leaves may not be the look you're after in a game, so the next logical extension to this example is to add leaves.

If it's a tree that's going to be close to the player, then it may be worth utilizing a particle technique to display each leaf individually.

On the other hand, if the tree is at some distance from the player, or a non-photorealistic look is what you're after, modeling entire branches of leaves with large textured polygons is another approach that might be worth investigating.

4
Creating Water and Sky

In this chapter we will cover:

- ▶ Creating water within the HiDef profile
- ▶ Building skyboxes within the Reach profile
- ▶ Building skyboxes within the HiDef profile
- ▶ Cloud generation within the Reach profile

Introduction

Just like in a landscape painting, background elements such as sky, clouds, and water seem to add atmosphere and depth to a scene. They help to provide both visual complexity and a sense that your players are interacting with merely a portion of a much larger dynamic environment.

Water can be used to supply natural-looking barriers to players roaming, while a well lit sky can be amazingly effective at boosting what would otherwise appear to be a simplistic and unnatural scene into an artistic force of emotional impact.

Creating water within the HiDef profile

It goes without saying that in real life, water is everywhere! So it's not surprising how often the need to have it present in our games arises.

Similar to how the appearance of water can vary in real life, the techniques used to simulate the look of water in a game can vary quite widely, depending on the situation.

For example, a pool of water on the roadside might be achieved with a simple flat reflection, whereas a close-up inspection of water being poured from a jug into a glass might require a complex set of light and physics simulations running in the background.

In this section, we're going to aim for somewhere around a third of the way up the complexity scale. We'll use a method of drawing water that forms the basis of most of the water display techniques you'll see in 3D games these days, and should hopefully form a comfortable base for you to customize and advance upon in the future.

Getting ready

This recipe requires an image as a basis for the seemingly random ripples that appear on the water's surface. The more random and abstract, the better, but anything will suffice; from a picture of the neighborhood cat to something like the following texture:

How to do it...

To add water to your game:

1. Add a new **effect** file to your content project named `ShallowWater.fx`, and define the input matrices, vectors, and textures that will dictate the behavior of the water effect:

    ```
    float4x4 World;
    float4x4 View;
    float4x4 Projection;
    texture Reflection;
    float4x4 ReflectionView;
    texture Refraction;
    float3 CameraPosition;
    float3 LightDirection;
    float WaterAnimation;
    texture RandomMap;
    ```

2. Define the samplers for the reflected and refracted textures along with the one for the source of pseudo-randomness for the shaders:

```
sampler ReflectionSampler = sampler_state{
    Texture = <Reflection>;
    MinFilter = LINEAR;
    MagFilter = LINEAR;
    MipFilter = LINEAR;
    AddressU  = CLAMP;
    AddressV  = CLAMP;
};

sampler RefractionSampler = sampler_state{
    Texture = <Refraction>;
    MinFilter = LINEAR;
    MagFilter = LINEAR;
    MipFilter = LINEAR;
    AddressU  = CLAMP;
    AddressV  = CLAMP;
};

sampler RandomSampler = sampler_state{
    Texture = <RandomMap>;
    MinFilter = LINEAR;
    MagFilter = LINEAR;
    MipFilter = LINEAR;
    AddressU  = MIRROR;
    AddressV  = MIRROR;
};
```

3. Create the structures used to pass information to and from the shaders:

```
struct VertexShaderInput
{
    float4 Position : POSITION0;
};

struct VertexShaderOutput
{
    float4 Position : POSITION0;
    float4 Position3D : TEXCOORD1;
    float4 Texture : TEXCOORD2;
    float2 RandomSamplingPosition:  TEXCOORD3;
};
```

4. Add a new vertex shader to calculate the screen, world, texture, and reflected positions of each vertex:

```
VertexShaderOutput VertexShaderFunction(VertexShaderInput input)
{
    VertexShaderOutput output = (VertexShaderOutput)0;

    float4 worldPosition = mul(input.Position, World);
    float4 viewPosition = mul(worldPosition, View);
    output.Position = mul(viewPosition, Projection);
    output.Position3D = worldPosition;

    float4x4 reflectionViewProjection = mul(
                     ReflectionView, Projection);
    float4x4 worldReflectionViewPosition = mul(
                     World, reflectionViewProjection);
    output.Texture = mul(
            input.Position, worldReflectionViewPosition);
    output.RandomSamplingPosition =
            output.Position3D.xz / 10.0f;
    return output;
}
```

5. Begin a new pixel shader which will assemble and render the various textures into one cohesive water effect:

```
float4 PixelShaderFunction(VertexShaderOutput input) : COLOR0
{
```

6. Calculate the height of an imaginary wave at each point in the image so the amount of distortion to be applied to the reflected and refracted textures can be calculated more realistically:

```
float waveHeight = 0.025f;
float3 randomOne = (tex2D(
                RandomSampler,input.RandomSamplingPosition -
                WaterAnimation * 1.5)
                -0.5f) *2.0f;
float3 randomTwo = (tex2D(
                RandomSampler,input.RandomSamplingPosition +
                WaterAnimation)
                -0.5f) *2.0f;
float3 waveOffset;
waveOffset.y = waveHeight * 20.0f;
waveOffset.xz = ((randomOne + randomTwo) /2.0f) * waveHeight;
```

7. Determine the reflected color of the given point by a lookup of the associated texture color for a point offset by the amount of wave distortion:

```
float2 reflectedCoords;
reflectedCoords.x = input.Texture.x/input.Texture.w/2.0f +
                    0.5f;
reflectedCoords.y = input.Texture.y/input.Texture.w/2.0f +
                    0.5f;

float4 reflectiveColor = tex2D(ReflectionSampler,
                    reflectedCoords + waveOffset.xz);
```

8. Perform a calculation for the refracted color, similar to what was done for the reflected color:

```
float2 refractedCoords;
refractedCoords.x = input.Texture.x/input.Texture.w/2.0f +
                    0.5f;
refractedCoords.y = -input.Texture.y/input.Texture.w/2.0f +
                    0.5f;

float4 refractiveColor = tex2D(RefractionSampler,
                    refractedCoords + waveOffset.xz);
```

9. Add a small amount of additional color to the refracted color to roughly approximate any discoloration within the water itself:

```
float4 dullColor = float4(0.1f, 0.2f, 0.3f, 1.0f);
refractiveColor = lerp(refractiveColor, dullColor, 0.5f);
```

10. Using the difference in angle between the surface normal of the water at a particular point and the viewing position, calculate the ratio of how much refraction versus reflection is visible:

```
float3 eyeVector = normalize(CameraPosition -
                                input.Position3D);
float3 normalVector = normalize(waveOffset);
float fresnelTerm = dot(eyeVector, normalVector);

float4 combinedColor = lerp(reflectiveColor,
                            refractiveColor,
                            fresnelTerm);
```

11. Calculate the amount of specular highlight by determining the respective angles between the viewing position, the surface normal, and the direction of lighting:

```
float3 reflectionVector = -reflect(LightDirection,
                                normalVector);
float specular = dot(normalize(reflectionVector),
```

```
                          normalize(eyeVector));
     specular = pow(specular, 256);
```

12. Return the resulting color and complete the pixel shader definition:

```
     return combinedColor + specular;
     }
```

13. Specify a technique that indicates the use of the two newly-defined shaders:

```
     technique Technique1
     {
         pass Pass1
         {

             VertexShader = compile vs_2_0 VertexShaderFunction();
             PixelShader = compile ps_2_0 PixelShaderFunction();
         }
     }
```

14. Within your game's initialization code, create two new render targets along with an instance of the `ShallowWater` effect defined earlier:

```
     pp = GraphicsDevice.PresentationParameters;
     refractionTarget = new RenderTarget2D(
                     GraphicsDevice,
                     GraphicsDevice.Viewport.Width ,
                     GraphicsDevice.Viewport.Height,
                     false,
                     pp.BackBufferFormat,
                     pp.DepthStencilFormat);
     reflectionTarget = new RenderTarget2D(
                     GraphicsDevice,
                     GraphicsDevice.Viewport.Width,
                     GraphicsDevice.Viewport.Height,
                     false,
                     pp.BackBufferFormat,
                     pp.DepthStencilFormat);

     waterEffect = Content.Load<Effect>("ShallowWater");
     waterEffect.Parameters["Reflection"].SetValue(
                                     reflectionTarget);
     waterEffect.Parameters["Refraction"].SetValue(
                                     refractionTarget);
     waterEffect.Parameters["RandomMap"].SetValue(
                 content.Load<Texture2D>("Random"));
```

15. Create a plane from two triangles that the water effect will be painted onto:

```
var factory = new
VertexPositionNormalTextureGeometricBufferFactory();

var waterHeight = 0.75f;
var backwardLeft = Vector3.Up * waterHeight +
                    Vector3.Backward + Vector3.Left;
var backwardRight = Vector3.Up * waterHeight +
                    Vector3.Backward + Vector3.Right;
var forwardLeft = Vector3.Up * waterHeight +
                    Vector3.Forward + Vector3.Left;
var forwardRight = Vector3.Up * waterHeight +
                    Vector3.Forward + Vector3.Right;

var topLeft = new Vector2(0, 0);
var topRight = new Vector2(1, 0);
var bottomRight = new Vector2(1, 1);
var bottomLeft = new Vector2(0, 1);

factory.AddPane(
    forwardLeft, topLeft,
    forwardRight, topRight,
    backwardRight, bottomRight,
    backwardLeft, bottomLeft);

buffer = factory.Create(GraphicsDevice);
```

16. In the `Update()` method of your game, populate the inputs of the `ShallowWater` shader in a manner similar to the following:

```
waterEffect.Parameters["LightDirection"].SetValue(
        Vector3.Normalize(Vector3.Up + Vector3.Forward));
waterEffect.Parameters["View"].SetValue(cameraView);
waterEffect.Parameters["Projection"].SetValue(
        camera.Projection);
waterEffect.Parameters["ReflectionView"].SetValue(
        camera.View);
waterEffect.Parameters["CameraPosition"].SetValue(
        camera.Position);
waterEffect.Parameters["WaterAnimation"].SetValue(
    (float)gameTime.TotalGameTime.TotalSeconds / 50);
waterEffect.Parameters["World"].SetValue(
        Matrix.CreateTranslation(Vector3.Zero));
```

17. Calculate the reflected view by flipping the camera's position and angle to the other side of the water's surface. Here's an example of calculating a camera's view and the associated reflected view:

```
var cameraRotation = Matrix.CreateRotationX(cameraPitchAngle)
                        * Matrix.CreateRotationY(cameraYawAngle);

var rotationOffset = Vector3.Transform(
                        Vector3.Forward, cameraRotation);

var target = Position + rotationOffset;

var rotatedUp = Vector3.Transform(
                        Vector3.Up, cameraRotation);

View = Matrix.CreateLookAt(Position, target, rotatedUp);

float waterHeight = 0.75f;

var reflectedCameraPosition = Position;
reflectedCameraPosition.Y = -Position.Y + waterHeight * 2f;

var reflectedTarget = target;
reflectedTarget.Y = -target.Y + waterHeight * 2;

var cameraRight = Vector3.Transform(Vector3.Right,
                                    cameraRotation);
var inverseUp = Vector3.Cross(
                    cameraRight,
                    reflectedTarget - reflectedCameraPosition);

ReflectedView = Matrix.CreateLookAt(
                    reflectedCameraPosition,
                    reflectedTarget,
                    inverseUp);
```

18. Calculate a rough approximation of the refracted view by offsetting the angle and position of the camera slightly:

```
var refractedCameraRotation = Matrix.CreateRotationX(
                    cameraPitchAngle +
                    MathHelper.ToRadians(-2)) *
                    Matrix.CreateRotationY(cameraYawAngle);
var refractedPosition = Vector3.Transform(
                        Vector3.Backward,
                        refractedCameraRotation) +
```

```
                              target;

RefractedView = Matrix.CreateLookAt(
                    refractedPosition, target, rotatedUp);
```

19. Render the scene into the reflection render target from the perspective of the reflected view in the `Draw()` method of your game, using the previously defined reflected transformation:

```
graphicsDevice.SetRenderTarget(reflectionTarget);
sceneObject.Draw(world, ReflectedView, projection);
```

20. Render a refracted view of the scene into the refraction render target:

```
graphicsDevice.SetRenderTarget(refractionTarget);
sceneObject.Draw(world, RefractedView, projection);
```

21. Set the render target to `null`, and render the scene as normal to the screen:

```
graphicsDevice.SetRenderTarget(null);
sceneObject.Draw(world, View, projection);
```

22. Draw the water plane onto the screen using the water shader:

```
buffer.Draw(waterEffect);
```

How it works...

What may initially appear to be quite a complex effect is, in fact, a combination of six simpler elements: **reflection, refraction, tinting, Fresnel effect, surface distortion**, and **specular highlighting**. These are discussed here:

▸ **Reflection**: Reflection is achieved by rendering the scene from the perspective of a camera that is in a mirror position to the regular camera position under the water's surface, focused on the same point, as shown in the following illustration:

▶ **Refraction**: A very rough approximation of refraction can be achieved by rendering the scene from a position slightly forward of the regular camera position, as shown in the following illustration:

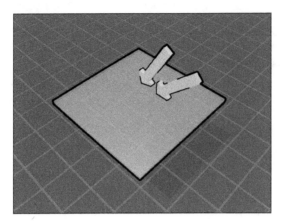

▶ **Tinting**: To aid in the illusion of either the depth or the chemical composition of the water, a small amount of tint is added, as shown in the following illustration:

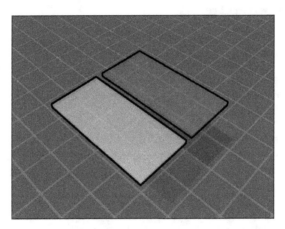

▶ **Fresnel effect**: Imagine yourself standing in the middle of a flat and straight stretch of highway, and in the distance you can see a small puddle of water. If you attempt to describe exactly what such a puddle of water would look like, there's a very good chance it would look like a mirror reflection of the sky.

Now imagine yourself standing over the puddle and looking straight down at it. Instead of seeing an almost perfect reflection of the sky, you can now see straight through to the road surface beneath, with only a small amount of reflection around the edges.

This effect, where the amount of reflection is relative to the position of the viewer in relation to the normal of the surface, is known as the Fresnel effect (pronounced "fra-nel" with a silent "s") and, while being quite subtle, can add a lot to the perceived realism of a watery or metallic scene, as shown in the following illustration:

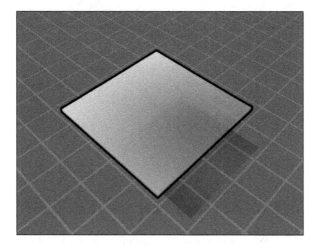

▸ **Surface distortion**: To produce the distortion effect commonly associated with waves in water, we could perform some complex calculations to trace the light path as it passes through the peaks and troughs of a virtual wave. It turns out though that a very simple distortion is enough to fool the human eye. We take multiple samples of the random texture and combine them together to produce a distortion map, indicating how far or close from a given pixel we should sample the underlying background texture, as shown in the following illustration:

▸ **Specular highlighting**: Finally, we have specular highlights which both simulate the reflective nature of water and help to reinforce the illusion that there are waves passing across the surface, as shown in the following illustration:

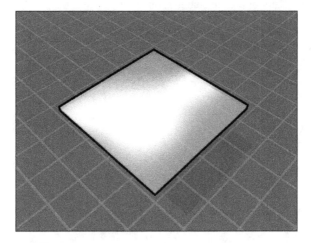

With all of these smaller effects mixed together, we find ourselves with a passable facsimile of water, as shown in the following screenshot:

There's more...

Even though the steps presented here will produce a reasonably realistic result, there are two edge cases that may undermine the effect and are worth taking note of.

The first is concerning structures or landscape that may obscure the bottom of the water container when you're rendering the refraction texture.

If a piece of the surrounding scenery does end up being captured in the reflection texture, then you'll end up with what appears to be a wavy underwater duplicate of the scenery.

The second edge case is almost identical with the accidental inclusion of surrounding scenery when capturing the reflection texture.

Accidentally capturing surrounding scenery sitting beneath the water line will result in a confusing "double reflection" artifact, which can seriously undermine the overall effect.

The approach to address both edge cases is that you should try only to capture the scenery elements that are on one side or the other of the water line, but _not both_.

This can usually be achieved through use of a relatively simple height threshold in your custom shaders for rendering scenery.

Shallow water

The pattern of light formed on elements below water is commonly referred to as **caustics**, and can really help to enhance the realism of the water effect.

Caustics can be achieved in a variety of ways from a simple set of overlapping textures to real-time ray tracing of light paths.

Deep water

In this example, the waves were small enough, they could therefore be faked through just the simulated side effects of a bumpy surface, such as distortions and specular highlights.

With larger sized waves, as one might find in the open ocean, these simulated side effects aren't going to be enough, and actual distortions of the surface are going to be required.

Building skyboxes within the Reach profile

What would a world, virtual or otherwise, be without a sky?

In this section, we'll be adding a sky to our scene with the rather simplistic method of wrapping the world in a box, and "painting" the inside of the box to make it look like the world around us, as demonstrated in the following screenshot:

Getting ready

This recipe requires a skybox texture, as shown in the following:

The exact orientation and position of the panels for each direction isn't important, although you will need to adjust the coordinates specified in step 4 of the following recipe to match your particular skybox texture.

How to do it...

To render a skybox within the Reach profile:

1. Add a collection of helper methods to convert the given corner of a texture coordinate measured in pixels into the ratio, from zero to one, that the graphics infrastructure prefers to deal with:

    ```
    private static Vector2 ScaledLeft(
        Rectangle portion, Rectangle whole)
    ```

```
{
    return Vector2.UnitX * portion.Left / whole.Width;
}

private static Vector2 ScaledRight(
    Rectangle portion, Rectangle whole)
{
    return Vector2.UnitX * portion.Right / whole.Width;
}

private static Vector2 ScaledTop(
    Rectangle portion, Rectangle whole)
{
    return Vector2.UnitY * portion.Top / whole.Width;
}

private static Vector2 ScaledBottom(
    Rectangle portion, Rectangle whole)
{
    return Vector2.UnitY * portion.Bottom / whole.Width;
}
```

2. Create a new instance of the `BasicEffect` class specifically for rendering of the sky, and load the sky texture into it:

```
effect = new BasicEffect(GraphicsDevice)
{
    Texture = Content.Load<Texture2D>("skybox"),
    TextureEnabled = true,
    EmissiveColor = Color.White.ToVector3()
};
```

3. Define the corners of the sky cube in 3D space for easy reference in the later construction:

```
var size = 200f;

var topForwardLeft = (Vector3.Up + Vector3.Forward +
                    Vector3.Left) * size;
var topForwardRight = (Vector3.Up + Vector3.Forward +
                    Vector3.Right) * size;
var topBackwardLeft = (Vector3.Up + Vector3.Backward +
                    Vector3.Left) * size;
var topBackwardRight = (Vector3.Up + Vector3.Backward +
                    Vector3.Right) * size;
var bottomForwardLeft = (Vector3.Down + Vector3.Forward +
```

```
                                Vector3.Left) * size;
var bottomForwardRight = (Vector3.Down + Vector3.Forward +
                         Vector3.Right) * size;
var bottomBackwardLeft = (Vector3.Down + Vector3.Backward +
                         Vector3.Left) * size;
var bottomBackwardRight = (Vector3.Down + Vector3.Backward +
                          Vector3.Right) * size;
```

4. Specify the dimensions and positions of each of the faces of the sky texture:

```
var textureArea = new Rectangle(0, 0,
                          effect.Texture.Width,
                          effect.Texture.Height);

var forwardArea = new Rectangle(0, 0, 255, 255);
var rightArea = new Rectangle(256, 0, 255, 255);
var backwardArea = new Rectangle(256 *2, 0, 255, 255);
var leftArea = new Rectangle(256 * 3, 0, 255, 255);
var bottomArea = new Rectangle(256 * 4, 0, 255, 255);
var topArea = new Rectangle(256 * 5, 0, 255, 255);
```

5. Construct the top face of the cube, making sure that it's defined so it's facing inwards, towards the game area:

```
var factory = new
    VertexPositionNormalTextureGeometricBufferFactory();

factory.AddPane(
    topForwardRight,
    ScaledBottom(topArea, textureArea) +
        ScaledRight(topArea, textureArea),
    topForwardLeft,
    ScaledBottom(topArea, textureArea) +
        ScaledLeft(topArea, textureArea),
    topBackwardLeft,
    ScaledTop(topArea, textureArea) +
        ScaledLeft(topArea, textureArea),
    topBackwardRight,
    ScaledTop(topArea, textureArea) +
        ScaledRight(topArea, textureArea));
```

6. Add the bottom, upward-facing pane:

```
factory.AddPane(
    bottomForwardLeft,
    ScaledBottom(bottomArea, textureArea) +
        ScaledRight(bottomArea, textureArea),
```

```
    bottomForwardRight,
    ScaledBottom(bottomArea, textureArea) +
        ScaledLeft(bottomArea, textureArea),
    bottomBackwardRight,
    ScaledTop(bottomArea, textureArea) +
        ScaledLeft(bottomArea, textureArea),
    bottomBackwardLeft,
    ScaledTop(bottomArea, textureArea) +
        ScaledRight(bottomArea, textureArea)
    );
```

7. Continue by defining the left- and right-hand side panes of the cube:

```
factory.AddPane(
    topBackwardLeft,
    ScaledTop(leftArea, textureArea) +
        ScaledLeft(leftArea, textureArea),
    topForwardLeft,
    ScaledTop(leftArea, textureArea) +
        ScaledRight(leftArea, textureArea),
    bottomForwardLeft,
    ScaledBottom(leftArea, textureArea) +
        ScaledRight(leftArea, textureArea),
    bottomBackwardLeft,
    ScaledBottom(leftArea, textureArea) +
        ScaledLeft(leftArea, textureArea)
    );

factory.AddPane(
    topForwardRight,
    ScaledTop(rightArea, textureArea) +
        ScaledLeft(rightArea, textureArea),
    topBackwardRight,
    ScaledTop(rightArea, textureArea) +
        ScaledRight(rightArea, textureArea),
    bottomBackwardRight,
    ScaledBottom(rightArea, textureArea) +
        ScaledRight(rightArea, textureArea),
    bottomForwardRight, ScaledBottom(rightArea, textureArea) +
        ScaledLeft(rightArea, textureArea)
    );
```

8. Complete the cube with the definition of the forward and backward panes:

```
factory.AddPane(
    topBackwardRight,
    ScaledTop(backwardArea, textureArea) +
        ScaledLeft(backwardArea, textureArea),
    topBackwardLeft,
    ScaledTop(backwardArea, textureArea) +
        ScaledRight(backwardArea, textureArea),
    bottomBackwardLeft,
    ScaledBottom(backwardArea, textureArea) +
        ScaledRight(backwardArea, textureArea),
    bottomBackwardRight,
        ScaledBottom(backwardArea, textureArea) +
        ScaledLeft(backwardArea, textureArea)
    );

factory.AddPane(
    topForwardLeft,
    ScaledTop(forwardArea, textureArea) +
        ScaledLeft(forwardArea, textureArea),
    topForwardRight,
    ScaledTop(forwardArea, textureArea) +
        ScaledRight(forwardArea, textureArea),
    bottomForwardRight,
    ScaledBottom(forwardArea, textureArea) +
        ScaledRight(forwardArea, textureArea),
    bottomForwardLeft,
    ScaledBottom(forwardArea, textureArea) +
        ScaledLeft(forwardArea, textureArea)
    );
```

9. In the `Draw()` method of your game, set the sky cube so that it remains at the same distance from the player's viewpoint throughout the game. For example:

```
effect.World = Matrix.CreateTranslation(camera.Position);
```

10. Render the sky cube using the previously defined `BasicEffect`:

```
buffer.Draw(effect);
```

How it works...

This effect is really just the act of sticking your player inside a giant box that has been painted a sky color on the inside, and its effectiveness comes down to two elements.

The first is how well your chosen sky texture seamlessly folds into a cube shape. As long as the cube is large enough, and the seam is aligned close enough, then the actual geometry of the cube will seemingly disappear into irrelevance as the open wonder of the pictured scene is revealed.

The second is ensuring the background remains as a distant piece of scenery. This is achieved in step 9 of this recipe, where the skybox is always kept centered over the camera.

Building skyboxes within the HiDef profile

As you progress into the more advanced 3D graphics techniques, you might find that you want to start applying special effects to your surrounding scenery. Even though the technique demonstrated in the earlier *Skyboxes within the Reach profile* recipe of this chapter certainly does what it is designed to do, it doesn't provide much help when writing shaders and effects to be applied over it.

What we need is a way to move from the simple, pre-textured polygon towards something where we have more direct control over the process via a shader. Luckily enough that's exactly what we'll be doing in this recipe.

Getting ready

This recipe requires a skybox texture as shown in the following:

The exact position of the panels for each direction within the image isn't important, although you will need to adjust the coordinates specified in step 3 of the recipe to match your particular skybox texture.

How to do it...

To render a skybox within the HiDef profile:

1. Create a new **Content Pipeline Extension Library** project to your solution.

2. Add a new content processor class named `CubemapProcessor.cs` to the newly created project:

```
[ContentProcessor]
public class CubemapProcessor : ContentProcessor<TextureContent,
TextureCubeContent>
```

```
    {
    }
```

3. Override the `Process()` method so it reads in a 2-dimensional bitmap image file and converts it to a 3-dimensional cube map:

```
public override TextureCubeContent Process(
  TextureContent input,
  ContentProcessorContext context)
{

    input.ConvertBitmapType(typeof(PixelBitmapContent<Color>));
    var image = (PixelBitmapContent<Color>)input.Faces[0][0];
    var cubemap = new TextureCubeContent();

    cubemap.Faces[(int)CubeMapFace.NegativeZ] = CreateFace(
    image, new Rectangle(0, 0, 255, 255), true, false);
    cubemap.Faces[(int)CubeMapFace.PositiveX] = CreateFace(
        image, new Rectangle(256, 0, 255, 255), true, false);
    cubemap.Faces[(int)CubeMapFace.PositiveZ] = CreateFace(
      image, new Rectangle(256 * 2, 0, 255, 255), true, false);
    cubemap.Faces[(int)CubeMapFace.NegativeX] = CreateFace(
      image, new Rectangle(256 * 3, 0, 255, 255), true, false);
    cubemap.Faces[(int)CubeMapFace.NegativeY] = CreateFace(
      image, new Rectangle(256 * 4, 0, 255, 255), true, false);
    cubemap.Faces[(int)CubeMapFace.PositiveY] = CreateFace(
      image, new Rectangle(256 * 5, 0, 255, 255), true, false);

    return cubemap;
}
```

4. Add a helper method to copy the various faces embedded within the bitmap across to the cube map:

```
const int cubemapSize = 255;
static BitmapContent CreateFace(
    PixelBitmapContent<Color> source,
    Rectangle sourceRegion,
    bool flipHorizontally,
    bool flipVertically)
{
    PixelBitmapContent<Color> result;
    result = new PixelBitmapContent<Color>(
                cubemapSize, cubemapSize);
    Rectangle destinationRegion = new Rectangle(
                0, 0, cubemapSize, cubemapSize);
```

```
        for (var y = 0; y < sourceRegion.Height; y++)
        {
            for (var x = 0; x < sourceRegion.Width; x++)
            {
                var sourceX = sourceRegion.Left + x;
                if (flipHorizontally)
                {
                    sourceX = sourceRegion.Right - x;
                }

                var sourceY = sourceRegion.Top + y;
                if (flipVertically)
                {
                    sourceY = sourceRegion.Bottom - y;
                }

                var sourceColor = source.GetPixel(
                                    sourceX, sourceY);
                result.SetPixel(
                    destinationRegion.Left + x,
                    destinationRegion.Y + y,
                    sourceColor);
            }
        }
        return result;
    }
```

5. Add a reference to the newly created content processor project to your game's content project.

6. Add the skybox texture to the content project and set it's `Processor` property to be the `CubeMapProcessor`.

7. Create a new effect file in your content project named `Skybox.fx`. Within the newly created file, define the matrices and vector that form the input to the shaders and will define where the skybox is in the world and what it displays:

```
float4x4 World;
float4x4 View;
float4x4 Projection;
float3 CameraPosition;
Texture SkyBoxTexture;
```

8. Create a sampler to allow the shaders to read the cube texture's contents:

```
samplerCUBE SkyBoxSampler = sampler_state
{
    texture = <SkyBoxTexture>;
```

```
        magfilter = LINEAR;
        minfilter = LINEAR;
        mipfilter = LINEAR;
        AddressU = Mirror;
        AddressV = Mirror;
    };
```

9. Define the structures used to pass data between the shaders:

    ```
    struct VertexShaderInput
    {
        float4 Position : POSITION0;
    };

    struct VertexShaderOutput
    {
        float4 Position : POSITION0;
        float3 TextureCoordinate : TEXCOORD0;
    };
    ```

10. Create the vertex shader, which will apply the usual world-to-screen transformation of coordinates, but keep the skybox centered on the player's viewpoint:

    ```
    VertexShaderOutput VertexShaderFunction(VertexShaderInput input)
    {
        VertexShaderOutput output;

        float4 worldPosition = mul(input.Position, World);
        float4 viewPosition = mul(worldPosition, View);
        output.Position = mul(viewPosition, Projection);

        float4 vertexPosition = mul(input.Position, World);
        output.TextureCoordinate = vertexPosition -
                CameraPosition;

        return output;
    }
    ```

11. Add a pixel shader to retrieve the associated texture for a given viewing angle:

    ```
    float4 PixelShaderFunction(VertexShaderOutput input) : COLOR0
    {
        float3 rayDirection = normalize(input.TextureCoordinate);
        return texCUBE(SkyBoxSampler, rayDirection );
    }
    ```

12. Construct a technique to plug the shaders together into a single callable unit:

```
technique Technique1
{
    pass Pass1
    {
        VertexShader = compile vs_2_0 VertexShaderFunction();
        PixelShader = compile ps_2_0 PixelShaderFunction();
    }
}
```

13. In your game, create a new instance of the skybox effect when the game loads:

```
effect = content.Load<Effect>("skybox");
effect.Parameters["SkyBoxTexture"].SetValue(
        content.Load<Texture>("skybox_texture"));
```

14. Map out the corners of a cube of sufficient size to fill the game world's sky:

```
var size = 200f;

var topForwardLeft = (Vector3.Up + Vector3.Forward +
                    Vector3.Left) * size;
var topForwardRight = (Vector3.Up + Vector3.Forward +
                    Vector3.Right) * size;
var topBackwardLeft = (Vector3.Up + Vector3.Backward +
                    Vector3.Left) * size;
var topBackwardRight = (Vector3.Up + Vector3.Backward +
                    Vector3.Right) * size;
var bottomForwardLeft = (Vector3.Down + Vector3.Forward +
                    Vector3.Left) * size;
var bottomForwardRight = (Vector3.Down + Vector3.Forward +
                    Vector3.Right) * size;
var bottomBackwardLeft = (Vector3.Down + Vector3.Backward +
                    Vector3.Left) * size;
var bottomBackwardRight = (Vector3.Down + Vector3.Backward +
                    Vector3.Right) * size;

var topLeft = new Vector2(0, 0);
var topRight = new Vector2(1, 0);
var bottomRight = new Vector2(1, 1);
var bottomLeft = new Vector2(0, 1);
```

15. Create the top and bottom panes of the cube:

```
var factory = new
VertexPositionNormalTextureGeometricBufferFactory();
```

```
factory.AddPane(
    topForwardRight, topLeft,
    topForwardLeft,topRight,
    topBackwardLeft, bottomRight,
    topBackwardRight, bottomLeft);

factory.AddPane(
    bottomForwardLeft, topLeft,
        bottomForwardRight, topRight,
    bottomBackwardRight, bottomRight,
    bottomBackwardLeft, bottomLeft
    );
```

16. Add the left- and right-hand side panes:

```
factory.AddPane(
    topBackwardLeft, topLeft,
    topForwardLeft, topRight,
    bottomForwardLeft, bottomRight,
    bottomBackwardLeft, bottomLeft
    );

factory.AddPane(
    topForwardRight, topLeft,
    topBackwardRight,topRight,
    bottomBackwardRight, bottomRight,
    bottomForwardRight, bottomLeft
    );
```

17. Complete the cube by adding the forward and backward panes:

```
factory.AddPane(
    topBackwardRight, topLeft,
    topBackwardLeft,topRight,
    bottomBackwardLeft,bottomRight,
    bottomBackwardRight, bottomLeft
    );

factory.AddPane(
    topForwardLeft, topLeft,
    topForwardRight, topRight,
    bottomForwardRight, bottomRight,
```

```
    bottomForwardLeft, bottomLeft
    );

buffer = factory.Create(graphicsDevice);
```

18. In the `Draw()` method of your game, update the parameters of the skybox effect:

```
effect.Parameters["View"].SetValue(camera.View);
effect.Parameters["Projection"].SetValue(camera.Projection);
effect.Parameters["CameraPosition"].SetValue(camera.Position);
effect.Parameters["World"].SetValue(
    Matrix.CreateTranslation(camera.Position));
```

19. Draw the shape using the skybox effect:

```
buffer.Draw(effect);
```

How it works...

With the built-in `texCUBE` function available for call in the pixel shader doing most of heavy lifting in terms of texture mapping, the biggest element left for us to deal with is to manipulate the skybox texture into a format that the `texCUBE` function can deal with.

Inside the custom processor of the content pipeline, we read-in the flat, 2D texture file, and copy and paste each panel of the cube texture into place.

Within our game, all we need to do is render a large piece of geometry with a custom `texCUBE` enhanced shader and voila! One skybox is rendered.

There's more...

If you're constructing your own skybox texture maps with one of the larger, more established 3D modeling packages, there's a reasonable chance that it may be able to export the rendered image out directly in the cube map format. This would bypass the need for the custom **content pipeline** import function included in this recipe.

Cloud generation within the Reach profile

Sometimes a 2D image of cloud just isn't going to cut it.

Maybe your game needs some fluffy, white, 3D clouds to fly through or there is some dramatic and dynamic change of weather.

In either case, knowing how to generate a 3D cloud programmatically is a good place to start.

Getting ready

A cloud particle texture is required for this recipe.

Since it will be replicated and rotated repeatedly to make up a cloud, any random collection of white or grey dots on a transparent background should do the job nicely, as seen here:

How to do it...

To start rendering your own in-game clouds:

1. Create a new class named `ReachCloud`:

   ```
   class ReachCloud
   {
   ```

2. Create the instance-level variables to hold the details common to all the particles that go towards making up the cloud:

   ```
   SpriteBatch spriteBatch;
   Texture2D cloudParticleTexture;
   Vector2 cloudParticleTextureOrigin;
   const float cloudDensity = 2f;
   const float scale = 1f;
   ```

3. Add the instance-level variables to describe the location and color of each particle:

   ```
   Dictionary<Vector3, int> depthFromLightByRelativePosition;
   private Dictionary<int, Color> colorByDepth;
   public Matrix World;
   ```

4. Create a constructor that creates instances of the spritebatch and texture, along with the collection of cloud particle details:

   ```
   public ReachCloud(GraphicsDevice graphicsDevice, Texture2D
   cloudParticleTexture)
   {
       spriteBatch = new SpriteBatch(graphicsDevice);
       this.cloudParticleTexture = cloudParticleTexture;
       cloudParticleTextureOrigin = new Vector2(
               cloudParticleTexture.Width,
               cloudParticleTexture.Height) / 2;
   ```

```
    var metaballSizeByPosition = CreateMetaballs();
    CalculateParticleCloud(metaballSizeByPosition);
    PopulateColorByDepth();
}
```

5. Add a method to create a collection of metaballs that describe the shape of the cloud:

```
private static Dictionary<Vector3, int> CreateMetaballs()
{
    var metaballSizeByPosition = new Dictionary
                                      <Vector3, int>();
    metaballSizeByPosition[new Vector3(0, 2, 0)] = 5;
    metaballSizeByPosition[new Vector3(-3, 0, 0)] = 4;
    metaballSizeByPosition[new Vector3(3, 0, 0)] = 4;
    metaballSizeByPosition[new Vector3(0, 0, -3)] = 4;
    metaballSizeByPosition[new Vector3(0, 0, 3)] = 4;
    metaballSizeByPosition[new Vector3(-5, 0, 0)] = 3;
    metaballSizeByPosition[new Vector3(5, 0, 0)] = 3;
    metaballSizeByPosition[new Vector3(-7, 0, 0)] = 2;
    metaballSizeByPosition[new Vector3(7, 0, 0)] = 2;
    return metaballSizeByPosition;
}
```

6. Include the method that will take the shape as defined by metaballs, and calculate the associated particle positions:

```
private void CalculateParticleCloud(Dictionary<Vector3, int>
metaballSizeByPosition)
{
    var particleQueue = new Queue<Vector3>();
    var uniqueParticles = new HashSet<Vector3>();
    depthFromLightByRelativePosition = new Dictionary<Vector3,
int>();

    for (var y = -10; y < 10; y++)
    {
        for (var z = -10; z < 10; z++)
        {
            for (var x = -10; x < 10; x++)
            {
                var position = new Vector3(x, y, z);
                EnqueueIfContainedByMetaballs(metaballSizeByPositi
on, particleQueue, uniqueParticles, position);
            }
        }
    }
```

```
        CalculateParticleDepth(particleQueue, uniqueParticles);
    }
```

7. Define a helper method to determine whether an individual position is within the cloud shape and, if so, note it for later calculations:

```
private static void EnqueueIfContainedByMetaballs(
    Dictionary<Vector3, int> metaballSizeByPosition,
    Queue<Vector3> particleQueue,
    HashSet<Vector3> uniqueParticlePositions,
    Vector3 position)
{


    foreach (var metaballPositionSizePair
                in metaballSizeByPosition)
    {
        var metaballSizeSquared = Math.Pow(
                    metaballPositionSizePair.Value, 2);
        var metaballPosition = metaballPositionSizePair.Key;

        if (Vector3.DistanceSquared(
            position, metaballPosition) <=
                    metaballSizeSquared)
        {
            uniqueParticlePositions.Add(position);
            particleQueue.Enqueue(position);
            break;
        }

    }
}
```

8. Add a method to calculate the depth of each particle from the perspective of a given lighting direction for later use in lighting calculations:

```
private void CalculateParticleDepth(
    Queue<Vector3> pending, HashSet<Vector3> all)
{
    var lightDirection = new Vector3(-1, 1, 1);
    while (pending.Count > 0)
    {
        var position = pending.Dequeue();
        var neighborsPosition = position + lightDirection;
```

```
        if (!all.Contains(neighborsPosition))
        {
            depthFromLightByRelativePosition.Add(position, 0);
            continue;
        }

        int neighborsDepth;
        if (!depthFromLightByRelativePosition.TryGetValue(
                neighborsPosition, out neighborsDepth))
        {
            pending.Enqueue(position);
            continue;
        }

        depthFromLightByRelativePosition.Add(
            position, neighborsDepth + 1);
    }
}
```

9. Include a method to populate the mapping from particle depth to lighting tint:

```
private void PopulateColorByDepth()
{
    var shallowColor = Color.FromNonPremultiplied(
                        255, 255, 255, 30);
    var deepColor = Color.FromNonPremultiplied(
                        50, 50, 50, 30);
    colorByDepth = new Dictionary<int, Color>();

    var maxDepth = 10;
    for (var depth = 0; depth < maxDepth; depth++)
    {
        var ratio = ((float)depth) / ((float)maxDepth);
        colorByDepth[depth] = Color.Lerp(
            shallowColor, deepColor, ratio);
    }
}
```

10. Begin a `Draw()` method by adding some tests to check whether the particles, after scaling, are going to be of a suitable size to draw, and exit early if they are not:

```
public void Draw(
    Matrix view, Matrix projection, Viewport viewport)
{

    var scaleTestPositionOne = viewport.Project(
```

```
        Vector3.Transform(Vector3.Right, World),
        projection,
        view,
        Matrix.Identity);
    if (scaleTestPositionOne.Z < 0)
    {
        return;
    }

    var scaleTestPositionTwo = viewport.Project(
        Vector3.Transform(Vector3.Up, World),
        projection,
        view,
        Matrix.Identity);
    var projectedScale = Vector3.Distance(scaleTestPositionOne,
scaleTestPositionTwo) / (cloudParticleTexture.Height * 2);
    if (projectedScale > 5f)
    {
        return;
    }
```

11. Add the start of a loop to iterate through each of the particles and draw them:

```
spriteBatch.Begin(
    SpriteSortMode.Deferred,
    BlendState.AlphaBlend, null,
    DepthStencilState.DepthRead, null);

var rotation = 0f;
foreach (var relativePositionDepthFromLightPair in
        depthFromLightByRelativePosition)
{
```

12. For each particle, calculate the rotation, scale, and position on the screen:

```
rotation += 0.1234f;
var displayScale = scale / 5f * projectedScale;

var relativePosition = relativePositionDepthFromLightPair.Key;
var position = Vector3.Transform(
    relativePosition / (10f * cloudDensity), World);
var projectedPosition = viewport.Project(
    position, projection, view, Matrix.Identity);
var screenPosition = new Vector2(
    projectedPosition.X, projectedPosition.Y);
```

13. Look up the associated lighting tint for each particle, and draw the particle on the screen:

```
var depthFromLight = relativePositionDepthFromLightPair.Value;
var tint = colorByDepth[depthFromLight];

spriteBatch.Draw(
    cloudParticleTexture, screenPosition,
    null, tint, rotation, cloudParticleTextureOrigin,
    displayScale,
    SpriteEffects.None, projectedPosition.Z);
```

14. Complete both the loop and the `Draw()` method:

```
    }

    spriteBatch.End();
}
```

15. To your game class, add an instance-level variable to hold a collection of clouds:

```
List<ReachCloud> clouds;
```

16. Within the `LoadContent()` method, create a collection of clouds:

```
clouds = new List<ReachCloud>();
for (var x = -2; x < 2; x++)
{
    var cloud = new ReachCloud(
                GraphicsDevice,
                Content.Load<Texture2D>("CloudParticle"))
    {
        World = Matrix.CreateTranslation(
                Vector3.Up * 2 +
                Vector3.Left * x * 2 +
                Vector3.Forward * 2)
    };
    clouds.Add(cloud);
}
```

17. Draw each one of the clouds inside your game class's `Draw()` method:

```
foreach (var cloud in clouds)
{
    cloud.Draw(
        camera.View,
        camera.Projection,
        GraphicsDevice.Viewport);
}
```

How it works...

I find it easiest to imagine this recipe in terms of a sculpture made out of a lattice of cloud particles.

We start with a blueprint defined in terms of **metaballs**.

If you've not dealt with them previously, metaballs are simply a location in space, and a radius of "influence defined".

In this case, we iterate through every position in a 3-dimensional lattice, adding a cloud particle to each point on the lattice that is under sufficient "influence" from one or more metaballs. The calculation to determine the amount of "influence" can be seen in step 7 of this recipe.

Once we have a lattice of cloud particles, we color them in terms of how many particles separate them from the nearest light source. This will simulate the darker color that thick portions of clouds tend to take on, as seen here:

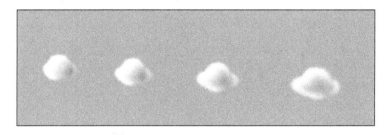

In much the same way that the particles in the *Smoke within the Reach profile* recipe of *Chapter 1, Applying Special Effects*, were drawn, pre-calculating the mapping from 3D world coordinates to 2D screen coordinates within our C# game code means that using the `SpriteBatch.Draw()` method to communicate with the graphics card can be significantly more efficient in its attempt to draw large numbers of the same texture.

There's more...

A set of identical clouds may be fine for a demonstration, but is unlikely to look appropriate in any game trying for a more realistic appearance.

For a more interesting effect, try moving the metaball creation process across to something a little more random.

For example, for a little more realism, generate a collection of metaballs of various sizes, and then move them towards the center by varying degrees dependant on their size.

This should help create an effect similar to that of a fluffy, white, cumulus cloud.

Billboarding

Even with the techniques presented in this recipe, the large number of particles required to create clouds make them a relatively expensive endeavor to both produce and draw. Any chance to avoid having to do so is usually an attractive proposition. Therefore, if you're rendering clouds that are unlikely to change orientation relative to the player, maybe because of distance, then rendering a cloud to a billboard and displaying the billboard until the orientation or distance does change significantly, can provide you with a notable increase in efficiency.

A deeper explanation of billboards, along with an example, can be found in the *Rendering crowds* recipe of *Chapter 6, Playing with Animation*.

See also

▸   *Smoke within the Reach profile* recipe of *Chapter 1, Applying Special Effects*.

5
Non-Player Characters

In this chapter we will cover:

- ▶ A* pathfinding
- ▶ Character state machines
- ▶ Constructing dialogue
- ▶ Decentralizing behavior

Introduction

This chapter is all about adding intelligence and personality to the **Non-Player Characters** (**NPCs**) that inhabit your world, or at least adding enough of an approximation to satisfy the requirements of the game.

Need a gruff old-timer who quickly grows tired of too many questions and storms out of the room in disgust? By the end of this chapter, you should find yourself with the architectural building blocks to know how to construct such an unsavory character.

This chapter also includes a brief exploration into the realm of decentralized behavior, which can be a useful way to model everything from a flock of birds to a traffic jam.

A* pathfinding

Finding one's way from point A to point B can seem like an obvious enough task, but doing it in a way that appears vaguely natural tends to be a little less obvious.

The A* (pronounced "A star") family of algorithms comes from various attempts to improve upon Edsger Dijkstra's algorithm for solving the shortest path problem on a connected graph of nodes. It has become the default method of pathfinding in modern gaming.

Presented here is a simple variation of the A* algorithm, which demonstrates the core theme present in all the A* variations. This is a good starting point from which to tailor a solution optimized for your particular situation.

Getting ready

This recipe requires three, 20 x 20 pixel textures to represent a patch of ground, a segment of undecided path, and the final selection of path.

How to do it...

1. Add a class to hold the map of the landscape to be navigated:

```
class Map
{
    Rectangle arena = new Rectangle(0, 0, 20, 20);

    public int Width
    {
        get
        {
            return arena.Width;
        }
    }

    public int Height
    {
        get
        {
            return arena.Height;
        }
    }
```

2. Initialize the map with the addition of some obstructive walls:

```
List<Rectangle> walls;

public Map()
{
    walls = new List<Rectangle>()
    {
        new Rectangle(13,0,1,5),
```

```
            new Rectangle(13,5,3,1),
            new Rectangle(13,7,1,4),
            new Rectangle(5,5,6,1),
            new Rectangle(10,6,1,5)
    };
}
```

3. Complete the class with the addition of a method to indicate if a particular spot on the map is occupied by an obstruction such as a wall:

```
public bool IsObstructionAt(Point mapPosition)
{
    if (!arena.Contains(mapPosition))
    {
        return true;
    }

    foreach (var wall in walls)
    {
        if (wall.Contains(mapPosition))
        {
            return true;
        }
    }

    return false;
}
```

4. Add a new class to represent a point along a path and the estimated cost involved in taking it:

```
class GuideNode
{
    public GuideNode Parent;
    public Point Position;
    public int PathLength;
    public int Cost;

    public GuideNode(GuideNode parent,
        Point position,
        Point destination,
        float estimatedDistanceWeighting)
    {
        Parent = parent;
        Position = position;
```

```
        if (parent != null)
        {
            PathLength = parent.PathLength + 1;
        }

        var manhattanDistance =
                (Math.Abs(position.X - destination.X) +
                 Math.Abs(position.Y - destination.Y));

        Cost = (int)(PathLength +
            (estimatedDistanceWeighting *
                manhattanDistance));
    }
}
```

5. Begin a new class to perform the pathfinding with the creation of a node to represent the starting position:

```
class PathFinder
{
    private List<GuideNode> openNodes = new List<GuideNode>();
    private HashSet<Point> openPositions = new HashSet<Point>();
    private HashSet<Point> closedPositions = new HashSet<Point>();
    public Point Start;
    public Point End;
    private Map map;
    private float estimatedDistanceWeighting;

    public PathFinder(Point start,
        Point end,
        Map map,
        bool diagonalsEnabled,
        float estimatedDistanceWeighting)
    {
        Start = start;
        End = end;
        this.map = map;
        this.estimatedDistanceWeighting =
estimatedDistanceWeighting;

        var startNode = new GuideNode(
            null,
            start,
            end,
            estimatedDistanceWeighting);
```

```
        openNodes.Add(startNode);

        GenerateSearchOffsets(diagonalsEnabled);
    }
```

6. Add a method to generate the commonly used offsets of directions to be searched from each node:

```
private List<Point> searchOffsets = new List<Point>();

private void GenerateSearchOffsets(bool diagonalsEnabled)
{
    searchOffsets.Add(new Point(0, -1));
    searchOffsets.Add(new Point(-1, 0));
    searchOffsets.Add(new Point(1, 0));
    searchOffsets.Add(new Point(0, 1));

    if (diagonalsEnabled)
    {
        searchOffsets.Add(new Point(-1, -1));
        searchOffsets.Add(new Point(1, -1));
        searchOffsets.Add(new Point(1, 1));
        searchOffsets.Add(new Point(-1, 1));
    }
}
```

7. Begin a new method which will take the next node that is estimated to be closest to the destination and consider the possible moves from that point onwards:

```
public void ConsiderMove()
{
    openNodes.Sort((a, b) => { return
                    a.Cost.CompareTo(b.Cost); });
    var node = ExtractAndCloseNextNonPathNode();
```

8. Iterate through each possible direction, calculating the neighboring position in each direction:

```
foreach (var offset in searchOffsets)
{
    var possiblePosition = new Point(
            node.Position.X + offset.X,
            node.Position.Y + offset.Y);
```

9. Ignore the neighboring position if it's obstructed, off the map, pending consideration, or has already been considered:

```
if (openPositions.Contains(possiblePosition) ||
    closedPositions.Contains(possiblePosition))
{
    continue;
}

if (map.IsObstructionAt(possiblePosition))
{
    continue;
}
```

10. Close the loop and the method with the addition of the neighboring position to the list of positions to be considered:

```
            var possibility = new GuideNode(
                node,
                possiblePosition,
                End,
                estimatedDistanceWeighting);

            openNodes.Add(possibility);
            openPositions.Add(possibility.Position);
        }
    }
```

11. Add a method to move a node from the list of nodes that are pending consideration to the list of nodes that have been considered:

```
private GuideNode ExtractAndCloseNextNonPathNode()
{
    var nodeIndex = 0;
    while (openNodes[nodeIndex].Position == End)
    {
        nodeIndex++;
    }
    var node = openNodes[nodeIndex];
    openNodes.RemoveAt(nodeIndex);
    openPositions.Remove(node.Position);
    closedPositions.Add(node.Position);
    return node;
}
```

12. Include properties to indicate if a path has been found and, if so, what it is:

```
public List<Point> Path
{
    get
    {
        var path = new List<Point>();
        if (!PathFound)
        {
            return path;
        }

        var node = openNodes[0];
        while (node != null)
        {
            path.Insert(0, node.Position);
            node = node.Parent;
        }

        return path;
    }
}

public bool PathFound
{
    get
    {
        return (openNodes[0].Position == End);
    }
}
```

13. Continue with two additional properties to indicate which points are pending consideration and which have already been considered:

```
public HashSet<Point> PointsPendingConsideration
{
    get
    {
        var points = new HashSet<Point>();
        foreach (var node in openNodes)
        {
            points.Add(node.Position);
        }
```

```
                return points;
            }
        }


    public HashSet<Point> ConsideredPoints
    {
        get
        {
            var points = new HashSet<Point>();
            foreach (var point in closedPositions)
            {
                points.Add(point);
            }

            return points;
        }
    }
```

14. In your game class, load the textures and create the map and a new instance of `PathFinder`:

```
SpriteBatch spriteBatch;
Texture2D block;
Texture2D circle;
Texture2D openCircle;
Map map;
PathFinder pathFinder;

protected override void LoadContent()
{
    spriteBatch = new SpriteBatch(GraphicsDevice);
    block = Content.Load<Texture2D>("block");
    circle = Content.Load<Texture2D>("circle");
    openCircle = Content.Load<Texture2D>("opencircle");

    map = new Map();

    pathFinder = new PathFinder(
        start:new Point(3, 12),
        end:new Point(15, 2),
        map:map,
        diagonalsEnabled:true,
        estimatedDistanceWeighting: 5);
}
```

15. In the `Update()` method of your game, have the pathfinder consider a move upon the user hitting the Space bar:

```
KeyboardState lastKeyboard;

protected override void Update(GameTime gameTime)
{
    var keyboard = Keyboard.GetState();

    if (!pathFinder.PathFound &&
        keyboard.IsKeyDown(Keys.Space) &&
        lastKeyboard.IsKeyUp(Keys.Space))
    {
        pathFinder.ConsiderMove();
    }

    lastKeyboard = keyboard;
    base.Update(gameTime);
}
```

16. Begin drawing by determining whether a completed path has been found or not, and locating the associated data:

```
protected override void Draw(GameTime gameTime)
{
    List<Point> path = null;
    HashSet<Point> considered = null;
    HashSet<Point> pendingConsiderations = null;
    var pathFound = pathFinder.PathFound;
    if (pathFound)
    {
        path = pathFinder.Path;
    }
    else
    {
        considered = pathFinder.ConsideredPoints;
        pendingConsiderations =
            pathFinder.PointsPendingConsideration;
    }
```

17. Complete the `Draw()` method by iterating through each position on the map and drawing the details on the screen:

```
    GraphicsDevice.Clear(Color.Black);
    var displayScale = 20;
    spriteBatch.Begin();
```

```
            for (var y = 0; y < map.Height; y++)
            {
                for (var x = 0; x < map.Width; x++)
                {
                    var mapPosition = new Point(x, y);
                    var displayPosition = new Vector2(
                            x * displayScale,
                            y * displayScale);

                    DrawMap(mapPosition, displayPosition);
                    DrawPath(path,
                            considered,
                            pendingConsiderations,
                            mapPosition,
                            displayPosition);
                    DrawStartEnd(mapPosition, displayPosition);
                }
            }

        spriteBatch.End();

        base.Draw(gameTime);
    }
```

18. Add a method to draw the map:

```
    private void DrawMap(Point mapPosition, Vector2 displayPosition)
    {
        var displayColor = Color.DarkKhaki;
        if (map.IsObstructionAt(mapPosition))
        {
            displayColor = Color.Wheat;
        }

        spriteBatch.Draw(block, displayPosition, displayColor);
    }
```

19. Include a method to draw the start and end positions of the trek:

```
    private void DrawStartEnd(Point mapPosition, Vector2
    displayPosition)
    {
        if (mapPosition == pathFinder.Start ||
            mapPosition == pathFinder.End)
        {
            spriteBatch.Draw(openCircle, displayPosition, Color.
```

```
Black);
        }
    }
```

20. Complete the class with the addition of a method to draw the path:

```csharp
private void DrawPath(
    List<Point> path,
    HashSet<Point> considered,
    HashSet<Point> pendingConsiderations,
    Point mapPosition,
    Vector2 displayPosition)
{
    if (pathFinder.PathFound)
    {
        if (path.Contains(mapPosition))
        {
            spriteBatch.Draw(
                circle,
                displayPosition,
                Color.Blue);
        }
    }
    else
    {
        if (considered.Contains(mapPosition))
        {
            spriteBatch.Draw(
                circle,
                displayPosition,
                Color.Brown);
        }
        else if (pendingConsiderations.Contains(mapPosition))
        {
            spriteBatch.Draw(
                openCircle,
                displayPosition,
                Color.Brown);
        }
    }
}
```

How it works...

The A* family of algorithms is based around the notion of building up a tree of possible steps to take towards a given destination, in search for the shortest path in an acceptable amount of time.

What defines "shortest" and "acceptable" depends on a particular situation and can be quite varied from one game to the next.

In this particular case, we're measuring shortest in terms of what's been referred to by some as the **Manhattan distance**, and an "acceptable" time period as something that could be calculated within a few seconds.

If one imagines a diagonal line connecting the start and destination points, the Manhattan distance would be the two additional lines required to form a right angle triangle, as shown in the following illustration, and gains its name from the similar shape of a path one might traverse in the city of Manhattan:

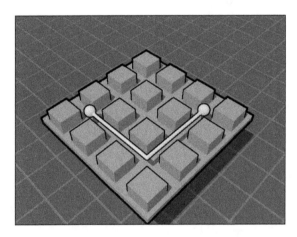

The A* algorithm is a heuristic algorithm. This essentially means it's designed to deliver the best effort at a good solution within the time permitted, rather than an exhaustive search for the best possible solution over a much longer period of time.

The quality of the path found can be directly tied back to the quality of the guess made by the algorithm over the distance between any given spot and the goal. The better the guess, the better the final path.

In the case of this recipe, the number of steps from the start, and the Manhattan distance to the destination, determines the guess of how far a point is from the destination.

How these two numbers are combined to generate the overall "fitness" of a particular point can be seen in the constructor of the GuideNode class.

There's more...

To calculate a path that's shorter, smoother, or quicker, try altering the `estimatedDistanceWeighting` parameter passed into the pathfinding algorithm.

This number determines whether more focus is given to minimizing the known distance covered or the predicted distance to travel and, in more simplistic terms, tends to determine how much time is spent searching for an optimal solution, rather than rushing for the first option available.

Distance estimation

Another option that can significantly alter the quality of the path found is how the distance to the destination is estimated.

If you're implementing a game that involves different types of terrain, it might be worthwhile weighting the estimate depending on the types of terrain that lie between a given point and the destination.

See also

▸ The *Decentralizing behavior* recipe in this chapter, for other ways to navigate

Character state machines

Defining a character's temperament and possible actions in the form of a finite state machine is a simple but effective way to simulate emotion, personality, and those subtle quirks that hint at humanity.

In this recipe, we're going to create a pretty simple example in the form of a security guard who gets progressively more or less excitable depending on whether he can hear or see the hero of the game.

Just like a real person might react, the guard doesn't instantly jump into full-blown anger upon the smallest noise, nor does he instantly calm down upon losing sight of the hero.

Getting ready

This recipe requires only an XNA-compatible font of your choosing.

How to do it...

To create your own character state machine:

1. Add a new `SpriteFont` to your solution, named `Text`.

2. Create a class to represent the emotional state of a character:

```
class StateNode
{
    public string Id;
```

3. Complete the class by including a list of possible nodes to transit to, along with a method to determine the first transition that is applicable:

```
public List<StateTransition> Transitions =
                    new List<StateTransition>();

public StateNode Next()
{
    foreach (var transition in Transitions)
    {
        if (transition.Prerequisite())
        {
            if (transition.OnTransition != null)
            {
                transition.OnTransition();
            }
            return transition.Node;
        }
    }
    return this;
}
}
```

4. Add a class to hold the details of a given transition:

```
class StateTransition
{
    public StateNode Node;
    public Func<bool> Prerequisite;
    public Action OnTransition;
}
```

5. Create a class to represent a guard NPC:

```
class Guard
{
    private StateNode node;
```

6. In the constructor, begin by defining all the possible emotional states for the guard:

```
public Guard()
{
    var bored = new StateNode() { Id = "Bored" };
    var sleeping = new StateNode() { Id = "Sleeping" };
    var nervous = new StateNode() { Id = "Nervous" };
    var angry = new StateNode() { Id = "Angry" };
```

7. Define the possible transitions for when the guard is bored:

```
bored.Transitions.Add(new StateTransition() {
    Node = angry,
    Prerequisite = () => {
        return HeroSpotted; } });

bored.Transitions.Add(new StateTransition() {
    Node = nervous,
    Prerequisite = () => {
        return NoiseHeard; } });

bored.Transitions.Add(new StateTransition() {
    Node = sleeping,
    Prerequisite = () => {
        return (timeInNode > 5); } });
```

8. Map out the possible transitions for when the guard is nervous:

```
nervous.Transitions.Add(new StateTransition()
{
    Node = angry,
    Prerequisite = () =>
    {
        return HeroSpotted;
    }
});
nervous.Transitions.Add(new StateTransition()
{
    Node = angry,
    Prerequisite = () =>
    {
        return NoiseHeard;
    }
});
nervous.Transitions.Add(new StateTransition()
{
    Node = bored,
```

```
                    Prerequisite = () =>
                    {
                         return (timeInNode > 5);
                    }
          });
```

9. Complete the constructor by mapping out the possible transitions for when
    the guard is angry, and have the guard's default emotional state set to bored:

```
          angry.Transitions.Add(new StateTransition()
          {
               Node = angry,
               Prerequisite = () =>
               {
                    return NoiseHeard;
               },
               OnTransition = () =>
               {
                    timeInNode = 0;
               }
          });
          angry.Transitions.Add(new StateTransition()
          {
               Node = angry,
               Prerequisite = () =>
               {
                    return HeroSpotted;
               },
               OnTransition = () =>
               {
                    timeInNode = 0;
               }
          });
          angry.Transitions.Add(new StateTransition()
          {
               Node = nervous,
               Prerequisite = () =>
               {
                    return (timeInNode > 5);
               }
          });

          node = bored;
     }
```

10. Add an `Update()` method to calculate the guard's emotional state:

```
public bool HeroSpotted = false;
public bool NoiseHeard = false;
private double timeInNode;
StateNode lastNode;

public void Update(GameTime gameTime)
{
    node = node.Next();

    HeroSpotted = false;
    NoiseHeard = false;

    if (node != lastNode)
    {
        timeInNode = 0;
    }

    timeInNode += gameTime.ElapsedGameTime.TotalSeconds;
    lastNode = node;
}
```

11. Finish the `guard` class with a property to return the `Id` of the current emotional state:

```
public string State
{
    get
    {
        return node.Id;
    }
}
```

12. In your game code, load up the font and a new instance of `guard`:

```
SpriteFont textFont;
Guard guard;

protected override void LoadContent()
{
    spriteBatch = new SpriteBatch(GraphicsDevice);
    textFont = Content.Load<SpriteFont>("Text");
    guard = new Guard();
}
```

13. Adjust the `Update()` method so that upon hitting the corresponding key on the keyboard, the guard will either "see" the hero or "hear" a strange noise:

```
KeyboardState lastKeyboard;
protected override void Update(GameTime gameTime)
{
    var keyboard = Keyboard.GetState();

    if (lastKeyboard.IsKeyDown(Keys.H) &&
        keyboard.IsKeyUp(Keys.H))
    {
        guard.HeroSpotted = true;
    }

    if (lastKeyboard.IsKeyDown(Keys.N) &&
        keyboard.IsKeyUp(Keys.N))
    {
        guard.NoiseHeard = true;
    }

    guard.Update(gameTime);

    lastKeyboard = keyboard;
    base.Update(gameTime);
}
```

14. Update the `Draw()` method to display the guard's current emotional state:

```
protected override void Draw(GameTime gameTime)
{
    GraphicsDevice.Clear(Color.CornflowerBlue);

    spriteBatch.Begin();
    spriteBatch.DrawString(
        textFont, guard.State, Vector2.Zero, Color.White);
    spriteBatch.End();

    base.Draw(gameTime);
}
```

How it works...

This recipe relies upon building up a graph of nodes connected by one or more criteria (known more formally as predicates) as seen here:

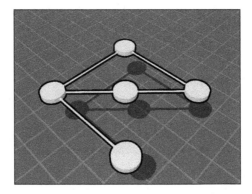

The predicates are defined in terms of lambda expressions that are evaluated against the various attributes of the character or the surrounding world in each update cycle.

This means the NPC can move from state to state, but only ever being in one state at a time, and the current state being determined by the previous state.

There's more...

A character's state can be the basis for much more than just a single line of text.

Everything from the dialogue spoken to the choice of animation for a character can be based on its state.

Try mixing the state machine presented in this recipe along with the dialogue system, also presented in this chapter, to produce characters that can alter their conversations depending on how they feel, and vice versa.

Scripting

If your game's characters are getting quite complex, or you're lucky enough to have a team member dedicated to the creation of such things, you may want to investigate defining a character's state through a script file instead of hardcoding it in C#.

Animation

It's not just conversations that can be constructed in a node-based state machine fashion.

The animation cycles derived from a character's state may also have their own states. This can lead to far more complex and interesting combinations.

See also

▸ *Constructing dialogue* recipe in this chapter.

▸ *Applying animation with the SkinnedEffect* recipe in *Chapter 6, Playing with Animation*

Constructing dialogue

Whether divulging small nuggets of information, engaging in trade, or just adding that little bit of texture, for gaming genres such as the role-playing game, the ability to converse with characters in the surrounding world is often at the heart of the storytelling process.

In this recipe, we're going to examine a technique for constructing dialogue trees loosely based on the **Gang of Four** command pattern.

Getting ready

An XNA-compatible font of your choice is all that's required for this recipe.

How to do it...

To create a dialogue engine:

1. Add a new `SpriteFont` to the solution named `Dialogue`.

2. Create an interface to define how to interact with an NPC during conversation:

    ```
    interface ChatSupplier
    {
        IEnumerable<ChatOptionDisplayable> ChatOptions
            { get; }
        void Select(ChatOptionDisplayable chatOption);
    }
    ```

3. Define the options that can be presented by an NPC in a conversation:

    ```
    interface ChatOptionDisplayable
    {
        float DisplayHeight { get; set; }
        string Text { get; }
        bool PreviouslySelected { get; set; }
    }
    ```

4. Create a specific implementation of the chat options for our scenario:

```
class ChatOption : ChatOptionDisplayable
{
    public float DisplayHeight { get; set; }
    public string Text { get; set; }
    public bool PreviouslySelected { get; set; }

    public Func<bool> IsVisible;
    public Action Respond;
}
```

5. Add the beginning of a new class to enable the player to select one of the options presented by an NPC:

```
class ChatSelector
{
    SpriteBatch spriteBatch;
    SpriteFont font;
    Rectangle chatArea;
    List<ChatOptionDisplayable> options;
    ChatSupplier supplier;

    public ChatSelector(
        ChatSupplier chatable,
        GraphicsDevice graphicsDevice,
        SpriteFont font,
        Rectangle chatArea)
    {
        this.supplier = chatable;
        this.font = font;
        this.chatArea = chatArea;

        spriteBatch = new SpriteBatch(graphicsDevice);
        PopulateOptions(chatable, font);
    }

    private void PopulateOptions(
        ChatSupplier chatable,
        SpriteFont font)
    {
        options = new List<ChatOptionDisplayable>();
        options.AddRange(chatable.ChatOptions);
        CalculateOptionHeights();
    }
```

```
private void CalculateOptionHeights()
{
    foreach (var option in options)
    {
        option.DisplayHeight =
            font.MeasureString(option.Text).Y /
            1.4f;
    }
}
```

6. Start the `Update()` method with a read of the keyboard state:

```
int selectedOptionIndex = 0;
KeyboardState lastKeyboard;

public void Update(GameTime gameTime)
{
    if (options.Count == 0)
    {
        return;
    }

    var keyboard = Keyboard.GetState();
```

7. Change the selected option depending upon the user hitting the up or down cursor keys:

```
if (keyboard.IsKeyDown(Keys.Down) &&
    lastKeyboard.IsKeyUp(Keys.Down) &&
    selectedOptionIndex < (options.Count - 1))
{
    selectedOptionIndex++;
}

if (keyboard.IsKeyDown(Keys.Up) &&
    lastKeyboard.IsKeyUp(Keys.Up) &&
    selectedOptionIndex > 0)
{
    selectedOptionIndex--;
}
```

8. If the user selects the current option, send it to the NPC and load up the resulting set of options:

```
if (keyboard.IsKeyDown(Keys.Space) &&
    lastKeyboard.IsKeyUp(Keys.Space))
{
```

```
        var selectedLine = options[selectedOptionIndex];
        supplier.Select(selectedLine);

        options.Clear();
        selectedLine.PreviouslySelected = true;
        options.AddRange(supplier.ChatOptions);

        CalculateOptionHeights();
        selectedOptionIndex = 0;
    }
```

9. Complete the `Update()` method by adding the calculations for determining how tall it is, in preparation for being displayed on screen:

```
        var optionIndex = 0;
        optionScrollVerticalOffset = 0;
        while (optionIndex != selectedOptionIndex)
        {
            optionIndex++;
            var selectedLine = options[selectedOptionIndex];
            optionScrollVerticalOffset -=
                    selectedLine.DisplayHeight;
        }
        lastKeyboard = keyboard;
    }
```

10. Add the `Draw()` method to display the options on screen:

```
    float optionScrollVerticalOffset;

    public void Draw()
    {
        spriteBatch.Begin();
        var textPosition = new Vector2(chatArea.Left, 0);
        var displayHeightTotal = 0f;

        for (var optionIndex = 0;
             optionIndex < options.Count; optionIndex++)
        {
            var option = options[optionIndex];

            textPosition.Y = chatArea.Top +
                            optionScrollVerticalOffset +
                            displayHeightTotal;

            Color optionColor = Color.Brown;
```

```
            if (optionIndex == selectedOptionIndex)
            {
                optionColor = Color.Black;
            }
            else if (option.PreviouslySelected)
            {
                optionColor = Color.DarkOrchid;
            }

            spriteBatch.DrawString(
                font,
                option.Text,
                    textPosition,
                optionColor);

            displayHeightTotal += option.DisplayHeight;
        }

        spriteBatch.End();
    }
```

11. Create a new class to display the dialogue response of the NPC:

```
class ChatLog
{
    private SpriteBatch spriteBatch;
    private SpriteFont font;
    private Rectangle displayArea;

    public ChatLog(GraphicsDevice graphicsDevice,
        SpriteFont font,
        Rectangle displayArea)
    {
        spriteBatch = new SpriteBatch(graphicsDevice);
        this.font = font;
        this.displayArea = displayArea;

        origin = new Vector2(displayArea.X, displayArea.Y);
    }
```

12. Provide the ability to log new lines of text to the display:

```
private List<ChatLogEntry> logs = new List<ChatLogEntry>();

public void Display(Color color, string text)
{
```

```
    logs.Add(new ChatLogEntry() { Text = text, Color = color, Life
= 1 });
}
```

13. Slowly "age" any displayed log items over time and cull any that have expired:

```
public void Update(GameTime gameTime)
{
    for (var logIndex = logs.Count - 1;
            logIndex >= 0;
            logIndex--)
    {
        var log = logs[logIndex];
        log.Life -= (float)(gameTime.ElapsedGameTime.TotalSeconds
/ 3f);
        if (log.Life < 0)
        {
            logs.RemoveAt(logIndex);
        }
    }
}
```

14. Display the log items on screen, eventually fading the older ones to complete transparency:

```
Vector2 origin;
Vector2 offset;

public void Draw()
{
    offset.Y = displayArea.Bottom;
    foreach (var log in logs)
    {
        offset.Y -= font.MeasureString(log.Text).Y;
    }

    spriteBatch.Begin();
    foreach (var log in logs)
    {
        spriteBatch.DrawString(
            font,
            log.Text,
            origin + offset,
            Color.Lerp(
                Color.Transparent,
                log.Color,
                log.Life));
```

```
                offset.Y += font.MeasureString(log.Text).Y;
        }
        spriteBatch.End();
    }
```

15. Define the `ChatLogEntry` class and the data that will be held for each line:

```
class ChatLogEntry
{
    public string Text;
    public Color Color;
    public float Life;
}
```

16. Create the beginnings of a new NPC class to provide some conversation:

```
class Jane : ChatSupplier
{
    private List<ChatOption> allChatOptions;

    private bool hasAskedAboutName;
    private bool isShopping;
    private List<string> inventory;

    private Color janeColor = Color.Blue;
```

17. Add a constructor and the start of the definition for the chat options:

```
public Jane(ChatLog log)
{
    allChatOptions = new List<ChatOption>()
    {
```

18. Begin the chat options with a simple option that will be available whenever the player and the NPC aren't involved in a shopping transaction:

```
new ChatOption() {
    Text = "Am I a banana?",
    IsVisible = () => { return !isShopping; },
    Respond = () => {
        log.Display(janeColor, "No. You are not a banana...\n...as
far as I know.");
    }
},
```

19. Add chat options relating to asking for the NPC's name the first time, and subsequently after:

```
new ChatOption() {
    Text = "Who are you?",
```

```
        IsVisible = () => { return !isShopping &&
                                    !hasAskedAboutName; },
        Respond = () => {
            hasAskedAboutName = true;
            log.Display(janeColor, "My name is Jane.");
        }
    },
    new ChatOption() {
        Text = "Who are you... again?",
        IsVisible = () => { return !isShopping &&
                                    hasAskedAboutName; },
        Respond = () => {
            hasAskedAboutName = true;
            log.Display(janeColor, "Sigh. My name is Jane.");
        }
    },
```

20. Finish the initial population of the chat options with an option to shop if there's any inventory available to be sold:

```
    new ChatOption() {
        Text = "Anything to sell?",
        IsVisible = () => { return !isShopping; },
        Respond = () => {
            if (inventory.Count == 0)
            {
                log.Display(janeColor, "No. Sorry.");
            }
            else
            {
                isShopping = true;
                log.Display(janeColor, "Certainly! What would you
like to buy?");
            }
        }
    },
};
```

21. Populate the inventory with items to sell:

```
inventory = new List<string>()
{
    "book",
    "spoon",
    "goat"
};
```

22. Create an associated chat option for each inventory item:

```
foreach (var inventoryItem in inventory)
{
    var item = inventoryItem;
    allChatOptions.Add(new ChatOption()
    {
        Text = "The " + item + ".",
        IsVisible = () =>
        {
            return isShopping &&
                    inventory.Contains(item);
        },
        Respond = () =>
        {
            log.Display(janeColor, "Yes. Here you go. One " + item
+ ". Anything else?");
            inventory.Remove(item);
        }
    });
}
```

23. Close out the method by adding the option to stop shopping:

```
allChatOptions.Add(new ChatOption()
    {
        Text = "No thanks.",
        IsVisible = () =>
        {
            return isShopping;
        },
        Respond = () =>
        {
            log.Display(janeColor, "Okay.");
            isShopping = false;
        }
    });
}
```

24. Implement the `ChatSupplier` interface through the addition of the method to retrieve the current chat options and the method to select one of them:

```
public IEnumerable<ChatOptionDisplayable> ChatOptions
{
    get
    {
        return from chatOption in allChatOptions
```

```
                    where chatOption.IsVisible()
                    select chatOption;
        }
    }

    public void Select(ChatOptionDisplayable chatOption)
    {
        ((ChatOption)chatOption).Respond();
    }
}
```

25. In your game code, add the initialization of the two UI elements and the NPC, `Jane`:

```
SpriteBatch spriteBatch;
ChatLog chatLog;
ChatSelector chatSelector;
Jane jane;

protected override void LoadContent()
{
    spriteBatch = new SpriteBatch(GraphicsDevice);
    chatLog = new ChatLog(
                GraphicsDevice,
                Content.Load<SpriteFont>("Dialogue"),
                new Rectangle(100,50,600,100));
    jane = new Jane(chatLog);
    chatSelector = new ChatSelector(
                        jane,
                        GraphicsDevice,
                        Content.Load<SpriteFont>("Dialogue"),
                        new Rectangle(100, 300, 600, 200));
}
```

26. Include the two UI elements in the `Update()` method:

```
protected override void Update(GameTime gameTime)
{
    chatSelector.Update(gameTime);
    chatLog.Update(gameTime);

    base.Update(gameTime);
}
```

27. Render the two UI elements to the screen:

```
protected override void Draw(GameTime gameTime)
{
    GraphicsDevice.Clear(Color.Wheat);
```

```
        chatSelector.Draw();
        chatLog.Draw();

        base.Draw(gameTime);
    }
```

How it works...

The essence of this recipe is really just the construction of a list and the player's selection of one of the list items.

Each time the NPC is asked for a list of possible conversation options, each option's suitability is checked via the `IsVisible` lambda expression contained within it, based upon the state of the character and the world around it.

If an option is deemed to be visible, then it is included in the list of options presented to the player.

When the player selects an option, the action stored in the `Respond` property is executed, usually resulting in some sort of change within the character and text-based reply.

There's more...

How involved or complex a character's dialogue is depends on the particular game. The more "world-aware" a character is, the more complex, interesting, and realistic it can be in your game.

Scripting

As with the *Character state machine* recipe presented in this chapter, there's value to be found in switching across to script files to define possible states over hardcoding them in C#.

Moving to script files can mean an easier time, both for anyone who has to write the dialogue and anyone responsible for maintaining the C# code, in the long term.

See also

- ▶ *Character state machine* recipe in this chapter.
- ▶ *Creating pie menus* recipe in *Chapter 8, Receiving Player Input*.
- ▶ *"Design Patterns: Elements of Reusable Object-Orientated Software" (ISBN 978-0-201-63361-0), Erich Gamma, Richard Helm, Ralph Johnson* and *John Vlissides; Addison–Wesley publishing.*

Decentralizing behavior

In the real world, the behavior demonstrated by a group as a whole can be quite different and surprisingly complex when compared to the behavior of its members. Given our own predilection as humans to organize ourselves in hierarchies, it can be tempting to imagine there's always a central, controlling, intelligence overseeing and directing each member's actions in harmony with its peers.

For group behavior, such as a flock of birds flying in formation or ants foraging for food, research would tend to suggest that no centralized controlling intelligence is required, and that such feats can be achieved through each member of the group following a relatively simple set of rules.

Getting ready

This recipe requires a plain white texture file, preferably small and only a few pixels in height and width.

How to do it...

To create your own example of decentralized behavior:

1. Add an enumeration to describe the various states an ant can be in:

```
enum AntMode
{
    FollowingPheromone,
    LookingForFood,
    ReturningToNestWithFood
}
```

2. Define the class to hold data regarding a patch of land:

```
class Patch
{
    public bool Nest;
    public float NestScent;
    public int Food;
    public float Pheromone;
}
```

3. Add a class to specify the behavior and state of an ant:

```
class Ant
{
    public int WorldWidth;
    public int WorldHeight;
```

```
        public Point Position;
        public AntMode Mode;

    public void Update(
        Patch[, ,] patches,
        int current,
        Random random,
        GameTime gameTime)
    {

        var currentPatch = patches[
                current,
                Position.X, Position.Y];

        switch (Mode)
        {
```

4. Define the case for what should happen when an ant is attempting to follow a pheromone trail:

```
        case AntMode.FollowingPheromone:
            if (!TryMoveTowardsPheromone(patches, current))
            {
                Mode = AntMode.LookingForFood;
            }
            break;
```

5. Add the case for what an ant should do when searching for food:

```
        case AntMode.LookingForFood:
            int food;
            if (TryFindFood(patches, current, out food))
            {
                Mode = AntMode.ReturningToNestWithFood;
            }
            else
            {
                MoveRandomly(random);
            }
            break;
```

6. Complete the method by specifying what should happen when an ant is returning to the nest with food:

```
        case AntMode.ReturningToNestWithFood:
            if (currentPatch.Nest)
            {
```

```
                Mode = AntMode.FollowingPheromone;
            }
            else if (TryMoveTowardsNest(patches, current))
            {
                currentPatch.Pheromone += 1;
            }
            else
            {
                MoveRandomly(random);
            }
            break;
    }
}
```

7. Begin a new method that dictates that the ant should search for food by looking in each neighboring patch of land:

```
private bool TryFindFood(
    Patch[, ,] patches,
    int current,
    out int food)
{

    for (var offsetY = -1; offsetY <= 1; offsetY++)
    {
        for (var offsetX = -1; offsetX <= 1; offsetX++)
        {
```

8. Ignore the patch of land if it's either under the ant or off the edge of the known world:

```
if (offsetY == 0 && offsetX == 0)
{
    continue;
}

var neighborX = Position.X + offsetX;
if (neighborX < 0 || neighborX >= WorldWidth)
{
    continue;
}
var neighborY = Position.Y + offsetY;
if (neighborY < 0 || neighborY >= WorldHeight)
{
    continue;
}
```

9. Complete the method by removing any food that is found from the patch:

```
var neighborPatch = patches[
        current,
        neighborX, neighborY];
if (neighborPatch.Food > 0)
{
        neighborPatch.Food -= 1;
        food = 1;
        return true;
    }
  }
}
food = 0;
return false;
}
```

10. Create a new method to try and find the next patch of land that's on the path to following the pheromone trail:

```
private bool TryMoveTowardsPheromone(Patch[, ,] patches, int
current)
{

    var deltaX = 0;
    var deltaY = 0;
    var patch = patches[current, Position.X, Position.Y];
    var smallestNestScent = patch.NestScent;
    var smallerNestScentFound = false;

    for (var offsetY = -3; offsetY <= 3; offsetY++)
    {
        for (var offsetX = -3; offsetX <= 3; offsetX++)
        {
```

11. Ignore any patches that are directly under the ant or off of the map:

```
if (offsetY == 0 && offsetX == 0)
{
    continue;
}
var neighborX = Position.X + offsetX;
if (neighborX < 0 || neighborX >= WorldWidth)
{
    continue;
}
var neighborY = Position.Y + offsetY;
```

```
if (neighborY < 0 || neighborY >= WorldHeight)
{
    continue;
}
```

12. Likewise, ignore any patches that don't have some pheromone present:

```
var neighborPatch = patches[current, neighborX, neighborY];

var neighborPheromone = neighborPatch.Pheromone;
if (neighborPheromone == 0)
{
    continue;
}
```

13. Complete the loops by taking note of the patch that had traces of pheromone and the lowest scent of the nest:

```
        var neighbourNestScent = neighborPatch.NestScent;
        if (neighbourNestScent < smallestNestScent)
        {
            smallestNestScent = neighbourNestScent;
            smallerNestScentFound = true;
            deltaX = Math.Sign(offsetX);
            deltaY = Math.Sign(offsetY);
        }

    }
}
```

14. Finish the method by returning whether a suitable patch was found:

```
    if (!smallerNestScentFound)
    {
        return false;
    }

    Position.X += deltaX;
    Position.Y += deltaY;
    return true;
}
```

15. Add a method to try and find the next patch, which is on the path back to the nest:

```
private bool TryMoveTowardsNest(Patch[, ,] patches, int current)
{
    var strongestScent = float.MinValue;
    var scentFound = false;
```

```
var nextX = 0;
var nextY = 0;

for (var y = -1; y <= 1; y++)
{
    for (var x = -1; x <= 1; x++)
    {
```

16. Ignore any patches that are either off the edge of the map, or directly under the ant:

```
if (y == 0 && x == 0)
{
    continue;
}
var neighborX = Position.X + x;
if (neighborX < 0 || neighborX >= WorldWidth)
{
    continue;
}
var neighborY = Position.Y + y;
if (neighborY < 0 || neighborY >= WorldHeight)
{
    continue;
}
```

17. Finish the loops by selecting the patch that has the strongest scent of the nest:

```
var neighborPatch = patches[
        current,
        neighborX, neighborY];
if (neighborPatch.NestScent <= strongestScent)
{
    continue;
}
strongestScent = neighborPatch.NestScent;
scentFound = true;
nextX = neighborX;
nextY = neighborY;
    }
}
```

18. Complete the method by returning with any matching patch found:

```
if (!scentFound)
{
    return false;
}
```

```
        Position.X = nextX;
        Position.Y = nextY;
        return true;
    }
```

19. Add a method to move to a randomly selected neighboring patch on the map:

```
int deltaX;
int deltaY;

private void MoveRandomly(Random random)
{
    if (random.NextDouble() < 0.2f)
    {
        deltaX = random.Next(-1, 2);
        deltaY = random.Next(-1, 2);
    }

    var validMove = false;
    var nextX = deltaX + Position.X;
    var nextY = deltaY + Position.Y;
    validMove = (!(nextX == 0 && nextY == 0) &&
                    nextX >= 0 && nextX < WorldWidth &&
                    nextY >= 0 && nextY < WorldHeight);
    if (validMove)
    {
        Position.X = nextX;
        Position.Y = nextY;
    }
}
```

20. In your game class, define the variables to hold the state of the ants, patches, food placement, and whether the various airborne factors are going to be displayed:

```
Texture2D block;
Rectangle blockDrawArea;
List<Point> allDirections;
int worldWidth = 100;
int worldHeight = 100;

Patch[, ,] patches;
int previousPatchIndex = 0;
int nextPatchIndex = 1;

List<Ant> ants;
```

```
        List<Vector2> foodCentres = new List<Vector2>() {
                new Vector2(90, 50),
                new Vector2(10, 20),
                new Vector2(50,90) };
        Vector2 currentPosition = Vector2.Zero;

        Random random = new Random();

        double lastUpdateTime;
        bool showGases = false;
```

21. Alter your game's content loading to include the setup of the ant simulation:

```
protected override void LoadContent()
{
        spriteBatch = new SpriteBatch(GraphicsDevice);

        block = Content.Load<Texture2D>("block");
        blockDrawArea = new Rectangle(0, 0, 5, 5);

        PopulateAllDirections();

        SetupAnts();
        SetupPatches();
}
```

22. In the regular update of the game loop, ensure that the ant and patch simulated parts are updated roughly every tenth of a second:

```
protected override void Update(GameTime gameTime)
{
        if (gameTime.TotalGameTime.TotalSeconds - lastUpdateTime >
                0.0125)
        {
            UpdatePatches(CopyFood, AgePheromone);

            foreach (var ant in ants)
            {
                ant.Update(
                    patches,
                    nextPatchIndex,
                    random,
                    gameTime);
            }
```

```
            SwapPreviousWithNext();
            lastUpdateTime = gameTime.TotalGameTime.TotalSeconds;
        }

        base.Update(gameTime);
    }
```

23. Include a method to set up the ants:

```
    private void SetupAnts()
    {
        ants = new List<Ant>();
        for (var antIndex = 0; antIndex < 100; antIndex++)
        {
            var ant = new Ant()
            {
                WorldWidth = worldWidth,
                WorldHeight = worldHeight,
                Position = new Point(
                    random.Next(0, worldWidth),
                    random.Next(0, worldHeight))
            };
            ants.Add(ant);
        }
    }
```

24. For the simulation, set up two sets of patches so that during the update cycle, its possible to easily distinguish between the previous state and the next state of each patch:

```
    private void SetupPatches()
    {
        patches = new Patch[2, worldWidth, worldHeight];


        for (var y = 0; y < worldHeight; y++)
        {
            for (var x = 0; x < worldWidth; x++)
            {
                var patch = new Patch();
                patches[previousPatchIndex, x, y] = patch;

                if (y == 50 && x == 50)
                {
                    patch.NestScent = 2500;
                    patch.Nest = true;
```

```
            }
            else
            {
                patch.NestScent = 0;
                patch.Nest = false;
            }

            var alternate = new Patch();
            patches[nextPatchIndex, x, y] = alternate;
        }
    }

    var nestScentHasReachedEdge = false;
    do
    {
        UpdatePatches(
            CopyNestDetails,
            DiffuseNestScent,
            CopyFood,
            CreateFood);
        SwapPreviousWithNext();
        var patch = patches[previousPatchIndex, 0, 0];
        nestScentHasReachedEdge = (patch.NestScent > 0.01f);
    } while (!nestScentHasReachedEdge);
}
```

25. Add some helper methods to populate the relative directions' table and swap patches:

```
private void PopulateAllDirections()
{
    allDirections = new List<Point>();
    for (var y = -1; y <= 1; y++)
    {
        for (var x = -1; x <= 1; x++)
        {
            if (y == 0 &&
                x == 0)
            {
                continue;
            }

            allDirections.Add(new Point(x, y));
        }
    }
}
```

```
    }

    private void SwapPreviousWithNext()
    {
        previousPatchIndex = 1 - previousPatchIndex;
        nextPatchIndex = 1 - nextPatchIndex;
    }
```

26. Add the logic to update the patches through a series of patch updating methods referred to as `patchUpdaters`:

```
private void UpdatePatches(
params Action<Patch, Patch, int, int>[] patchUpdaters)
{
    for (var y = 0; y < worldHeight; y++)
    {
        for (var x = 0; x < worldWidth; x++)
        {
            var previousPatch = patches[
                                    previousPatchIndex, x, y];
            var nextPatch = patches[nextPatchIndex, x, y];

            foreach (var patchUpdater in patchUpdaters)
            {
                patchUpdater(previousPatch, nextPatch, x, y);
            }
        }
    }
}
```

27. Include the first two of the patch updaters that, in this case, deal with the setup and movement of food across patches:

```
private void CreateFood(
    Patch previousPatch, Patch nextPatch, int x, int y)
{
    currentPosition.X = x;
    currentPosition.Y = y;

    foreach (var foodCentre in foodCentres)
    {
        if (
        Vector2.Distance(foodCentre, currentPosition) < 10 &&
            random.NextDouble() > 0.997)
        {
            nextPatch.Food += 1;
```

```
            }
        }
    }

    private void CopyFood(
        Patch previousPatch, Patch nextPatch, int x, int y)
    {
        nextPatch.Food = previousPatch.Food;
    }
```

28. Next, add the patch updater that diffuses the scent of a particular patch in all valid directions:

```
private void DiffuseNestScent(
    Patch previousPatch,
    Patch nextPatch,
    int x, int y)
{
    var combinedTotal = previousPatch.NestScent;
    var combinedCount = 1;
    for (var directionIndex = 0;
        directionIndex < allDirections.Count;
        directionIndex++)
    {
        var direction = allDirections[directionIndex];

        var testY = y + direction.Y;
        if (testY < 0 || testY >= worldHeight)
        {
            continue;
        }

        var testX = x + direction.X;
        if (testX < 0 || testX >= worldWidth)
        {
            continue;
        }

        var previousNeighbour = patches[
                previousPatchIndex, testX, testY];
        var value = previousNeighbour.NestScent;
        combinedTotal += value;
        combinedCount++;
    }
    nextPatch.NestScent = combinedTotal / combinedCount;
}
```

29. Add a patch updater to ensure that the next set of patches has the same ant nests as the previous:

```
private void CopyNestDetails(
    Patch previousPatch, Patch nextPatch, int x, int y)
{
    nextPatch.Nest = previousPatch.Nest;
    nextPatch.NestScent = previousPatch.NestScent;
}
```

30. Complete the patch updaters with one that ages the ant's deposited pheromone over time:

```
private void AgePheromone(
    Patch previousPatch, Patch nextPatch, int x, int y)
{
    var pheromone = previousPatch.Pheromone;

    if (pheromone <= float.Epsilon)
    {
        pheromone = 0f;
    }
    else
    {
        pheromone *= 0.6f;
    }

    nextPatch.Pheromone = pheromone;
}
```

31. Begin the `Draw()` method by rendering the ground, food, and pheromones:

```
protected override void Draw(GameTime gameTime)
{
    GraphicsDevice.Clear(Color.CornflowerBlue);
    spriteBatch.Begin();
    for (var y = 0; y < patches.GetLength(2); y++)
    {
        blockDrawArea.Y = y * blockDrawArea.Height;
        for (var x = 0; x < patches.GetLength(1); x++)
        {
            blockDrawArea.X = x * blockDrawArea.Width;

            var patch = patches[previousPatchIndex, x, y];
            var patchColor = Color.Black;
            if (patch.Food > 1)
            {
```

```
                patchColor = Color.Green;
            }
            else if (showGases)
            {
                patchColor = Color.Lerp(
                            patchColor,
                            Color.Brown,
                            patch.NestScent);
                if (patch.Pheromone >= float.Epsilon)
                {
                    patchColor = Color.Lerp(
                            patchColor,
                            Color.Blue,
                            0.25f);
                }
            }
            spriteBatch.Draw(
                block,
                blockDrawArea,
                patchColor);
        }
    }
```

32. Complete the draw method by rendering the ants:

```
    foreach (var ant in ants)
    {
        blockDrawArea.X = ant.Position.X *
                            blockDrawArea.Width;
        blockDrawArea.Y = ant.Position.Y *
                            blockDrawArea.Height;
        Color antColor = Color.White;
        if (showGases)
        {
            switch (ant.Mode)
            {
                case AntMode.ReturningToNestWithFood:
                    antColor = Color.Yellow;
                    break;
```

```
                }
            }
            spriteBatch.Draw(block, blockDrawArea, antColor);
        }

        spriteBatch.End();

        base.Draw(gameTime);
    }
```

How it works...

This recipe centers on a simplified model of how ants seem to locate food in the wild, visually represented in the following image:

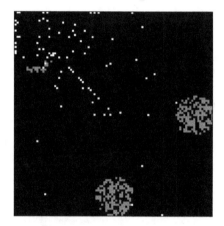

An ant may start off by wandering aimlessly around on the hunt for food.

Upon finding some food, it will pick it up and navigate its way back to the nest, by using smell. As it travels back home, it emits a pheromone indicating that it has found food.

Upon dropping the food off at the nest, the ant may detect the presence of the aforementioned pheromone from either itself or another ant, and follow it back to the point where food was originally found.

In the real world, ants seem to be able to detect the age of the pheromone in the air and follow it back to where it's oldest, but in order to keep things as simple as possible, this recipe opts for a mix of where the nest scent is weakest and the pheromone is present.

There's more...

Decentralized behavior is an entire research discipline unto itself. How and what you choose to model in such a fashion is almost limitless. However, the best results generally tend to occur with a larger number of group members.

If you have a situation where the individual movements of a group member aren't ultimately that important (such as a resource collecting unit's in an RTS or animals flocking), then opting for a decentralized approach can make for easier and more resilient behavior.

See also

▶ *"Turtles, Termites and Traffic Jams" (ISBN 978-0262680936), Mitchel Resnick. MIT Press*

6
Playing with Animation

In this chapter we will cover:

- ▶ Applying animation with SkinnedEffect
- ▶ Motion capture with Kinect
- ▶ Integrating rag doll physics
- ▶ Rendering crowds

Introduction

A quick review of any of the major modeling packages, along with a number of popular helper libraries, will confirm that the animation of 3D models is both a common and popular requirement in games production.

Given that the main task of animation is covered elsewhere so regularly, this chapter takes a slightly different approach by highlighting what lies at the foundation of some common animation techniques; namely two different ways of generating it, how it can be applied to one or many models in a performant fashion.

Applying animation with SkinnedEffect

The XNA framework comes pre-bundled with an effect that allows the GPU to take a fair portion of the burden of animating meshes away from the CPU. There are freely available examples, both from Microsoft and others, on how to import animation data from various modeling packages into a format suitable for XNA and said effect.

One aspect that I haven't seen covered in quite as much detail is how one actually interacts with such an effect in the simplest possible manner and how the effect manages to do what it does.

The chapter will hopefully fill both gaps.

Getting ready

This example utilizes the `GeometricBuffer` classes detailed in the procedural modeling recipes of *Chapter 3, Procedural Modeling*, but any library or modeling package that can deal with a mesh constructed from a custom vertex type will do.

How to do it...

To begin your exploration of the `SkinnedEffect`:

1. Add a new vertex type that includes weighting information:

```
public struct VertexPositionNormalTextureWeightBlend : IVertexType
{
    public Vector3 Position;
    public Vector3 Normal;
    public Vector2 TextureCoordinate;
    public Vector4 BoneWeights;
    public Vector4 BlendIndices;

    public readonly static VertexDeclaration VertexDeclaration =
new VertexDeclaration
    (
        new VertexElement(0, VertexElementFormat.Vector3,
            VertexElementUsage.Position, 0),
        new VertexElement(sizeof(float) *3,
            VertexElementFormat.Vector3,
            VertexElementUsage.Normal, 0),
        new VertexElement(sizeof(float) *(3 + 3),
            VertexElementFormat.Vector2,
            VertexElementUsage.TextureCoordinate, 0),
        new VertexElement(sizeof(float) *(3 + 3 + 2),
            VertexElementFormat.Vector4,
            VertexElementUsage.BlendWeight, 0),
        new VertexElement((sizeof(float) * (3 + 3 + 2 + 4)),
            VertexElementFormat.Vector4,
            VertexElementUsage.BlendIndices, 0)
    );
```

```
public VertexPositionNormalTextureWeightBlend(
    Vector3 position,
    Vector3 normal,
    Vector2 textureCoordinate,
    Vector4 boneWeights,
    Vector4 blendIndices)
{
    Position = position;
    Normal = normal;
    TextureCoordinate = textureCoordinate;
    BoneWeights = boneWeights;
    BlendIndices = blendIndices;
}

VertexDeclaration IVertexType.VertexDeclaration
{
    get
    {
        return VertexDeclaration;
    }
}
}
```

2. Create a new factory class to ease the construction of meshes made from the new vertex type:

```
public class
VertexPositionNormalTextureWeightBlendGeometricBufferFactory : Geo
metricBufferFactory<VertexPositionNormalTextureWeightBlend>
{
    public void AddTriangle(
        Vector3 vertex1,
        Vector2 textureCoordinate1,
        Vector4 weight1, Vector4 blendIndex1,
        Vector3 vertex2,
        Vector2 textureCoordinate2,
        Vector4 weight2, Vector4 blendIndex2,
        Vector3 vertex3, Vector2 textureCoordinate3,
        Vector4 weight3, Vector4 blendIndex3)
    {
        var planar1 = vertex2 - vertex1;
        var planar2 = vertex1 - vertex3;
        var normal = Vector3.Normalize(
                        Vector3.Cross(planar1, planar2));
```

```
            AddTriangle(
                new VertexPositionNormalTextureWeightBlend(
                    vertex1,
                    normal,
                    textureCoordinate1,
                    weight1, blendIndex1),
                new VertexPositionNormalTextureWeightBlend(
                    vertex2,
                    normal,
                    textureCoordinate2,
                    weight2, blendIndex2),
                new VertexPositionNormalTextureWeightBlend(
                    vertex3,
                    normal,
                    textureCoordinate3,
                    weight3, blendIndex3));
        }

        public void AddTriangle(
            VertexPositionNormalTextureWeightBlend vertex1,
            VertexPositionNormalTextureWeightBlend vertex2,
            VertexPositionNormalTextureWeightBlend vertex3)
        {
            vertices.Add(vertex1);
            vertices.Add(vertex2);
            vertices.Add(vertex3);
        }

    }
```

3. In your game, create the instance-level variables to hold the buffers for the triangle to display, the matrices for the camera, and the effect that will render the animation:

```
Matrix world;
Matrix view;
Matrix projection;
SkinnedEffect effect;

GeometricBuffer<VertexPositionNormalTextureWeightBlend> buffer;
```

4. In the `LoadContent()` method, load the camera matrices as follows:

```
world = Matrix.CreateTranslation(Vector3.Zero);
view = Matrix.CreateLookAt(
                Vector3.Backward * 3 + Vector3.Up,
                Vector3.Zero,
```

```
                         Vector3.Up);
    projection = Matrix.CreatePerspectiveFieldOfView(
                         MathHelper.ToRadians(60f),
                         GraphicsDevice.Viewport.AspectRatio,
                         0.002f, 200f);
```

5. Create an instance of the `SkinnedEffect`:

```
effect = new SkinnedEffect(GraphicsDevice);
effect.World = world;
effect.View = view;
effect.Projection = projection;
effect.EnableDefaultLighting();
```

6. Set the number of weights that will influence each vertex to two:

```
effect.WeightsPerVertex = 2;
```

7. Create a triangle with weightings set for each vertex as follows:

```
var factory = new
VertexPositionNormalTextureWeightBlendGeometricBufferFactory();
factory.AddTriangle(
    vertex1:new Vector3(-1, 0, 0),
    textureCoordinate1: new Vector2(0, 1),
    weight1: new Vector4(1, 0, 0, 0),
    blendIndex1: new Vector4(0, 0, 0, 0),

    vertex2: new Vector3(0, 1, 0),
    textureCoordinate2: new Vector2(0.5f, 0),
    weight2: new Vector4(0.5f, 0.5f, 0, 0),
    blendIndex2: new Vector4(0, 1, 0, 0),

    vertex3: new Vector3(1, 0, 0),
    textureCoordinate3: new Vector2(1, 1),
    weight3: new Vector4(1, 0, 0, 0),
    blendIndex3: new Vector4(1, 0, 0, 0));

buffer = factory.Create(GraphicsDevice);
```

8. Begin the `Update()` method with two variables that cycle between positive one and negative one:

```
float offsetOne = 0f;
float deltaOne = 1f;
float offsetTwo = 0f;
float deltaTwo = -1f;

protected override void Update(GameTime gameTime)
```

```
{
    offsetOne += deltaOne *
        (float)gameTime.ElapsedGameTime.TotalSeconds;
    if (offsetOne > 1f || offsetOne < -1f)
    {
        deltaOne = -deltaOne;
    }

    offsetTwo += deltaTwo *
        (float)gameTime.ElapsedGameTime.TotalSeconds;
    if (offsetTwo > 1f || offsetTwo < -1f)
    {
        deltaTwo = -deltaTwo;
    }
```

9. Finish updating through the setting of the bone transforms:

```
effect.SetBoneTransforms(new Matrix[] {
    Matrix.CreateTranslation(new Vector3(offsetOne,0,0)),
    Matrix.CreateTranslation(new Vector3(0,offsetTwo,0)) });
```

10. Complete the `Draw()` method by drawing the triangle:

```
buffer.Draw(effect);
```

Upon executing the code you should hopefully find yourself with one animated triangle similar to the following:

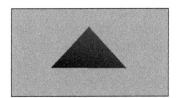

How it works...

The `SkinnedEffect` allows for up to 72 vertices to be associated with up to four transformations each. By setting up how much each transformation affects a given vertex and then adjusting the transformations over time, a reasonably efficient method of animation can be achieved.

When the vertex array is constructed, an additional four-dimensional vector is supplied. This specifies the indices of which transformations will affect the vertex and by how much.

Upon each update, a freshly calculated list of influential transformations is supplied to the GPU; allowing it to go through and recalculate the position of each vertex.

By only transmitting a single copy of the vertex buffer and the bare minimum of animation data to the GPU a great deal of efficiency can be gained from both the succinct communication to and the specialized hardware of the GPU.

Motion capture with Kinect

With the ease and availability of a high-quality motion capture device, such as the Kinect, close at hand for many people, it seems only sensible to apply some of its impressive horsepower towards solving one of the common problems of game development: the collection of realistic animation data.

This recipe will illustrate how to communicate with a Kinect device so that you can do anything from capturing your own body movements for character animation in a forthcoming game or as a basis for capturing player's movements in released games.

Getting ready

This recipe assumes that a Kinect device is attached to your PC and the Kinect for Windows SDK is installed. As the SDK was in beta at the time of writing, there may be some small differences between what's presented here and the preferred method of operation in later API, but hopefully the overall concepts will still be evident.

The SDK can be found at `http://www.kinectforwindows.org`

A texture to indicate the position of skeletal joints on screen is also required. It can be of any size or shape but I would recommend using a small white dot as an easy starting point.

How to do it...

To start your own Kinect-based adventures:

1. Create a new `Observer` class to hold the Kinect-specific logic as follows:

   ```
   class Observer
   {
   ```

2. Add instance variables to hold references to any Kinect devices attached along with the texture used to display joint markers:

   ```
   private GraphicsDevice graphicsDevice;
   private Texture2D marker;
   private Vector2 markerOrigin;

   private KinectSensor sensor;
   private Texture2D colourImage;
   ```

```
public Observer(GraphicsDevice graphicsDevice, ContentManager
content)
{
    this.graphicsDevice = graphicsDevice;
    marker = content.Load<Texture2D>("circle");
    markerOrigin = new Vector2(
        marker.Width / 2, marker.Height / 2);
    KinectSensor.KinectSensors.StatusChanged +=
        this.KinectsStatusChanged;
    FindFirstAvailableKinect();
}
```

3. Create a method to find the first Kinect device available for use:

```
private void FindFirstAvailableKinect()
{
```

4. As there's a possibility that Kinect devices may be attached or detached during the execution of this code, make sure any reference to a previously connected device is cleaned up correctly:

```
if (sensor != null)
{
    sensor.AllFramesReady -= new EventHandler<AllFramesReadyEventA
rgs>(sensor_AllFramesReady);
    lastImageFormat = ColorImageFormat.Undefined;
    sensor = null;
}
```

5. Complete the method by iterating through any connected devices and enabling the various image-based data streams available:

```
foreach (var kinectSensor in KinectSensor.KinectSensors)
    {
        if (kinectSensor.Status == KinectStatus.Connected)
        {
            sensor = kinectSensor;
            sensor.AllFramesReady += new EventHandler<AllFramesRea
dyEventArgs>(sensor_AllFramesReady);

            if (!sensor.ColorStream.IsEnabled)
            {
                sensor.ColorStream.Enable(
                ColorImageFormat.RgbResolution640x480Fps30);
            }
            if (!sensor.DepthStream.IsEnabled)
            {
                sensor.DepthStream.Enable();
```

```
        }
        if (!sensor.SkeletonStream.IsEnabled)
        {
            sensor.SkeletonStream.Enable();
        }
        if (!sensor.IsRunning)
        {
            sensor.Start();
        }
        return;
      }
    }
    sensor = null;
}
```

6. Add an event handler to store the details of any image data that becomes available between updates:

```
private bool allFramesReady = false;
private AllFramesReadyEventArgs allFramesEventArgs;

void sensor_AllFramesReady(object sender, AllFramesReadyEventArgs
e)
{
    allFramesEventArgs = e;
    allFramesReady = true;
}
```

7. Create a handler so that when the status of a Kinect device changes, a fresh search for available devices is initiated:

```
private void KinectsStatusChanged(
     object sender, StatusChangedEventArgs e)
{
    FindFirstAvailableKinect();
}
```

8. Add an `Update()` method to check for the presence of any new image data and read it in as required:

```
public void Update(GameTime gameTime)
{
    if (allFramesReady)
    {
        var skeletonFrame = allFramesEventArgs.
OpenSkeletonFrame();
        var depthFrame = allFramesEventArgs.OpenDepthImageFrame();
        var imageFrame = allFramesEventArgs.OpenColorImageFrame();
```

```
        if (imageFrame != null)
        {
            Read(imageFrame);
        }

        if (skeletonFrame != null &&
            depthFrame != null)
        {
            Read(skeletonFrame, depthFrame);
        }
        allFramesReady = false;
    }
}
```

9. Insert a method to convert the color image data supplied by the Kinect into a format that the XNA framework can consume and display easily:

```
private ColorImageFormat lastImageFormat = ColorImageFormat.
Undefined;
private byte[] pixelData;
private Color[] colorData;

private void Read(ColorImageFrame imageFrame)
{

    var haveNewFormat = lastImageFormat != imageFrame.Format;

    if (haveNewFormat)
    {
        pixelData = new byte[imageFrame.PixelDataLength];
        colourImage = new Texture2D(
            graphicsDevice,
            imageFrame.Width, imageFrame.Height,
            false, SurfaceFormat.Color);
        colorData = new Color[imageFrame.Width *
            imageFrame.Height];
    }

    imageFrame.CopyPixelDataTo(pixelData);
    for (int i = 0; i < pixelData.Length; i += 4)
    {
        var b = pixelData[i];
        var g = pixelData[i + 1];
        var r = pixelData[i + 2];
```

```
        var color = new Color(r, g, b);
        colorData[i / 4] = color;
    }


    colourImage.SetData(colorData);


}
```

10. Begin a new method to read in the skeletal data supplied by the Kinect by copying said data into an array:

```
public Dictionary<int,
    Dictionary<
        JointType,
        ColorImagePoint>> PointByJointBySkeleton = new
    Dictionary<int,
        Dictionary<JointType, ColorImagePoint>>();

private Skeleton[] skeletonData;
private HashSet<int> recentlyRefreshedSkeletons = new
HashSet<int>();
private List<int> allSkeletonTrackingIds = new List<int>();

private void Read(
    SkeletonFrame skeletonFrame,
    DepthImageFrame depthFrame)
{
    if (skeletonData == null ||
        skeletonData.Length !=
            skeletonFrame.SkeletonArrayLength)
    {
        skeletonData =
          new Skeleton[skeletonFrame.SkeletonArrayLength];
    }
    skeletonFrame.CopySkeletonDataTo(skeletonData);
```

11. Iterate through any tracked skeletons; mapping the three-dimensional joint data into the corresponding color image locations:

```
recentlyRefreshedSkeletons.Clear();
foreach (Skeleton skeleton in skeletonData)
{
    if (skeleton.TrackingState != SkeletonTrackingState.Tracked)
    {
        continue;
```

```
    }

    Dictionary<JointType, ColorImagePoint> pointByJoint;
    if (!PointByJointBySkeleton.TryGetValue(
            skeleton.TrackingId, out pointByJoint))
    {
        pointByJoint = new Dictionary<
                            JointType, ColorImagePoint>();
        PointByJointBySkeleton[skeleton.TrackingId] =
          pointByJoint;
    }

    foreach (Joint joint in skeleton.Joints)
    {
        if (joint.TrackingState != JointTrackingState.Tracked)
        {
            pointByJoint.Remove(joint.JointType);
            continue;
        }
        var depthPoint =
            depthFrame.MapFromSkeletonPoint(joint.Position);
        var colorPoint =
            depthFrame.MapToColorImagePoint(
                depthPoint.X, depthPoint.Y,
                sensor.ColorStream.Format);
        pointByJoint[joint.JointType] = colorPoint;
        recentlyRefreshedSkeletons.Add(skeleton.TrackingId);
    }
}
```

12. Complete the method by cleaning up any joint position data that wasn't refreshed in the current update:

```
allSkeletonTrackingIds.Clear();
allSkeletonTrackingIds.AddRange(
    PointByJointBySkeleton.Keys);
foreach (var id in allSkeletonTrackingIds)
{
    if (!recentlyRefreshedSkeletons.Contains(id))
    {
        PointByJointBySkeleton.Remove(id);
    }
}
}
```

13. Finish the class by providing the ability for it to draw the color image stream from the Kinect with any tracked skeleton joints overlaid:

```
Vector2 displayPoint;

public void Draw(SpriteBatch spriteBatch)
{
    if (colourImage == null)
    {
        return;
    }

    spriteBatch.Draw(colourImage, Vector2.Zero, Color.White);
    foreach (var jointTypePointSkeletonPair
        in PointByJointBySkeleton)
    {
        var pointByJoint = jointTypePointSkeletonPair.Value;

        foreach (var jointTypePointPair in pointByJoint)
        {
            var point = jointTypePointPair.Value;
            displayPoint.X = point.X;
            displayPoint.Y = point.Y;
            spriteBatch.Draw(
                marker, displayPoint, null, Color.White,
                0, markerOrigin, 0.5f,
                SpriteEffects.None, 0);
        }
    }
}
```

14. In your game class, create an instance of the `Observer` class along with a `SpriteBatch` to help with the onscreen rendering:

```
SpriteBatch spriteBatch;
Observer recorder;

protected override void LoadContent()
{
    spriteBatch = new SpriteBatch(GraphicsDevice);
    recorder = new Observer(GraphicsDevice, Content);
}
```

15. Update the `Observer` instance upon each update cycle:

```
protected override void Update(GameTime gameTime)
{
    recorder.Update(gameTime);
    base.Update(gameTime);
}
```

16. Draw the Kinect color stream with any tracked skeletons:

```
protected override void Draw(GameTime gameTime)
{
    GraphicsDevice.Clear(Color.CornflowerBlue);
    spriteBatch.Begin();

    recorder.Draw(spriteBatch);

    spriteBatch.End();
    base.Draw(gameTime);
}
```

How it works...

Two of the Kinect's more noticeable outputs are a color video and a depth stream.

By capturing the imagery from these two streams and applying some specialized hardware heuristics built into the Kinect device, we're able to extract the actual or implied positions of a player's significant body parts.

As can be observed in the code, the bulk of the work is done by the Kinect hardware and SDK, leaving only some device management and a small amount of image conversion for our code to perform.

There's more...

This recipe only covers how to collect the data from the Kinect device; not the many ways one may find on how to use the said data once it's been collected.

A dictionary of skeletal points from the `Observer` instance is exposed upon each update cycle. This might form a good basis for either recording animations to file for later playback or analyzing them immediately to determine player gestures.

Under voice command

The Kinect and its SDK have some equally powerful directional speech analysis capabilities that can significantly enhance either the ease of recording animation, through being able to say key phrases such as 'start' and 'stop', or the level of interaction available to your players by being able to give vocal commands directly to game characters.

Integrating rag doll physics

Particularly in the realm of computer games, attempting to pre-generate absolutely every bit of animation required by characters in a game is not always going to yield the most efficient use of developer's or artist's time.

Sometimes we want an animation to be able to react in real time to the environment around it and the introduction of a physics engine is a popular way of achieving that.

As writing a physics engine is complicated enough to warrant a number of books by itself, it's far more common for games to utilize third-party physics engines rather than for developers to construct their own.

With this in mind, the following recipe demonstrates how to integrate one specific physics engine in the hope that the general principles involved in integrating just about any of the other physics engines available will be indicated.

Getting ready

This recipe relies upon both the `GeometricBuffer` classes discussed in *Chapter 3, Procedural Modeling*, and the BEPU physics engine available for free at `http://bepu. squarespace.com`, although other mesh containers and physics engines should be relatively easy to substitute in as required.

How to do it...

To begin animating your own rag doll characters:

1. Create a class to render a box shape to the screen:

```
class BoxDisplay
{
    private GeometricBuffer<VertexPositionNormalTexture> buffer;

    public BoxDisplay(GeometricBuffer<VertexPositionNormalTexture>
buffer, Color diffuseColor)
    {
        this.buffer = buffer;
        DiffuseColor = diffuseColor;
    }

    public Matrix World = Matrix.Identity;
```

```
        public Color DiffuseColor;

        public void Draw(BasicEffect effect)
        {
            effect.DiffuseColor = DiffuseColor.ToVector3();
            effect.World = World;
            buffer.Draw(effect);
        }
    }
}
```

2. Create a factory class to produce display boxes:

```
class BoxDisplayFactory
{
```

3. Add a method to create new display box instances of a given color:

```
public static BoxDisplay Create(
    GraphicsDevice graphicsDevice,
    ContentManager content,
    Color diffuseColor)
{
```

4. Map out the vertex and texture positions:

```
var topForwardLeft = (Vector3.Up +
        Vector3.Forward + Vector3.Left) / 2f;
var topForwardRight = (Vector3.Up +
        Vector3.Forward + Vector3.Right) /2f;
var topBackwardLeft = (Vector3.Up +
        Vector3.Backward + Vector3.Left) /2f;
var topBackwardRight = (Vector3.Up +
        Vector3.Backward + Vector3.Right) /2f;
var bottomForwardLeft = (Vector3.Down +
        Vector3.Forward + Vector3.Left) /2f;
var bottomForwardRight = (Vector3.Down +
        Vector3.Forward + Vector3.Right) /2f;
var bottomBackwardLeft = (Vector3.Down +
        Vector3.Backward + Vector3.Left) /2f;
var bottomBackwardRight = (Vector3.Down +
        Vector3.Backward + Vector3.Right) / 2f;

var topLeft = new Vector2(0, 0);
var topRight = new Vector2(1, 0);
var bottomRight = new Vector2(1, 1);
var bottomLeft = new Vector2(0, 1);
```

5. Construct the various faces of the box:

```
var factory = new
VertexPositionNormalTextureGeometricBufferFactory();

factory.AddPane(
    topForwardLeft, topLeft,
    topForwardRight, topRight,
    topBackwardRight, bottomRight,
    topBackwardLeft, bottomLeft);

factory.AddPane(
        bottomForwardRight, topLeft,
    bottomForwardLeft, topRight,
    bottomBackwardLeft, bottomRight,
    bottomBackwardRight, bottomLeft
    );

factory.AddPane(
    topForwardLeft, topLeft,
    topBackwardLeft, topRight,
    bottomBackwardLeft, bottomRight,
    bottomForwardLeft, bottomLeft);

factory.AddPane(
    topBackwardRight, topLeft,
    topForwardRight, topRight,
    bottomForwardRight, bottomRight,
    bottomBackwardRight, bottomLeft);

factory.AddPane(
    topBackwardLeft, topLeft,
    topBackwardRight, topRight,
    bottomBackwardRight, bottomRight,
    bottomBackwardLeft, bottomLeft);

factory.AddPane(
    topForwardRight, topLeft,
    topForwardLeft, topRight,
    bottomForwardLeft, bottomRight,
    bottomForwardRight, bottomLeft);
```

6. Complete the method and class by converting the box faces into a buffer and feed it into a new instance of a `BoxDisplay`:

```
var buffer = factory.Create(graphicsDevice);
return new BoxDisplay(buffer, diffuseColor);
```

7. Add a class to simulate the ground via one large box represented both in graphical and physical form:

```
class Ground
{
    BoxDisplay boxDisplay;
    Box box;

    public Ground(
        GraphicsDevice graphicsDevice, ContentManager content,
        Space space)
    {
        box = new Box(new Vector3(0, -7, 0), 30, 10, 30);
        space.Add(box);
        boxDisplay = BoxDisplayFactory.Create(
            graphicsDevice, content,
            Color.Brown);
    }

    public void Update()
    {
        boxDisplay.World = Matrix.CreateScale(
            new Vector3(box.Width, box.Height, box.Length)) *
            box.WorldTransform;
    }

    public void Draw(BasicEffect effect)
    {
        boxDisplay.Draw(effect);
    }
}
```

8. Create a class to simulate the various body parts of a rag doll:

```
class DollPart
{
```

9. Add a constructor to set up the physical and display aspects of the body part:

```
BoxDisplay boxDisplay;
Box box;
Matrix displaySizeTransform;
```

```
public DollPart(
    GraphicsDevice graphicsDevice,
    ContentManager content,
    Space space,
    Vector3 position, Vector3 size, float weight)
{
    box = new Box(position, size.X, size.Y, size.Z, weight);
    space.Add(box);

    boxDisplay = BoxDisplayFactory.Create(
                    graphicsDevice, content, Color.White);
    displaySizeTransform = Matrix.CreateScale(size);
}
```

10. Construct a property to aid in the setup of the physical portion of the part:

```
public Entity PhysicsEntity
{
    get
    {
        return box;
    }
}
```

11. Add a method to update the display transforms with the ones calculated by the physics engine:

```
public void Update()
{
    boxDisplay.World = displaySizeTransform *
                        box.WorldTransform;
}
```

12. Complete the class with a method to render the part to the screen:

```
public void Draw(BasicEffect effect)
{
    boxDisplay.Draw(effect);
}
```

13. Create a `Doll` class that will approximate a human physique:

```
class Doll
{
    List<DollPart> parts;

    public Doll(
```

```
        GraphicsDevice graphicsDevice,
        ContentManager content, Space space)
{

    parts = new List<DollPart>();

    DollPart pelvis;
    DollPart torsoTop;

    AddBody(graphicsDevice, content, space,
                out pelvis, out torsoTop);
    AddHead(graphicsDevice, content, space,
                torsoTop);
    AddArm(graphicsDevice, content, space,
                torsoTop, true);
    AddArm(graphicsDevice, content, space,
                torsoTop, false);
    AddLeg(graphicsDevice, content, space,
                pelvis, true);
    AddLeg(graphicsDevice, content, space,
                pelvis, false);


}
```

14. Begin a new method to add the various doll parts that go into making the body of the doll:

```
private void AddBody(
    GraphicsDevice graphicsDevice,
    ContentManager content, Space space,
    out DollPart pelvis, out DollPart torsoTop)
{
```

15. Add the creation of the pelvis and lower half of the torso region:

```
pelvis = new DollPart(graphicsDevice, content, space,
                new Vector3(0, 0, 0),
                new Vector3(.5f, .28f, .33f), 20);
parts.Add(pelvis);

var torsoBottom = new DollPart(graphicsDevice, content, space,
    pelvis.PhysicsEntity.Position + new Vector3(0, .3f, 0),
    new Vector3(.42f, .48f, .3f), 15);
parts.Add(torsoBottom);
```

16. Define the rules that dictate how the lower torso and pelvis should move in relation to each other:

```
CollisionRules.AddRule(
      pelvis.PhysicsEntity, torsoBottom.PhysicsEntity,
      CollisionRule.NoBroadPhase);

space.Add(new BallSocketJoint(
    pelvis.PhysicsEntity, torsoBottom.PhysicsEntity,
    pelvis.PhysicsEntity.Position +
        new Vector3(0, .1f, 0)));

space.Add(new TwistLimit(
    pelvis.PhysicsEntity, torsoBottom.PhysicsEntity,
    Vector3.Up, Vector3.Up,
    -MathHelper.Pi / 6, MathHelper.Pi / 6));

space.Add(new SwingLimit(
    pelvis.PhysicsEntity, torsoBottom.PhysicsEntity,
    Vector3.Up, Vector3.Up, MathHelper.Pi / 6));
var pelvisToTorsoBottomMotor = new AngularMotor(
    pelvis.PhysicsEntity, torsoBottom.PhysicsEntity);
pelvisToTorsoBottomMotor.Settings.VelocityMotor.Softness = .05f;
space.Add(pelvisToTorsoBottomMotor);
```

17. Complete the method by defining the upper torso and how it should move in relation to the lower torso:

```
    torsoTop = new DollPart(graphicsDevice, content, space,
        torsoBottom.PhysicsEntity.Position +
            new Vector3(0, .3f, 0),
        new Vector3(.5f, .38f, .32f), 20);
    parts.Add(torsoTop);

    space.Add(new BallSocketJoint(
        torsoBottom.PhysicsEntity, torsoTop.PhysicsEntity,
        torsoBottom.PhysicsEntity.Position +
            new Vector3(0, .25f, 0)));
    space.Add(new SwingLimit(
        torsoBottom.PhysicsEntity, torsoTop.PhysicsEntity,
        Vector3.Up, Vector3.Up, MathHelper.Pi / 6));

    space.Add(new TwistLimit(
        torsoBottom.PhysicsEntity, torsoTop.PhysicsEntity,
        Vector3.Up, Vector3.Up,
        -MathHelper.Pi / 6, MathHelper.Pi / 6));
```

```
    var torsoBottomToTorsoTopMotor = new AngularMotor(
        torsoBottom.PhysicsEntity, torsoTop.PhysicsEntity);
    torsoBottomToTorsoTopMotor.Settings.VelocityMotor.Softness =
.05f;
    space.Add(torsoBottomToTorsoTopMotor);

    CollisionRules.AddRule(
        torsoBottom.PhysicsEntity, torsoTop.PhysicsEntity,
        CollisionRule.NoBroadPhase);

}
```

18. Create a new method to add a leg to the doll:

```
private void AddLeg(
    GraphicsDevice graphicsDevice, ContentManager content,
    Space space, DollPart pelvis, bool isRightSide)
{
```

19. Add a thigh and how it relates to the pelvis:

```
var side = new Vector3(isRightSide ? 1 : -1,1,1);

var thigh = new DollPart(graphicsDevice, content, space,
    pelvis.PhysicsEntity.Position +
        new Vector3(.15f, -.4f, 0) * side,
    new Vector3(.23f, .63f, .23f), 10);
parts.Add(thigh);

CollisionRules.AddRule(
    pelvis.PhysicsEntity, thigh.PhysicsEntity,
    CollisionRule.NoBroadPhase);

space.Add(new BallSocketJoint(
    pelvis.PhysicsEntity, thigh.PhysicsEntity,
    pelvis.PhysicsEntity.Position +
        (new Vector3(.15f, -.1f, 0) * side)));

var pelvisToThighEllipseSwingLimit = new EllipseSwingLimit(
    pelvis.PhysicsEntity, thigh.PhysicsEntity,
    Vector3.Normalize(new Vector3(.2f, -1, -.6f) * side),
    MathHelper.Pi * .7f, MathHelper.PiOver4);
pelvisToThighEllipseSwingLimit.LocalTwistAxisB = Vector3.Down;
space.Add(pelvisToThighEllipseSwingLimit);
```

```
space.Add(new TwistLimit(
    pelvis.PhysicsEntity, thigh.PhysicsEntity,
    Vector3.Down, Vector3.Down,
    -MathHelper.Pi / 6, MathHelper.Pi / 6));

var pelvisToThighMotor = new AngularMotor(
    pelvis.PhysicsEntity, thigh.PhysicsEntity);
pelvisToThighMotor.Settings.VelocityMotor.Softness = .1f;
space.Add(pelvisToThighMotor);
```

20. Join a shin onto the thigh:

```
var shin = new DollPart(
    graphicsDevice, content, space,
    thigh.PhysicsEntity.Position +
        new Vector3(0, -.6f, 0),
    new Vector3(.21f, .63f, .21f), 7);
parts.Add(shin);

CollisionRules.AddRule(
    thigh.PhysicsEntity, shin.PhysicsEntity,
    CollisionRule.NoBroadPhase);

var thighToShinRevoluteJoint = new RevoluteJoint(
    thigh.PhysicsEntity, shin.PhysicsEntity,
    thigh.PhysicsEntity.Position +
        new Vector3(0, -.3f, 0), Vector3.Right);
thighToShinRevoluteJoint.Limit.IsActive = true;
thighToShinRevoluteJoint.Limit.MinimumAngle =
    -MathHelper.Pi * .8f;
thighToShinRevoluteJoint.Limit.MaximumAngle = 0;
thighToShinRevoluteJoint.Motor.IsActive = true;
thighToShinRevoluteJoint.Motor.Settings.VelocityMotor.Softness =
.2f;
space.Add(thighToShinRevoluteJoint);
```

21. Complete the leg and the method by adding a foot:

```
var foot = new DollPart(
        graphicsDevice, content, space,
        shin.PhysicsEntity.Position +
            new Vector3(0, -.35f, -.1f),
        new Vector3(.23f, .15f, .43f), 5);
parts.Add(foot);

CollisionRules.AddRule(
```

```
        shin.PhysicsEntity, foot.PhysicsEntity,
        CollisionRule.NoBroadPhase);

    space.Add(new BallSocketJoint(
        shin.PhysicsEntity, foot.PhysicsEntity,
        shin.PhysicsEntity.Position +
            new Vector3(0, -.3f, 0)));

    space.Add(new SwingLimit(
        shin.PhysicsEntity, foot.PhysicsEntity,
        Vector3.Forward, Vector3.Forward,
        MathHelper.Pi / 8));

    var footTwistLimit = new TwistLimit(
        shin.PhysicsEntity, foot.PhysicsEntity,
        Vector3.Down, Vector3.Forward,
        -MathHelper.Pi / 8, MathHelper.Pi / 8);
    footTwistLimit.SpringSettings.StiffnessConstant = 100;
    footTwistLimit.SpringSettings.DampingConstant = 500;
    space.Add(footTwistLimit);

    var shinToFootMotor = new AngularMotor(
            shin.PhysicsEntity, foot.PhysicsEntity);
    shinToFootMotor.Settings.VelocityMotor.Softness = .2f;
    space.Add(shinToFootMotor);
}
```

22. Create a new method to add an arm to the doll:

```
private void AddArm(
    GraphicsDevice graphicsDevice, ContentManager content,
    Space space, DollPart torsoTop, bool isRightSide)
{
```

23. Start the arm by attaching the upper arm:

```
var side = new Vector3(isRightSide ? 1 : -1, 1, 1);

var upperArm = new DollPart(
        graphicsDevice, content, space,
    torsoTop.PhysicsEntity.Position +
    (new Vector3(.46f, .1f, 0) * side),
    new Vector3(.52f, .19f, .19f), 6);
parts.Add(upperArm);

CollisionRules.AddRule(
```

```
    torsoTop.PhysicsEntity, upperArm.PhysicsEntity,
    CollisionRule.NoBroadPhase);

space.Add(new BallSocketJoint(
    torsoTop.PhysicsEntity, upperArm.PhysicsEntity,
    torsoTop.PhysicsEntity.Position +
        (new Vector3(.3f, .1f, 0) * side)));

space.Add(new EllipseSwingLimit(
    torsoTop.PhysicsEntity, upperArm.PhysicsEntity,
    Vector3.Right * side, MathHelper.Pi * .75f,
    MathHelper.PiOver2));

space.Add(new TwistLimit(
    torsoTop.PhysicsEntity, upperArm.PhysicsEntity,
    Vector3.Right *side, Vector3.Right *side,
    -MathHelper.PiOver2, MathHelper.PiOver2));

var torsoTopToArmMotor = new AngularMotor(
    torsoTop.PhysicsEntity, upperArm.PhysicsEntity);
torsoTopToArmMotor.Settings.VelocityMotor.Softness = .2f;
space.Add(torsoTopToArmMotor);
```

24. Attach a forearm to the upper arm:

```
var lowerArm = new DollPart(graphicsDevice, content, space,
    upperArm.PhysicsEntity.Position +
        (new Vector3(.5f, 0, 0) * side),
    new Vector3(.52f, .18f, .18f), 5);
parts.Add(lowerArm);

CollisionRules.AddRule(
    upperArm.PhysicsEntity, lowerArm.PhysicsEntity,
    CollisionRule.NoBroadPhase);

var upperArmToLowerArmSwivelHingeJoint = new SwivelHingeJoint(
        upperArm.PhysicsEntity, lowerArm.PhysicsEntity,
        upperArm.PhysicsEntity.Position +
            (new Vector3(.28f, 0, 0) * side),
        Vector3.Up);
upperArmToLowerArmSwivelHingeJoint.HingeLimit.IsActive = true;
upperArmToLowerArmSwivelHingeJoint.TwistLimit.IsActive = true;
upperArmToLowerArmSwivelHingeJoint.TwistLimit.MinimumAngle =
    -MathHelper.Pi / 8;
upperArmToLowerArmSwivelHingeJoint.TwistLimit.MaximumAngle =
```

```
        MathHelper.Pi / 8;
    upperArmToLowerArmSwivelHingeJoint.HingeLimit.MinimumAngle =
        0;
    upperArmToLowerArmSwivelHingeJoint.HingeLimit.MaximumAngle =
        MathHelper.Pi * .8f;
    space.Add(upperArmToLowerArmSwivelHingeJoint);

    var upperArmToLowerArmMotor = new AngularMotor(
            upperArm.PhysicsEntity, lowerArm.PhysicsEntity);
    upperArmToLowerArmMotor.Settings.VelocityMotor.Softness = .3f;
    space.Add(upperArmToLowerArmMotor);
```

25. Complete the method by appending a hand onto the end of the arm:

```
    var hand = new DollPart(graphicsDevice, content, space,
        lowerArm.PhysicsEntity.Position +
            (new Vector3(.35f, 0, 0) * side),
        new Vector3(.28f, .13f, .22f), 4);
    parts.Add(hand);

    CollisionRules.AddRule(
        lowerArm.PhysicsEntity, hand.PhysicsEntity,
        CollisionRule.NoBroadPhase);

    space.Add(new BallSocketJoint(
        lowerArm.PhysicsEntity, hand.PhysicsEntity,
        lowerArm.PhysicsEntity.Position +
            (new Vector3(.2f, 0, 0) * side)));

    space.Add(new EllipseSwingLimit(
        lowerArm.PhysicsEntity, hand.PhysicsEntity,
        Vector3.Right, MathHelper.PiOver2,
        MathHelper.Pi / 6));

    space.Add(new TwistLimit(
        lowerArm.PhysicsEntity, hand.PhysicsEntity,
        Vector3.Right * side, Vector3.Right * side,
        -MathHelper.Pi / 6, MathHelper.Pi / 6));

    var lowerArmToHandMotor = new AngularMotor(
        lowerArm.PhysicsEntity, hand.PhysicsEntity);
    lowerArmToHandMotor.Settings.VelocityMotor.Softness = .4f;
    space.Add(lowerArmToHandMotor);
}
```

26. Place a head and neck on the body:

```
private void AddHead(GraphicsDevice graphicsDevice, ContentManager
content, Space space,
    DollPart torsoTop)
{
    var neck = new DollPart(graphicsDevice, content, space,
        torsoTop.PhysicsEntity.Position +
            new Vector3(0, .2f, .04f),
        new Vector3(.19f, .24f, .2f), 5);
    parts.Add(neck);

    CollisionRules.AddRule(
        torsoTop.PhysicsEntity,
        neck.PhysicsEntity,
        CollisionRule.NoBroadPhase);
    space.Add(new BallSocketJoint(
        torsoTop.PhysicsEntity,
        neck.PhysicsEntity,
        torsoTop.PhysicsEntity.Position +
            new Vector3(0, .15f, .05f)));
    space.Add(new SwingLimit(
        torsoTop.PhysicsEntity,
        neck.PhysicsEntity,
        Vector3.Up, Vector3.Up, MathHelper.Pi / 6));
    space.Add(new TwistLimit(
        torsoTop.PhysicsEntity,
        neck.PhysicsEntity,
        Vector3.Up, Vector3.Up,
        -MathHelper.Pi / 8,
        MathHelper.Pi / 8));
    var torsoTopToNeckMotor = new AngularMotor(
            torsoTop.PhysicsEntity, neck.PhysicsEntity);
    torsoTopToNeckMotor.Settings.VelocityMotor.Softness = .1f;
    space.Add(torsoTopToNeckMotor);

    var head = new DollPart(graphicsDevice, content, space,
        neck.PhysicsEntity.Position +
            new Vector3(0, .22f, -.04f),
        new Vector3(.4f, .4f, .4f), 7);
    parts.Add(head);

    CollisionRules.AddRule(
        neck.PhysicsEntity, head.PhysicsEntity,
        CollisionRule.NoBroadPhase);
```

```
        space.Add(new BallSocketJoint(
            neck.PhysicsEntity, head.PhysicsEntity,
            neck.PhysicsEntity.Position +
                new Vector3(0, .1f, .05f)));
        space.Add(new TwistLimit(
            neck.PhysicsEntity, head.PhysicsEntity,
            Vector3.Up, Vector3.Up,
             -MathHelper.Pi / 8, MathHelper.Pi / 8));
        space.Add(new SwingLimit(
            neck.PhysicsEntity, head.PhysicsEntity,
            Vector3.Up, Vector3.Up, MathHelper.Pi / 6));
        var neckToHeadMotor = new AngularMotor(
            neck.PhysicsEntity, head.PhysicsEntity);
        neckToHeadMotor.Settings.VelocityMotor.Softness = .1f;
        space.Add(neckToHeadMotor);
    }
```

27. Finish the class through the addition of Update and Draw functionality:

```
public void Update()
{
    foreach (var part in parts)
    {
        part.Update();
    }
}
```

```
public void Draw(BasicEffect effect)
{
    foreach (var part in parts)
    {
        part.Draw(effect);
    }
}
```

28. In your game, create an instance of the physics engine along with the entities you wish to simulate and the effect used to render it:

```
Space space;
Ground ground;
Doll doll;
```

```
BasicEffect effect;

protected override void LoadContent()
{
    space = new Space();
    space.ForceUpdater.Gravity = new Vector3(0, -9.81f, 0);

    ground = new Ground(GraphicsDevice, Content, space);
    doll = new Doll(GraphicsDevice, Content, space);

    effect = new BasicEffect(GraphicsDevice)
    {
        View = Matrix.CreateLookAt(
            Vector3.Down + Vector3.Forward * 5,
            Vector3.Down + Vector3.Backward,
            Vector3.Up),
        Projection = Matrix.CreatePerspectiveFieldOfView(
            MathHelper.ToRadians(60f),
            GraphicsDevice.Viewport.AspectRatio,
            0.2f, 1000f)
    };
    effect.EnableDefaultLighting();
}
```

29. Upon each `Update` cycle, ask the physics engine to recalculate the state of the world and then update the associated display entities:

```
protected override void Update(GameTime gameTime)
{
    space.Update();
    ground.Update();
    doll.Update();

    base.Update(gameTime);
}
```

30. Complete the example by rendering the doll and ground to the screen:

```
protected override void Draw(GameTime gameTime)
{
    GraphicsDevice.Clear(Color.CornflowerBlue);

    ground.Draw(effect);
```

```
        doll.Draw(effect);

        base.Draw(gameTime);
    }
```

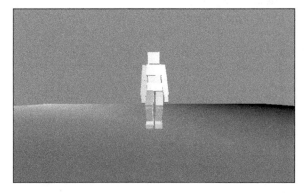

How it works...

The key to dealing with any physics engine is ensuring that an appropriate level of complexity is supplied in any model constructed within it and that a clear communication path exists out of it.

In the methods used to build up the rag doll, we can see that both a graphical representation and a physical representation of each body part is constructed with the `GeometricBuffer` holding the former and the BEPU `Space` collection holding the latter.

Upon each update cycle, the positions of each body part are read out of the physics engine and applied to the corresponding graphical elements.

The body parts of the rag doll are connected via constraints articulated to the physics engine in the form of joints and motors. These joints and motors allow us to specify that body parts shouldn't be able to pass through each other, bend in unnatural positions, or move too quickly in respect to the flesh and bone that fills a real world human body.

There's more...

In this example, the polygons used to describe the physical boundaries of the rag doll are close, bordering upon identical, in number and size to the ones used for the graphical representation. This need not always be so and is rarely true for anything but the most simplistic games involving physics engines.

It's not uncommon in a lot of commercial 3D titles, for example, for the graphical representation to consist of thousands of polygons but the associated physical representation to only number in the tens or hundreds at best. This way, the game designers can get a close enough simulation of a body's movement through the world without burning through unnecessary CPU cycles of physical complexity that add little or nothing to the enjoyment of the game.

Part time action

As good as physics engines may be, implementing all of a character's movements with one may not be the most efficient use of one's time. So, it might be useful to intermix physics with more traditional animation for the best of both worlds.

For example, the movements of a soldier within a game might be dictated by regular animation for the bulk of the game and then only swapping across to a rag doll physics engine model once the character is wounded or killed.

That way, the solider can walk across the floor in a natural fashion due to a regular animation cycle and then take a rather nasty fall down the stairs courtesy of the physics engine.

Rendering crowds

Rendering an individual character onscreen can be a costly exercise in and of itself, so the idea of rendering every member of a large crowd can sound positively insane in terms of overall performance.

The use of virtual billboards to "copy and paste" members of a crowd repeatedly throughout a space is one quite common way to reduce such an overhead.

Getting ready

This example relies upon the `GeometricBuffer` classes described in Chapter 3's procedural modeling recipes, but they are equally applicable to any method of holding and rendering meshes.

How to do it...

To render a crowd:

1. In your game, create the instance-level variables to hold the details for the camera, models, effects, and render targets that are going to be needed for rendering:

```
Vector3 cameraPosition = new Vector3(0, 2, 2);
Vector3 cameraTarget = Vector3.Zero;
Matrix world;
Matrix view;
Matrix projection;
BasicEffect personEffect;
AlphaTestEffect billboardEffect;
```

```
GeometricBuffer<VertexPositionNormalTexture> person;
GeometricBuffer<VertexPositionNormalTexture> billboard;
RenderTarget2D billboardTarget;
List<Matrix> personTranslations;
```

2. Add a method to populate the matrices associated with the "camera":

```
private void CreateCameraMatrices()
{
    world = Matrix.CreateTranslation(Vector3.Zero);
    view = Matrix.CreateLookAt(
                   cameraPosition, cameraTarget, Vector3.Up);
    projection = Matrix.CreatePerspectiveFieldOfView(
                   MathHelper.ToRadians(60f),
                   GraphicsDevice.Viewport.AspectRatio,
                   0.1f, 1000f);
}
```

3. Create a method to create the `RenderTarget` and `AlphaTestEffect` for the billboard:

```
private void CreateBillboard()
{
    billboardTarget = new RenderTarget2D(
      GraphicsDevice,
      512,
      512,
      false,
    GraphicsDevice.PresentationParameters.BackBufferFormat,
    GraphicsDevice.PresentationParameters.DepthStencilFormat);

    billboardEffect = new AlphaTestEffect(GraphicsDevice);
    billboardEffect.Texture = billboardTarget;
    billboardEffect.AlphaFunction = CompareFunction.Greater;
    billboardEffect.ReferenceAlpha = 128;
}
```

4. Begin the method for creating people by instantiating the `Effect` that will be used to render them to the billboard:

```
private void CreatePeople()
{
    personEffect = new BasicEffect(GraphicsDevice);
    personEffect.EnableDefaultLighting();
    personEffect.DiffuseColor = Color.Wheat.ToVector3();
    personEffect.World = Matrix.CreateTranslation(
        Vector3.Zero);
```

```
personEffect.Projection =
    Matrix.CreatePerspectiveFieldOfView(

            MathHelper.ToRadians(60f),
            GraphicsDevice.Viewport.AspectRatio,
            0.1f, 1000f);
```

5. Create the model representation of a person, which in this case will be
    a simple pyramid:

```
var personFactory = new
VertexPositionNormalTextureGeometricBufferFactory();
personFactory.AddTriangle(
    new Vector3(0.5f, 0f, -0.5f), new Vector2(0, 1),
    new Vector3(0, 0.5f, 0), new Vector2(0.5f, 0),
    new Vector3(-0.5f, 0f, -0.5f), new Vector2(1, 0));

personFactory.AddTriangle(
    new Vector3(-0.5f, 0f, 0.5f), new Vector2(0, 1),
    new Vector3(0, 0.5f, 0), new Vector2(0.5f, 0),
    new Vector3(0.5f, 0f, 0.5f), new Vector2(1, 0));

personFactory.AddTriangle(
    new Vector3(-0.5f, 0f, -0.5f), new Vector2(0, 1),
    new Vector3(0, 0.5f, 0), new Vector2(0.5f, 0),
    new Vector3(-0.5f, 0f, 0.5f), new Vector2(1, 0));

personFactory.AddTriangle(
    new Vector3(0.5f, 0f, 0.5f), new Vector2(0, 1),
    new Vector3(0, 0.5f, 0), new Vector2(0.5f, 0),
    new Vector3(0.5f, 0f, -0.5f), new Vector2(1, 0));

person = personFactory.Create(GraphicsDevice);
```

6. Complete the method by creating a list of world translations to hold the location
    of each person:

```
var random = new Random();
personTranslations = new List<Matrix>();

for (var peopleCount = 0; peopleCount < 500; peopleCount++)
{
    var translation = Matrix.CreateTranslation(new Vector3(
        10f - ((float)random.NextDouble() * 20f),
        0f,
        10f - ((float)random.NextDouble() * 20f)));
    personTranslations.Add(translation);
}
```

7. Call the newly-created content method from `LoadContent()`:

```
protected override void LoadContent()
{
    CreateCameraMatrices();
    CreateBillboard();
    CreatePeople();
}
```

8. Begin the `Update()` method by updating the position of the camera so it flies over the heads of the crowd:

```
protected override void Update(GameTime gameTime)
{
    cameraPosition += (Vector3.Backward + Vector3.Right) *
        (float)gameTime.ElapsedGameTime.TotalSeconds;
    view = Matrix.CreateLookAt(
        cameraPosition, cameraTarget, Vector3.Up);
```

9. Update the billboard so it's facing the camera and is in the right position relative to the camera:

```
var billboardTransform = Matrix.CreateBillboard(world.Translation,
cameraPosition, Vector3.Up, cameraTarget - cameraPosition);

var billboardFactory = new
VertexPositionNormalTextureGeometricBufferFactory();
billboardFactory.AddPane(
    Vector3.Transform(
        new Vector3(0.5f, 0.5f, 0),
        billboardTransform),
    new Vector2(0, 0),
    Vector3.Transform(
        new Vector3(-0.5f, 0.5f, 0),
        billboardTransform),
    new Vector2(1, 0),
    Vector3.Transform(
        new Vector3(-0.5f, -0.5f, 0),
        billboardTransform),
    new Vector2(1, 1),
    Vector3.Transform(
        new Vector3(0.5f, -0.5f, 0),
        billboardTransform),
```

```
        new Vector2(0, 1));
    billboard = billboardFactory.Create(GraphicsDevice);

    billboardEffect.View = view;
    billboardEffect.Projection = projection;
```

10. Complete the method by updating the camera position used to capture the image for the billboard to be of the same relative direction as the main camera position:

```
    personEffect.View = Matrix.CreateLookAt(
        Vector3.Normalize(cameraPosition) * 2f,
        Vector3.Zero,
        Vector3.Up);

    base.Update(gameTime);
}
```

11. Begin the `Draw()` method by rendering an image of a person into the `RenderTarget`:

```
protected override void Draw(GameTime gameTime)
{
    GraphicsDevice.SetRenderTarget(billboardTarget);

    GraphicsDevice.Clear(Color.Transparent);

    person.Draw(personEffect);
    GraphicsDevice.SetRenderTarget(null);
```

12. Complete the method by rendering a billboard textured with the image of a person at each person's location:

```
    GraphicsDevice.Clear(Color.CornflowerBlue);

    foreach (var personTranslation in personTranslations)
    {
        billboardEffect.World = personTranslation;
        billboard.Draw(billboardEffect);
    }
    base.Draw(gameTime);
}
```

How it works...

In this example, we're doing the equivalent of taking a photo of a typical crowd member, albeit a pyramid-shaped one in this case, and pasting copies of the photo up on billboards around the place to simulate a crowd.

Positioning of the "camera" used to take the photo of the prototypical crowd member is designed so it aligns with the approximate angle from which the main camera is positioned relative to billboard substitutes.

The `AlphaTestEffect` allows us to display a texture on polygon that contains transparent sections; hiding the fact that surrounding billboards are simple rectangular shapes.

In the `Update` cycle, the billboards are recreated so that they always face towards the camera, thereby helping to keep up the illusion that the two-dimensional image of a three-dimensional object is indeed three-dimensional.

There's more...

In this example, the representation was kept as simple as possible in order to concentrate on the core principles of how to utilize billboards and the `AlphaTest` effect.

On the assumption that you're going to want objects that look like people instead of pyramids and a crowd that consists of nothing but identical clones, you may want to expand out the complexity a little by rendering a selection of different people and randomly positioning them throughout the crowd.

7
Creating Vehicles

In this chapter we will cover:

- ▸ Applying simple car physics
- ▸ Implementing simple plane controls
- ▸ Rendering reflective materials within the Reach profile

Introduction

Depending on the particular game, the gap between simulation and reality may be quite large indeed, as the costs involved in both producing and running a highly accurate simulation may be significant and, possibly unintuitively, lead to a game that is less fun.

The trick is to find a level of simulation that matches your game's and its player's needs. This chapter is all about keeping things simple by providing just enough realism to make the player feel comfortable, but not so much as to trip either the player or ourselves up with unneeded complexity.

Applying simple car physics

In this example, we're going to tackle what I consider to be pretty close to the bare minimum of car physics: allowing the player to move forwards, backwards, left and right. No simulation of note will be included beyond the tracking of speed and location.

This sort of physics is usually well-suited for the simple, arcade type driving where you want the player to be able to focus on aspects other than the act of driving itself, such as dodging or shooting.

Getting ready

This recipe relies upon the Geometric Buffer classes discussed in *Chapter 3, Procedural Modeling*, to build the car mesh. Any representation, be it a 3D mesh or even a 2D image, can be substituted without issue though.

How to do it...

To create your own drivable car:

1. Create a new `Car()` class to hold the display and control logic for a car:

```
class Car
{
```

2. Add instance-level variables to hold the meshes and relative positions of the wheels:

```
GeometricBuffer<VertexPositionNormalTexture> carBuffer;
BasicEffect carEffect;
GeometricBuffer<VertexPositionNormalTexture> wheelBuffer;
BasicEffect wheelEffect;

Vector3 forwardLeftWheelOrigin;
Vector3 forwardRightWheelOrigin;
Vector3 backwardRightWheelOrigin;
Vector3 backwardLeftWheelOrigin;
```

3. Begin a constructor for the `Car()` class by mapping out some key positions on the car:

```
public Car(GraphicsDevice graphicsDevice)
{
    var topLeft = new Vector2(0, 0);
    var topRight = new Vector2(1, 0);
    var bottomRight = new Vector2(1, 1);
    var bottomLeft = new Vector2(0, 1);

    var chassisTopHeight = Vector3.Up;
    var chassisMidHeight = Vector3.Up * 0.5f;
    var chassisBottomHeight = Vector3.Up * 0.15f;
    var chassisForward = Vector3.Forward * 1.5f;
    var chassisScreenForward = Vector3.Forward;
    var chassisRoofForward = Vector3.Forward * 0.5f;
    var chassisRoofBackward = Vector3.Backward * 0.5f;
    var chassisScreenBackward = Vector3.Backward;
    var chassisBackward = Vector3.Backward * 1.5f;
    var chassisLeft = Vector3.Left * 0.5f;
```

```
var chassisRoofLeft = Vector3.Left * 0.3f;
var chassisRight = Vector3.Right * 0.5f;
var chassisRoofRight = Vector3.Right * 0.3f;
var wheelForward = (chassisForward +
                chassisScreenForward) / 2f;
var wheelBackward = (chassisBackward +
                chassisScreenBackward) / 2f;
```

4. Start creating the body mesh for the car by adding the front grill, hood, and front windscreen to the car:

```
var carFactory = new
VertexPositionNormalTextureGeometricBufferFactory();

carFactory.AddPane(
    chassisMidHeight + chassisForward + chassisRight,
    topLeft,
    chassisMidHeight + chassisForward + chassisLeft,
    topRight,
    chassisBottomHeight + chassisForward + chassisLeft,
    bottomRight,
    chassisBottomHeight + chassisForward + chassisRight,
    bottomLeft);

carFactory.AddPane(
    chassisMidHeight + chassisForward + chassisLeft,
    topRight,
    chassisMidHeight + chassisForward + chassisRight,
    topLeft,
    chassisBottomHeight + chassisForward + chassisRight,
    bottomLeft,
    chassisBottomHeight + chassisForward + chassisLeft,
    bottomRight);

carFactory.AddPane(
    chassisMidHeight + chassisForward + chassisLeft,
    topLeft,
    chassisMidHeight + chassisForward + chassisRight,
    topRight,
    chassisMidHeight + chassisScreenForward + chassisRight,
    bottomRight,
    chassisMidHeight + chassisScreenForward + chassisLeft,
    bottomLeft);

carFactory.AddPane(
```

```
        chassisMidHeight + chassisScreenForward + chassisRight,
        topRight,
        chassisMidHeight + chassisScreenForward + chassisLeft,
        topLeft,
        chassisBottomHeight + chassisScreenForward + chassisLeft,
        bottomLeft,
        chassisBottomHeight + chassisScreenForward + chassisRight,
        bottomRight);

    carFactory.AddPane(
        chassisMidHeight + chassisScreenForward + chassisLeft,
        topLeft,
        chassisMidHeight + chassisScreenForward + chassisRight,
        topRight,
        chassisTopHeight + chassisRoofForward + chassisRoofRight,
        bottomRight,
        chassisTopHeight + chasssRoofForward + chassisRoofLeft,
        bottomLeft);
```

5. Continue the car with the addition of two doors and a roof:

```
    carFactory.AddPane(
        chassisMidHeight + chassisScreenForward + chassisLeft,
        topLeft,
        chassisMidHeight + chassisScreenBackward + chassisLeft,
        topRight,
        chassisBottomHeight + chassisScreenBackward + chassisLeft,
        bottomRight,
        chassisBottomHeight + chassisScreenForward + chassisLeft,
        bottomLeft);

    carFactory.AddPane(
        chassisMidHeight + chassisScreenBackward + chassisRight,
        topRight,
        chassisMidHeight + chassisScreenForward + chassisRight,
        topLeft,
        chassisBottomHeight + chassisScreenForward + chassisRight,
        bottomLeft,
        chassisBottomHeight + chassisScreenBackward +
        chassisRight, bottomRight);

    carFactory.AddPane(
        chassisTopHeight + chassisRoofForward + chassisRoofLeft,
        topLeft,
        chassisTopHeight + chassisRoofForward + chassisRoofRight,
```

```
topRight,
chassisTopHeight + chassisRoofBackward + chassisRoofRight,
bottomRight,
chassisTopHeight + chassisRoofBackward + chassisRoofLeft,
 bottomLeft);
```

6. Add in the left- and right-hand side windows:

```
carFactory.AddTriangle(
    chassisMidHeight + chassisScreenForward + chassisLeft,
    bottomLeft,
    chassisTopHeight + chassisRoofForward + chassisRoofLeft,
    topRight,
    chassisMidHeight + chassisRoofForward + chassisLeft,
    bottomRight);

carFactory.AddPane(
    chassisTopHeight + chassisRoofForward + chassisRoofLeft,
    topLeft,
    chassisTopHeight + chassisRoofBackward + chassisRoofLeft,
    topRight,
    chassisMidHeight + chassisRoofBackward + chassisLeft,
    bottomRight,
    chassisMidHeight + chassisRoofForward + chassisLeft,
    bottomLeft);

carFactory.AddTriangle(
    chassisMidHeight + chassisRoofBackward + chassisLeft,
    bottomLeft,
    chassisTopHeight + chassisRoofBackward + chassisRoofLeft,
    topLeft,
    chassisMidHeight + chassisScreenBackward + chassisLeft,
    bottomRight);

carFactory.AddTriangle(
    chassisTopHeight + chassisRoofForward + chassisRoofRight,
    topRight,
    chassisMidHeight + chassisScreenForward + chassisRight,
    bottomLeft,
    chassisMidHeight + chassisRoofForward + chassisRight,
    bottomRight);

carFactory.AddPane(
    chassisTopHeight + chassisRoofBackward + chassisRoofRight,
    topRight,
```

```
        chassisTopHeight + chassisRoofForward + chassisRoofRight,
        topLeft,
        chassisMidHeight + chassisRoofForward + chassisRight,
        bottomLeft,
        chassisMidHeight + chassisRoofBackward + chassisRight,
        bottomRight);

    carFactory.AddTriangle(
        chassisTopHeight + chassisRoofBackward + chassisRoofRight,
        topLeft,
        chassisMidHeight + chassisRoofBackward + chassisRight,
        bottomLeft,
        chassisMidHeight + chassisScreenBackward + chassisRight,
        bottomRight);
```

7. Append a rear windscreen, and boot:

```
    carFactory.AddPane(
        chassisMidHeight + chassisScreenBackward + chassisLeft,
        topLeft,
        chassisMidHeight + chassisScreenBackward + chassisRight,
        topRight,
        chassisBottomHeight + chassisScreenBackward +
        chassisRight, bottomRight,
        chassisBottomHeight + chassisScreenBackward + chassisLeft,
        bottomLeft);

    carFactory.AddPane(
        chassisTopHeight + chassisRoofBackward + chassisRoofLeft,
        topLeft,
        chassisTopHeight + chassisRoofBackward + chassisRoofRight,
        topRight,
        chassisMidHeight + chassisScreenBackward + chassisRight,
        bottomRight,
        chassisMidHeight + chassisScreenBackward + chassisLeft,
        bottomLeft);

    carFactory.AddPane(
        chassisMidHeight + chassisScreenBackward + chassisLeft,
        topLeft,
        chassisMidHeight + chassisScreenBackward + chassisRight,
        topRight,
        chassisMidHeight + chassisBackward + chassisRight,
        bottomRight,
        chassisMidHeight + chassisBackward + chassisLeft,
        bottomLeft);
```

8. Complete the car body mesh with the tail assembly:

```
carFactory.AddPane(
    chassisMidHeight + chassisBackward + chassisLeft,
    topRight,
    chassisMidHeight + chassisBackward + chassisRight,
    topLeft,
    chassisBottomHeight + chassisBackward + chassisRight,
    bottomLeft,
    chassisBottomHeight + chassisBackward + chassisLeft,
    bottomRight);

carFactory.AddPane(
    chassisMidHeight + chassisBackward + chassisRight,
    topLeft,
    chassisMidHeight + chassisBackward + chassisLeft,
    topRight,
    chassisBottomHeight + chassisBackward + chassisLeft,
    bottomRight,
    chassisBottomHeight + chassisBackward + chassisRight,
    bottomLeft);

carBuffer = carFactory.Create(graphicsDevice);
```

9. Create a single mesh instance for a wheel that will be reused to display all four wheels:

```
var wheelFactory = new
VertexPositionNormalTextureGeometricBufferFactory();

var wheelRadius = 0.25f;
var wheelDepth = 0.1f;
var sliceCount = 16f;
var anglePerSlice = MathHelper.ToRadians(360f / sliceCount);
for (var sliceIndex = 0f;
    sliceIndex < sliceCount;
    sliceIndex++)
{
    var startAngle = sliceIndex * anglePerSlice;
    var endAngle = (sliceIndex + 1) * anglePerSlice;

    var outerEdgeStartPoint = new Vector3(
                    (float)Math.Sin(startAngle) *
                    wheelRadius,
                    (float)Math.Cos(startAngle) *
                    wheelRadius,
```

```
                                            0f);

        var outerEdgeEndPoint = new Vector3(
                            (float)Math.Sin(endAngle) *
                            wheelRadius,
                            (float)Math.Cos(endAngle) *
                            wheelRadius,
                            0f);

        var innerEdgeStartPoint = outerEdgeStartPoint +
                            (Vector3.Forward *
                            wheelDepth);

        var innerEdgeEndPoint = outerEdgeEndPoint +
                            (Vector3.Forward *
                            wheelDepth);

        wheelFactory.AddTriangle(
            Vector3.Zero, bottomLeft,
            outerEdgeStartPoint, topLeft,
            outerEdgeEndPoint, topRight);

        wheelFactory.AddPane(
            outerEdgeStartPoint, topLeft,
            innerEdgeStartPoint, topRight,
            innerEdgeEndPoint, bottomRight,
            outerEdgeEndPoint, bottomLeft);
    }
    wheelBuffer = wheelFactory.Create(graphicsDevice);
```

10. Calculate the relative position of the four wheels:

```
forwardLeftWheelOrigin = chassisBottomHeight +
                        wheelForward +
                        chassisLeft;
forwardRightWheelOrigin = chassisBottomHeight +
                        wheelForward +
                        chassisRight;
backwardRightWheelOrigin = chassisBottomHeight +
                        wheelBackward +
                        chassisRight;
backwardLeftWheelOrigin = chassisBottomHeight +
                        wheelBackward +
                        chassisLeft;
```

11. Complete the constructor by creating the effects used to render the body and wheels:

```
carEffect = new BasicEffect(graphicsDevice);
carEffect.EnableDefaultLighting();
carEffect.DiffuseColor = Color.Red.ToVector3();

wheelEffect = new BasicEffect(graphicsDevice);
wheelEffect.EnableDefaultLighting();
wheelEffect.DiffuseColor = Color.Gray.ToVector3();
}
```

12. Add some instance-level variables to hold the current physical state of the car:

```
Vector2 carLocation;
float carHeading;
float carSpeed;
float steeringAngle;
float wheelBaseLength = 2f;
Matrix world;
```

13. Begin the `Update()` method with the keyboard handling logic:

```
public void Update(GameTime gameTime)
{
    var dt = (float)gameTime.ElapsedGameTime.TotalSeconds;

    var keyboard = Keyboard.GetState();

    if (keyboard.IsKeyDown(Keys.Right))
    {
        steeringAngle += MathHelper.ToRadians(5) * dt * 50f;
    }
    if (keyboard.IsKeyDown(Keys.Left))
    {
        steeringAngle -= MathHelper.ToRadians(5) * dt * 50f;
    }
    steeringAngle *= .9f;

    if (keyboard.IsKeyDown(Keys.Up))
    {
        carSpeed = 10f * dt * 10f;
    }
    else if (keyboard.IsKeyDown(Keys.Down))
    {
        carSpeed = -10f * dt * 10f;
    }
```

```
        else
        {
            carSpeed *= .9f;
        }
```

14. Calculate the current position of the front and rear of the car:

```
var currentHeadingOffset = (wheelBaseLength / 2f) *
                    new Vector2(
                        (float)Math.Cos(carHeading),
                        (float)Math.Sin(carHeading));
var frontWheel = carLocation + currentHeadingOffset;
var backWheel = carLocation - currentHeadingOffset;
```

15. Extrapolate where the car will be next:

```
var nextHeadingOffset = carSpeed *
                dt *
                new Vector2(
                    (float)Math.Cos(carHeading),
                    (float)Math.Sin(carHeading));

var nextHeadingPlusSteeringOffset = carSpeed *
                dt *
                new Vector2(
                    (float)Math.Cos(carHeading +
                        steeringAngle),
                    (float)Math.Sin(carHeading +
                        steeringAngle));

backWheel += nextHeadingOffset;
frontWheel += nextHeadingPlusSteeringOffset;

carLocation = (frontWheel + backWheel) / 2f;
carHeading = (float)Math.Atan2(frontWheel.Y -
                    backWheel.Y,
                frontWheel.X -
                    backWheel.X);
```

16. Complete the method by updating the world transformation with the new position and rotation of the car:

```
world = Matrix.CreateRotationY(
            MathHelper.ToRadians(-90)) *
        Matrix.CreateRotationY(-carHeading) *
        Matrix.CreateTranslation(
            new Vector3(
```

```
            carLocation.X,
            0.15f,
            carLocation.Y));
}
```

17. Begin the `Draw()` method by rendering the car body:

```
public void Draw(Matrix view, Matrix projection)
{
    carEffect.World = world;
    carEffect.View = view;
    carEffect.Projection = projection;

    carBuffer.Draw(carEffect);
```

18. Update the wheel with the latest view and projection:

```
wheelEffect.View = view;
wheelEffect.Projection = projection;
```

19. Complete the method by rendering each wheel in turn with the previously constructed wheel mesh:

```
wheelEffect.World = Matrix.CreateRotationY(
                    MathHelper.ToRadians(-90) -
                    steeringAngle) *
                Matrix.CreateTranslation(
                    forwardLeftWheelOrigin) *
                world;
wheelBuffer.Draw(wheelEffect);
wheelEffect.World = Matrix.CreateRotationY(
                    MathHelper.ToRadians(90) -
                    steeringAngle) *
                Matrix.CreateTranslation(
                    forwardRightWheelOrigin) *
                world;
wheelBuffer.Draw(wheelEffect);
wheelEffect.World = Matrix.CreateRotationY(
                    MathHelper.ToRadians(90)) *
                Matrix.CreateTranslation(
                    backwardRightWheelOrigin) *
                world;
wheelBuffer.Draw(wheelEffect);
wheelEffect.World = Matrix.CreateRotationY(
                    MathHelper.ToRadians(-90)) *
```

```
                              Matrix.CreateTranslation(
                                  backwardLeftWheelOrigin) *
                              world;
          wheelBuffer.Draw(wheelEffect);


    }
```

20. Begin a new class to display the ground with the mesh and effect used to render it:

```
class Ground
{
    GeometricBuffer<VertexPositionNormalTexture> buffer;
    BasicEffect effect;
```

21. Add a constructor to create the mesh and the associated effect:

```
public Ground(GraphicsDevice graphicsDevice)
{
    var factory = new
VertexPositionNormalTextureGeometricBufferFactory();
    factory.AddPane(
        new Vector3(-50f, 0f, -50f), new Vector2(0, 0),
        new Vector3(50f, 0f, -50f), new Vector2(1, 0),
        new Vector3(50f, 0f, 50f), new Vector2(1, 1),
        new Vector3(-50f, 0f, 50f), new Vector2(0, 1));

    buffer = factory.Create(graphicsDevice);

    effect = new BasicEffect(graphicsDevice);
    effect.EnableDefaultLighting();
    effect.DiffuseColor = Color.Bisque.ToVector3();
    effect.World = Matrix.CreateTranslation(Vector3.Zero);
}
```

22. Complete the class with the addition of a `Draw()` method to render the ground:

```
public void Draw(Matrix view, Matrix projection)
{

    effect.View = view;
    effect.Projection = projection;
    buffer.Draw(effect);
}
```

23. In your game class, create some instance-level variables to hold the camera-related matrices along with instances of `car` and `ground`:

```
Matrix view;
Matrix projection;
Ground ground;
Car car;
```

24. Load up the camera matrices, and create instances of `Car` and `Ground` within the `LoadContent()` method:

```
protected override void LoadContent()
{
    view = Matrix.CreateLookAt(
                (Vector3.Backward * 10) + (Vector3.Up * 10),
                Vector3.Zero,
                Vector3.Up);

    projection = Matrix.CreatePerspectiveFieldOfView(
                MathHelper.ToRadians(60f),
                GraphicsDevice.Viewport.AspectRatio,
                0.2f, 100f);

    ground = new Ground(GraphicsDevice);
    car = new Car(GraphicsDevice);
}
```

25. Ensure that the car's position is being updated regularly:

```
protected override void Update(GameTime gameTime)
{
    car.Update(gameTime);
    base.Update(gameTime);
}
```

26. Finish by rendering `ground` and `car`:

```
protected override void Draw(GameTime gameTime)
{
    GraphicsDevice.Clear(Color.CornflowerBlue);

    ground.Draw(view, projection);
    car.Draw(view, projection);

    base.Draw(gameTime);
}
```

You should now be the proud owner of a drivable, albeit very minimalistic, car:

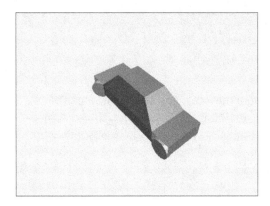

How it works...

The heart of this recipe is really in the calculation of the motion within the `Update()` method of the `Car` class.

We work out the current position of the front and rear axle of the car. From there we advance both points along the car's current heading, and then rotate the car around by the angle of the steering wheel.

To simulate the automatic return of the steering wheel, we continuously shrink the steering angle down in each update cycle.

There's more...

You may note that despite having a lot of detailed information available to us via the car's mesh, we actually only use a very small number of relatively independent variables to determine the car's movement.

This is intentional and has the dual advantage of making the code easier to replicate in other games and in 2D as well.

Getting more physical

If you're after slightly more realistic attributes in your game's driving, I would suggest making the move to a full-blown physics engine similar to the ones described in the *Integrating rag doll physics* recipe of *Chapter 6, Playing with Animation*, almost immediately. The math required to do a bad simulation of events, such as sliding and skidding, can be just as complex and involved as "proper" math, except that someone has already done most of the hard work with a third party physics engine.

See also

▶ _Integrating rag doll physics_ recipe of _Chapter 6, Playing with Animation_

Implementing simple plane controls

As with the previous recipe for car physics, this recipe is all about enough simulation to make the player feel involved (and hopefully enjoy themselves), but not so much as to either trip the player up in unnecessary detail or slow the game down to a crawl under the possibly heavy weight of a more rigorous simulation.

There is no stalling, wind shear, or trim adjustments here. Just the player turning left, right, up, or down, and powering towards fun.

Getting ready

This recipe relies upon the `GeometricBuffer` classes covered in _Chapter 3, Procedural Modeling_, to construct the plane, but any method of creating or supplying a 3D mesh should be sufficient.

How to do it...

To begin flying your own plane:

1. Begin a new `Plane()` class with instance-level variables to hold the rendering details:

```
class Plane
{
    GeometricBuffer<VertexPositionNormalTexture> buffer;
    BasicEffect effect;
```

2. Add a constructor and map out the key locations for creating the plane's mesh:

```
public Plane(GraphicsDevice graphicsDevice, ContentManager
content)
{
    var topLeft = new Vector2(0, 0);
    var topRight = new Vector2(1, 0);
    var bottomRight = new Vector2(1, 1);
    var bottomLeft = new Vector2(0, 1);

    var noseForward = Vector3.Forward * 2f;
    var bodyForward = Vector3.Forward;
```

```
var bodyBackward = Vector3.Backward * 2f;
var rudderForward = Vector3.Backward;
var bodyTop = Vector3.Up * 0.5f;
var bodyBottom = Vector3.Down * 0.5f;
var bodyLeft = Vector3.Left * 0.5f;
var bodyRight = Vector3.Right * 0.5f;
var wingLeft = Vector3.Left * 2f;
var wingRight = Vector3.Right * 2f;
var rudderTop = Vector3.Up;
```

3. Start the creation of the plane's mesh with the nose:

```
var factory = new
VertexPositionNormalTextureGeometricBufferFactory();

factory.AddTriangle(
    noseForward, topLeft,
    bodyForward + bodyTop + bodyRight, bottomRight,
    bodyForward + bodyTop + bodyLeft, bottomLeft);

factory.AddTriangle(
    noseForward, topLeft,
    bodyForward + bodyBottom + bodyLeft, bottomLeft,
    bodyForward + bodyBottom + bodyRight, bottomRight);

factory.AddTriangle(
    noseForward, topLeft,
    bodyForward + bodyTop + bodyLeft, topRight,
    bodyForward + bodyBottom + bodyLeft, bottomRight);

factory.AddTriangle(
    noseForward, topLeft,
    bodyForward + bodyBottom + bodyRight, bottomRight,
    bodyForward + bodyTop + bodyRight, topRight);
```

4. Create the body:

```
factory.AddPane(
    bodyForward + bodyTop + bodyLeft, topLeft,
    bodyForward + bodyTop + bodyRight, topRight,
    bodyBackward + bodyTop + bodyRight, bottomRight,
    bodyBackward + bodyTop + bodyLeft, bottomLeft);

factory.AddPane(
    bodyForward + bodyBottom + bodyRight, topRight,
    bodyForward + bodyBottom + bodyLeft, topLeft,
    bodyBackward + bodyBottom + bodyLeft, bottomLeft,
    bodyBackward + bodyBottom + bodyRight, bottomRight);
```

```
factory.AddPane(
    bodyForward + bodyTop + bodyLeft, topLeft,
    bodyBackward + bodyTop + bodyLeft, topRight,
    bodyBackward + bodyBottom + bodyLeft, bottomRight,
    bodyForward + bodyBottom + bodyLeft, bottomLeft);
factory.AddPane(
    bodyBackward + bodyTop + bodyRight, topRight,
    bodyForward + bodyTop + bodyRight, topLeft,
    bodyForward + bodyBottom + bodyRight, bottomLeft,
    bodyBackward + bodyBottom + bodyRight, bottomRight);
factory.AddPane(
    bodyBackward + bodyTop + bodyLeft, topLeft,
    bodyBackward + bodyTop + bodyRight, topRight,
    bodyBackward + bodyBottom + bodyRight, bottomRight,
    bodyBackward + bodyBottom + bodyLeft, bottomLeft);
```

5. Add the upper and lower surfaces of the two wings:

```
factory.AddTriangle(
    bodyForward + bodyLeft, topLeft,
    bodyBackward + bodyLeft, bottomRight,
    bodyBackward + wingLeft, bottomLeft);

factory.AddTriangle(
    bodyForward + bodyLeft, topLeft,
    bodyBackward + wingLeft, bottomLeft,
    bodyBackward + bodyLeft, bottomRight);

factory.AddTriangle(
    bodyForward + bodyRight, topLeft,
    bodyBackward + wingRight, bottomRight,
    bodyBackward + bodyRight, bottomLeft);

factory.AddTriangle(
    bodyForward + bodyRight, topLeft,
        bodyBackward + bodyRight, bottomLeft,
    bodyBackward + wingRight, bottomRight);
```

6. Attach a tail to complete the mesh:

```
factory.AddTriangle(
    rudderForward + bodyTop, bottomLeft,
    bodyBackward + rudderTop, topRight,
    bodyBackward + bodyTop, bottomRight);

factory.AddTriangle(
    bodyBackward + bodyTop, bottomLeft,
    bodyBackward + rudderTop, topLeft,
```

```
        rudderForward + bodyTop, bottomRight);
    buffer = factory.Create(graphicsDevice);
```

7. Complete the method by creating the effect used to render the mesh:

```
        effect = new BasicEffect(graphicsDevice);
        effect.EnableDefaultLighting();
        effect.DiffuseColor = Color.Red.ToVector3();
    }
```

8. Add some instance-level variables to hold the position and rotation of the plane:

```
Vector3 position;
float xAngle;
float yAngle;
float zAngle;
```

9. Begin the plane's `Update()` method with the keyboard handling logic:

```
public void Update(GameTime gameTime)
{
    var keyboard = Keyboard.GetState();
    if (keyboard.IsKeyDown(Keys.Up))
    {
        xAngle += MathHelper.ToRadians(-1f);
    }
    if (keyboard.IsKeyDown(Keys.Down))
    {
        xAngle += MathHelper.ToRadians(1f);
    }
    xAngle *= 0.99f;
    if (keyboard.IsKeyDown(Keys.Left))
    {
        zAngle += MathHelper.ToRadians(-1.5f);
        yAngle += MathHelper.ToRadians(1f);
    }
    if (keyboard.IsKeyDown(Keys.Right))
    {
        zAngle += MathHelper.ToRadians(-1.5f);
        yAngle += MathHelper.ToRadians(-1f);
    }
    zAngle *= 0.99f;
```

10. Calculate the new rotation and position of the plane:

```
var rotation = Matrix.CreateRotationX(xAngle) *
               Matrix.CreateRotationY(yAngle) *
               Matrix.CreateRotationZ(zAngle);
var delta = (float)gameTime.ElapsedGameTime.TotalSeconds *
            10f;
var velocity = Vector3.Transform(
                   Vector3.Forward * delta,
                   rotation);
position += velocity;
```

11. Complete the method by updating the world transformation with the new rotation and translation:

```
effect.World = rotation *
               Matrix.CreateTranslation(position);
}
```

12. Finish the class by adding a method to render the plane on to the screen:

```
public void Draw(Matrix view, Matrix projection)
{
    effect.View = view;
    effect.Projection = projection;

    buffer.Draw(effect);
}
```

13. In your game class, add some variables to hold the camera matrices and the `plane` instance:

```
Matrix view;
Matrix projection;
Plane plane;
```

14. Create the camera matrices and the instance of `plane` in the `LoadContent()` method:

```
protected override void LoadContent()
{
    view = Matrix.CreateLookAt(
        Vector3.Backward * 20 + Vector3.Up * 20,
        Vector3.Zero,
        Vector3.Up);

    projection = Matrix.CreatePerspectiveFieldOfView(
        MathHelper.ToRadians(60),
        GraphicsDevice.Viewport.AspectRatio,
        0.2f,
```

```
                100f);

            plane = new Plane(GraphicsDevice, Content);
        }
```

15. Ensure that the `plane` instance is updated regularly:

    ```
    protected override void Update(GameTime gameTime)
    {
        plane.Update(gameTime);

        base.Update(gameTime);
    }
    ```

16. Finish by rendering the `plane` instance on to the screen:

    ```
    protected override void Draw(GameTime gameTime)
    {
        GraphicsDevice.Clear(Color.CornflowerBlue);

        plane.Draw(view, projection);

        base.Draw(gameTime);
    }
    ```

Running the code should yield a very bare bones but navigable plane like the following:

How it works...

In this example, we're actually doing little more than simply rotating around a given point and moving forward in the resulting direction.

The trick is in the control of the rotation as demonstrated in the `Update()` method of the `Plane` class, where we can see that when the player indicates left or right, we're actually rotating the plane around both the y and z axes or, to put in aeronautical terms, we're both yawing and rolling the plane.

This gives the player the appropriate arcade or movie style-turning attributes that they might expect with just the use of two keys (or possibly a single thumbstick), without having to worry about the realities of things such as rudder control.

There's more...

Unlike the previous example concerning car physics, there's actually quite a lot of scope for expanding the "physics" with planes relatively easily, without needing to resort to a full-blown physics engine.

The main reason for this is that planes don't spend a lot of time in direct contact with other visible surfaces, and thus, common issues such as unwanted sliding are rarely perceptible to the player. So if you want to add a little extra, such as the ability to stall or dive at high speeds, there's a very good chance that the code involved won't be too arduous.

See also

▸   *Integrating rag doll physics* recipe of *Chapter 6, Playing with Animation*

Rendering reflective materials within the Reach profile

Given my relatively poor skill set in driving games, one of my more significant joys in such games is being able to stroll around a virtual car and delight in how the light plays off the smooth curves and elegant paintwork of it all.

Given the inclusion of dedicated viewing modes within games, such as Forza Motorsport and Grand Turismo, I can only assume that I'm not alone in such pursuits.

So how do we achieve similar visual appeal in our own games?

Well, in the case of cars, it's amazing what difference a shiny bit of paintwork can do, and in the case of virtual cars, that means knowing how to achieve reflective surfaces.

Getting ready

This example relies upon the `GeometricBuffer` and sphere creation classes covered in *Chapter 3, Procedural Modeling,* for mesh creation, although, any other mesh or form of mesh creation should work equally well.

It also relies upon the inclusion of a texture with the asset name of "Metallic". I would suggest a texture consisting of a single white pixel as a starting point, as this texture is really just included because the `EnvironmentMapEffect` effect being used doesn't have a textureless mode available like its `BasicEffect` peer does.

How to do it...

To start reflecting on your own virtual world:

1. Begin the class to render a metallic object with some instance-level variables containing the mesh, the effect, and the reflection texture:

```
class MetallicObject
{
    GeometricBuffer<VertexPositionNormalTexture> buffer;
    EnvironmentMapEffect effect;
    RenderTargetCube reflection;
```

2. Include two public fields containing the camera matrices for the reflected views:

```
public Matrix ReflectedView;
public Matrix ReflectedProjection;
```

3. Begin the constructor by creating the mesh:

```
public MetallicObject(
        GraphicsDevice graphicsDevice,
        ContentManager content)
{

    buffer = CreateSphere(graphicsDevice);
```

4. Create an instance of the texture cube to hold the reflected view of the surrounding environment:

```
reflection = new RenderTargetCube(
                    graphicsDevice,
                    8, false,
                    SurfaceFormat.Color,
                    DepthFormat.Depth16);
```

5. Instantiate the effect by setting it to display a red object in a well-lit room:

```
effect = new EnvironmentMapEffect(graphicsDevice);

effect.Texture = content.Load<Texture2D>("Metallic");
effect.DiffuseColor = Color.Red.ToVector3();

effect.EnableDefaultLighting();
effect.AmbientLightColor = Color.WhiteSmoke.ToVector3();
```

6. Set the reflection to be strong, with no specular highlights:

```
effect.EnvironmentMap = reflection;
effect.EnvironmentMapAmount = 1;
effect.EnvironmentMapSpecular = Vector3.Zero;
```

7. Position the object in the center of the world:

```
effect.World = Matrix.CreateTranslation(Vector3.Zero);
```

8. Complete the constructor by setting up the reflected projection to have a 90 degree field of view, so that each of the texture cube's face reflections interlock correctly:

```
    ReflectedProjection = Matrix.CreatePerspectiveFieldOfView(
        MathHelper.ToRadians(90),
        1f,
        0.2f,
        100f);
}
```

9. Add a method to set up the camera position and render the target for the capture of each one of the texture cube's reflected views:

```
public void BeginReflectionCapture(CubeMapFace cubeMapFace)
{
    effect.GraphicsDevice.SetRenderTarget(
        reflection,
        cubeMapFace);

    switch (cubeMapFace)
    {
        case CubeMapFace.NegativeX:
            ReflectedView = Matrix.CreateLookAt(
                Vector3.Zero,
                Vector3.Left,
                Vector3.Up);
            break;
        case CubeMapFace.PositiveX:
            ReflectedView = Matrix.CreateLookAt(
                Vector3.Zero,
                Vector3.Right,
                Vector3.Up);
            break;
        case CubeMapFace.NegativeY:
            ReflectedView = Matrix.CreateLookAt(
                Vector3.Zero,
                Vector3.Down,
                Vector3.Backward);
            break;
```

```
                case CubeMapFace.PositiveY:
                    ReflectedView = Matrix.CreateLookAt(
                        Vector3.Zero,
                        Vector3.Up,
                        Vector3.Forward);
                    break;
                case CubeMapFace.NegativeZ:
                    ReflectedView = Matrix.CreateLookAt(
                        Vector3.Zero,
                        Vector3.Forward,
                        Vector3.Up);
                    break;
                case CubeMapFace.PositiveZ:
                    ReflectedView = Matrix.CreateLookAt(
                        Vector3.Zero,
                        Vector3.Backward,
                        Vector3.Up);
                    break;
            }
        }
```

10. Create a method to mark the end of capture:

```
public void EndReflectionCapture()
{
    effect.GraphicsDevice.SetRenderTarget(null);
}
```

11. Complete the class by adding a method to render the object on screen:

```
public void Draw(Matrix view, Matrix projection)
{
    effect.View = view;
    effect.Projection = projection;
    buffer.Draw(effect);
}
```

12. Add a new Room class, for the display of a room to surround the metallic object, and add in some instance-level variables to hold the associated mesh and effect:

```
class Room
{
    GeometricBuffer<VertexPositionNormalTexture> buffer;
    BasicEffect effect;
```

13. Begin the constructor for the `Room` by mapping out the significant positions and dimensions:

```
public Room(GraphicsDevice graphicsDevice, ContentManager content)
{
    var halfRoomSize = 5f;
    var topForwardLeft = (Vector3.Up +
                          Vector3.Forward +
                          Vector3.Left) * halfRoomSize;
    var topForwardRight = (Vector3.Up +
                           Vector3.Forward +
                           Vector3.Right) * halfRoomSize;
    var topBackwardLeft = (Vector3.Up +
                           Vector3.Backward +
                           Vector3.Left) * halfRoomSize;
    var topBackwardRight = (Vector3.Up +
                            Vector3.Backward +
                            Vector3.Right) * halfRoomSize;
    var bottomForwardLeft = (Vector3.Down +
                             Vector3.Forward +
                             Vector3.Left) * halfRoomSize;
    var bottomForwardRight = (Vector3.Down +
                              Vector3.Forward +
                              Vector3.Right) * halfRoomSize;
    var bottomBackwardLeft = (Vector3.Down +
                              Vector3.Backward +
                              Vector3.Left) * halfRoomSize;
    var bottomBackwardRight = (Vector3.Down +
                               Vector3.Backward +
                               Vector3.Right) * halfRoomSize;

    var topLeft = new Vector2(0,0);
    var topRight = new Vector2(1,0);
    var bottomRight = new Vector2(1,1);
    var bottomLeft = new Vector2(0,1);
```

14. Construct the mesh:

```
var factory = new
VertexPositionNormalTextureGeometricBufferFactory();

factory.AddPane(
    bottomForwardLeft, topLeft,
    bottomForwardRight, topRight,
    bottomBackwardRight, bottomRight,
    bottomBackwardLeft, bottomLeft);
factory.AddPane(
```

```
        topForwardRight, topRight,
        topForwardLeft, topLeft,
        topBackwardLeft, bottomLeft,
        topBackwardRight, bottomRight);
    factory.AddPane(
        topForwardLeft, topLeft,
        topForwardRight, topRight,
        bottomForwardRight, bottomRight,
        bottomForwardLeft, bottomLeft);
    factory.AddPane(
        topForwardRight, topRight,
        topForwardLeft, topLeft,
        bottomForwardLeft, bottomLeft,
        bottomForwardRight, bottomRight);
    factory.AddPane(
        topBackwardLeft, topLeft,
        topForwardLeft, topRight,
        bottomForwardLeft, bottomRight,
        bottomBackwardLeft, bottomLeft);
    factory.AddPane(
        topForwardRight, topRight,
        topBackwardRight, topLeft,
        bottomBackwardRight, bottomLeft,
        bottomForwardRight, bottomRight);
    buffer = factory.Create(graphicsDevice);
```

15. Finish the constructor with the creation of the effect used to render the room:

```
    effect = new BasicEffect(graphicsDevice);
    effect.EnableDefaultLighting();
    effect.World = Matrix.CreateTranslation(Vector3.Zero);
    effect.DiffuseColor = Color.Wheat.ToVector3();
}
```

16. Complete the class by adding a `Draw()` method:

```
public void Draw(Matrix view, Matrix projection)
{
    effect.View = view;
    effect.Projection = projection;
    buffer.Draw(effect);
}
```

17. In your game class, add some instance-level variables to hold the camera matrices along with the room and metallic object instances:

```
Matrix view;
Matrix projection;

Room room;
MetallicObject metallicObject;
```

18. Load up the camera and scene objects within the `LoadContent()` method:

```
protected override void LoadContent()
{
    view = Matrix.CreateLookAt(
        Vector3.Backward * 5,
        Vector3.Zero,
        Vector3.Up);
    projection = Matrix.CreatePerspectiveFieldOfView(
        MathHelper.ToRadians(60f),
        GraphicsDevice.Viewport.AspectRatio,
        0.2f,
        1000f);

    room = new Room(GraphicsDevice, Content);
    metallicObject = new MetallicObject(
                            GraphicsDevice, Content);
}
```

19. Begin the `Draw()` method by rendering the surround scene into each of the faces of the texture cube used for reflection:

```
protected override void Draw(GameTime gameTime)
{
    foreach (CubeMapFace mapFace in
            Enum.GetValues(typeof(CubeMapFace)))
    {
        metallicObject.BeginReflectionCapture(mapFace);

        GraphicsDevice.Clear(Color.CornflowerBlue);
        room.Draw(
            metallicObject.ReflectedView,
            metallicObject.ReflectedProjection);

        metallicObject.EndReflectionCapture();
    }
```

20. Complete the method by rendering the entire scene to the screen:

```
GraphicsDevice.Clear(Color.CornflowerBlue);

room.Draw(view, projection);
metallicObject.Draw(view, projection);

base.Draw(gameTime);
}
```

Running the example should deliver a shiny object to the screen similar to the following:

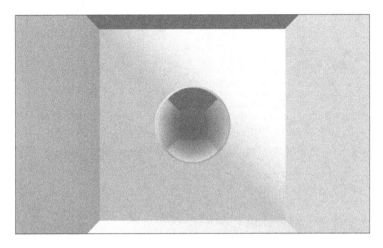

How it works...

In the *Creating water within the HiDef profile* recipe in *Chapter 4, Creating Water and Sky*, a virtual camera was set up to view the scene from the perspective of the reflected surface. The "reflected" scene was rendered to a render target and then used as a texture on the surface we wished to appear reflective.

Also, in the *Building skyboxes within the HiDef profile* recipe in *Chapter 4, Creating Water and Sky*, a texture cube was utilized where six textures were assembled to form an inwards-facing cube and used as a seamless backdrop for the scene.

This example can be thought of as a mix of these two concepts where we construct a texture cube made from the "reflected" renderings from the perspective of each face of the cube except, this time, no custom shader code is required. Everything that we need is built in.

We start by constructing a `RenderTargetCube`, which is similar to a regular `RenderTarget`, except instead of containing just one texture, a `RenderTargetCube` contains six textures set up in a cube formation, as suggested by its name.

In the `BeginReflectionCapture()` method of the `MetallicObject` class, we can see how a particular face of the cube is specified when we set the render target.

This means that we can iterate through each face of the cube and render the scene from the perspective of that particular face, capture the reflected scene, and build up to a complete mini-skybox representation of the surrounding world.

From there, it's just a case of feeding the texture cube along with a mesh into the `EnvironmentMapEffect`, and out pops a shiny rendered object.

There's more...

The `EnvironmentMapEffect` has a few other handy tricks up its sleeve, like the ability to render a specular map in addition to a reflection map. This means you can give your reflective surfaces the shiny highlights from light sources, such as the sun or headlights.

Another feature is the ability to increase the realism of your reflected surfaces by including what's known as the Fresnel effect, where how much refection you see is determined by the angle at which you view the surface.

For example, imagine seeing a puddle in the distance versus standing right over one. From one perspective you would mostly see the reflected sky, and from the other, you would mostly see the ground beneath the puddle.

The cost of reflecting

Reflections can be pretty costly in terms of performance so you may want to keep an active eye on minimizing their impact wherever possible.

For example, you may find you can drop the resolution for the reflected textures down quite low, without any noticeable impact on players. This is because the human eye isn't very picky at all when it comes to the accuracy of reflections. As long as the colors are roughly in the right place, most people won't notice.

Another possible saving is reducing the quality of what's being rendered in the reflected scenes. You might find that you can do away with any complex per-pixel lighting or texture effects for the reflected scene elements and go with the bare minimum.

If you've got models at multiple levels of detail, it's probably a good idea to go with the lowest polygon versions for the reflected scene elements.

Also, if you've got multiple shiny elements in the one scene, you might find you're able to use the same reflection across all of them. This can be especially handy in car racing games, where the action is so frantic that it's likely no one is going to notice minor details, such as all the cars sharing one reflection and none of the cars reflecting off of each other.

Last but not least, if you've got a scene where the only significant thing changing is the position of the camera or the rotation of the foreground object, you might be able to reuse the same reflection textures across multiple frames, possibly even an entire scene, thereby reducing the rendering cost to almost zero.

See also

> ▶ *Creating water within the HiDef profile* recipe in *Chapter 4, Creating Water and Sky*
>
> ▶ *Building skyboxes within the HiDef profile* recipe in *Chapter 4, Creating Water and Sky*

8
Receiving Player Input

In this chapter we will cover:

- ▸ Adding text fields
- ▸ Creating dialog wheels
- ▸ Dragging, dropping, and sliding

Introduction

One of the key aspects that separates a computer game from that of, for example, a movie, is its interactive nature and its ability to be influenced by the player to achieve a different outcome each and every time.

In this chapter, we will examine some different ways of capturing the player's intent that may not be immediately obvious or trivial to implement when we first set ourselves the challenge.

Adding text fields

I'm generally a big fan of having as few text fields in an application as possible, and this holds doubly true for a game but there are some occasions when receiving some sort of textual information from the player is required so in these regrettable occasions, a textbox or field may be an appropriate choice.

Unfortunately, a premade textbox isn't always available to us on any given gaming project, so sometimes we must create our own.

This recipe only relies upon the presence of a single `SpriteFont` file referring to any font at any desired size.

To start adding textboxes to your own games:

1. Add a `SpriteFont` to the solution named `Text`:

```xml
<?xml version="1.0" encoding="utf-8"?>
<XnaContent xmlns:Graphics=
"Microsoft.Xna.Framework.Content.Pipeline.Graphics">
  <Asset Type="Graphics:FontDescription">
    <FontName>Segoe UI Mono</FontName>
    <Size>28</Size>
    <Spacing>0</Spacing>
    <UseKerning>true</UseKerning>
    <Style>Regular</Style>
    <CharacterRegions>
      <CharacterRegion>
        <Start>&#32;</Start>
        <End>&#126;</End>
      </CharacterRegion>
    </CharacterRegions>
  </Asset>
</XnaContent>
```

2. Begin a new class to contain the text field logic, and embed a static mapping of the keyboard keys to their respective text characters:

```csharp
class Textbox
{

    private static Dictionary<Keys, char> characterByKey;
```

3. Create a static constructor to load the mapping of keys to characters:

```csharp
static Textbox()
{
    characterByKey = new Dictionary<Keys, char>()
    {
        {Keys.A, 'a'},
        {Keys.B, 'b'},
        {Keys.C, 'c'},
        {Keys.D, 'd'},
```

```
{Keys.E, 'e'},
{Keys.F, 'f'},
{Keys.G, 'g'},
{Keys.H, 'h'},
{Keys.I, 'i'},
{Keys.J, 'j'},
{Keys.K, 'k'},
{Keys.L, 'l'},
{Keys.M, 'm'},
{Keys.N, 'n'},
{Keys.O, 'o'},
{Keys.P, 'p'},
{Keys.Q, 'q'},
{Keys.R, 'r'},
{Keys.S, 's'},
{Keys.T, 't'},
{Keys.U, 'u'},
{Keys.V, 'v'},
{Keys.W, 'w'},
{Keys.X, 'x'},
{Keys.Y, 'y'},
{Keys.Z, 'z'},
{Keys.D0, '0'},
{Keys.D1, '1'},
{Keys.D2, '2'},
{Keys.D3, '3'},
{Keys.D4, '4'},
{Keys.D5, '5'},
{Keys.D6, '6'},
{Keys.D7, '7'},
{Keys.D8, '8'},
{Keys.D9, '9'},
{Keys.NumPad0, '0'},
{Keys.NumPad1, '1'},
{Keys.NumPad2, '2'},
{Keys.NumPad3, '3'},
{Keys.NumPad4, '4'},
{Keys.NumPad5, '5'},
{Keys.NumPad6, '6'},
{Keys.NumPad7, '7'},
{Keys.NumPad8, '8'},
{Keys.NumPad9, '9'},
{Keys.OemPeriod, '.'},
{Keys.OemMinus, '-'},
```

```
                  {Keys.Space, ' '}
          };
      }
```

4. Add the public instance fields that will determine the look and content of the display:

```
public StringBuilder Text;
public Vector2 Position;
public Color ForegroundColor;
public Color BackgroundColor;
public bool HasFocus;
```

5. Include instance-level references to the objects used in the rendering:

```
GraphicsDevice graphicsDevice;
SpriteFont font;
SpriteBatch spriteBatch;
RenderTarget2D renderTarget;
KeyboardState lastKeyboard;
bool renderIsDirty = true;
```

6. Begin the instance constructor by measuring the overall height of some key characters to determine the required height of the display, and create a render target to match:

```
public Textbox(GraphicsDevice graphicsDevice, int width,
SpriteFont font)
{
    this.font = font;

    var fontMeasurements = font.MeasureString("dfgjlJL");
    var height = (int)fontMeasurements.Y;

    var pp = graphicsDevice.PresentationParameters;
    renderTarget = new RenderTarget2D(graphicsDevice,
        width,
        height,
        false, pp.BackBufferFormat, pp.DepthStencilFormat);
```

7. Complete the constructor by instantiating the text container and `SpriteBatch`:

```
    Text = new StringBuilder();
    this.graphicsDevice = graphicsDevice;
    spriteBatch = new SpriteBatch(graphicsDevice);
}
```

8. Begin the `Update()` method by determining if we need to take any notice of the keyboard:

```
public void Update(GameTime gameTime)
{
    if (!HasFocus)
    {
        return;
    }
}
```

9. Retrieve all of the keys that are currently being depressed by the player and iterate through them, ignoring any that have been held down since the last update:

```
var keyboard = Keyboard.GetState();

foreach (var key in keyboard.GetPressedKeys())
{
    if (!lastKeyboard.IsKeyUp(key))
    {
        continue;
    }
}
```

10. Add the logic to remove a character from the end of the text, if either the *Backspace* or *Delete* key has been pressed:

```
if (key == Keys.Delete ||
    key == Keys.Back)
{
    if (Text.Length == 0)
    {
        continue;
    }

    Text.Length--;
    renderIsDirty = true;

    continue;
}
```

11. Complete the loop and the method by adding the corresponding character for any keys we recognize, taking note of the case as we do so:

```
        char character;
        if (!characterByKey.TryGetValue(key, out character))
        {
            continue;
        }
        if (keyboard.IsKeyDown(Keys.LeftShift) ||
```

```
                    keyboard.IsKeyDown(Keys.RightShift))
        {
            character = Char.ToUpper(character);
        }
        Text.Append(character);
        renderIsDirty = true;
    }


    lastKeyboard = keyboard;
}
```

12. Add a new method to render the contents of the text field to `RenderTarget` if it has changed:

```
public void PreDraw()
{
    if (!renderIsDirty)
    {
        return;
    }
    renderIsDirty = false;

    var existingRenderTargets = graphicsDevice.GetRenderTargets();

    graphicsDevice.SetRenderTarget(renderTarget);
    spriteBatch.Begin();
    graphicsDevice.Clear(BackgroundColor);
    spriteBatch.DrawString(
        font, Text,
        Vector2.Zero, ForegroundColor);
    spriteBatch.End();
    graphicsDevice.SetRenderTargets(existingRenderTargets);
}
```

13. Complete the class by adding a method to render the image of `RenderTarget` to the screen:

```
public void Draw()
{
    spriteBatch.Begin();
    spriteBatch.Draw(renderTarget, Position, Color.White);
    spriteBatch.End();
}
```

14. In your game's `LoadContent()` method, create a new instance of the text field:

```
Textbox textbox;

protected override void LoadContent()
{
    textbox = new Textbox(
        GraphicsDevice,
        400,
        Content.Load<SpriteFont>("Text"))
    {

        ForegroundColor = Color.YellowGreen,
        BackgroundColor = Color.DarkGreen,
        Position = new Vector2(100,100),
        HasFocus = true
    };
}
```

15. Ensure that the text field is updated regularly via your game's `Update()` method:

```
protected override void Update(GameTime gameTime)
{
    textbox.Update(gameTime);
    base.Update(gameTime);
}
```

16. In your game's `Draw()` method, let the text field perform its `RenderTarget` updates prior to rendering the scene including the text field:

```
protected override void Draw(GameTime gameTime)
{
    textbox.PreDraw();

    GraphicsDevice.Clear(Color.Black);

    textbox.Draw();

    base.Draw(gameTime);
}
```

Running the code should deliver a brand new textbox just waiting for some interesting text like the following:

How it works...

In the `Update()` method, we retrieve a list of all of the keys that are being depressed by the player at that particular moment in time.

Comparing this list to the list we captured in the previous update cycle allows us to determine which keys have only just been depressed.

Next, via a dictionary, we translate the newly depressed keys into characters and append them onto a `StringBuilder` instance.

We could have just as easily used a regular string, but due to the nature of string handling in .NET, the `StringBuilder` class is a lot more efficient in terms of memory use and garbage creation.

We could have also rendered our text directly to the screen, but it turns out that drawing text is a mildly expensive process, with each letter being placed on the screen as an individual image. So in order to minimize the cost and give the rest of our game as much processing power as possible, we render the text to `RenderTarget` only when the text changes, and just keep on displaying `RenderTarget` on screen during all those cycles when no changes occur.

There's more...

If you're constructing a screen that has more than one text field on it, you'll find the `HasFocus` state of the text field implementation to be a handy addition. This will allow you to restrict the keyboard input only to one text field at a time.

In the case of multiple text fields, I'd recommend taking a leaf from the operating system UI handbooks and adding some highlighting around the edges of a text field to clearly indicate which text field has focus.

Also, the addition of a visible text cursor at the end of any text within a text field with focus may help draw the player's eyes to the correct spot.

On the phone

If you do have access to a built-in text field control such as the one provided in the "Windows Phone XNA and Silverlight" project type, but still wish to render the control yourself, I recommend experimenting with enabling the prebuilt control, making it invisible, and feeding the text from it into your own text field display.

Creating dialog wheels

Games such as BioWare's Mass Effect series have propelled the dialog wheel style of option selection to the forefront of modern gaming UI.

While it's essentially a dropped-down list in terms of functionality, the ability for a player to easily select an option via a gamepad, and the possibility of developing a "muscle memory" for popular or regular options, makes it a compelling choice for console games developers.

Getting ready

This recipe requires a `SpriteFont` file along with six images, with each image containing one grayscale segment of the wheel.

Here's one example of a complete wheel:

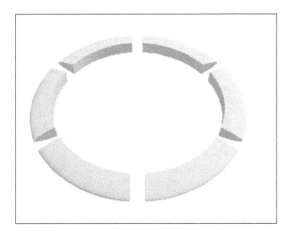

Here's one of the segment's images:

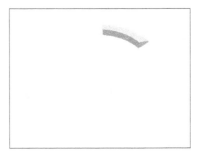

Note how the image of the individual segment hasn't been cropped or moved from its original position. Keeping each segment in place allows us to reconstruct the entire wheel easily by just layering the images directly on top of each other.

I constructed the example segments in a 3D rendering package, but any style of interlocking 2D imagery will do, as long as it follows a recognizable circular flow.

How to do it...

To add a dialogue wheel to your own game:

1. Add a `SpriteFont` file to the solution named `WheelText` along with an image for each segment:

```xml
<?xml version="1.0" encoding="utf-8"?>
<XnaContent xmlns:Graphics="Microsoft.Xna.Framework.Content.
Pipeline.Graphics">
  <Asset Type="Graphics:FontDescription">
    <FontName>Segoe UI Mono</FontName>
    <Size>14</Size>
    <Spacing>0</Spacing>
    <UseKerning>true</UseKerning>
    <Style>Bold</Style>
    <CharacterRegions>
      <CharacterRegion>
        <Start>&#32;</Start>
        <End>&#126;</End>
      </CharacterRegion>
    </CharacterRegions>
  </Asset>
</XnaContent>
```

2. Create a new class to hold the dialog wheel logic and add in some public fields to indicate its state:

```
class Wheel
{
    public bool IsDisplayed = false;
    public bool HasSelected = false;
    public int SelectedIndex = -1;
    public int FocusedSegmentIndex = 0;
```

3. Include some private instance variables to hold the remaining details:

```
private List<Texture2D> segments;
private SpriteFont font;
private List<Vector2> segmentTextOrigins;
private Vector2 segmentOrigin;
private List<string> segmentTexts;
private List<Vector2> textOffsets = new List<Vector2>();
private static Vector2 textShadowOffset = new Vector2(3, 3);
int lastPacketNumber;
GamePadState lastGamePadState;
Vector2 direction;
```

4. Add a constructor to take in the textures for the wheel, along with the text font and the significant positions:

```
public Wheel(
    List<Texture2D> segments,
    SpriteFont font,
    List<Vector2> segmentTextOrigins)
{
    this.segments = segments;
    this.font = font;
    this.segmentTextOrigins = segmentTextOrigins;

    segmentOrigin = new Vector2(
        segments[0].Width / 2,
        segments[0].Height / 2);
}
```

5. Create a method to indicate that the wheel should be displayed, taking in the text options, and calculating the horizontal alignment of each:

```
public void Display(List<string> segmentTexts)
{
    this.segmentTexts = segmentTexts;
    textOffsets.Clear();
    var halfTextCount = segmentTexts.Count / 2;
```

```
        for (var textIndex = 0;
            textIndex < segmentTexts.Count();
            textIndex++)
        {
            if (textIndex < halfTextCount)
            {
                textOffsets.Add(Vector2.Zero);
                continue;
            }
            var text = segmentTexts[textIndex];
            var textMeasurements = font.MeasureString(text);
            textOffsets.Add(new Vector2(-textMeasurements.X, 0));
        }
        IsDisplayed = true;
        HasSelected = false;
        SelectedIndex = -1;
    }
```

6. Add a corresponding method to cancel the display of the wheel:

```
public void Cancel()
{
    IsDisplayed = false;
}
```

7. Create an `Update()` method to check if the player has made any changes.
   If they have, whether it has been to select an item, or change item focus:

```
public void Update(GameTime gameTime)
{
    if (!IsDisplayed)
    {
        return;
    }

    var gamePad = GamePad.GetState(PlayerIndex.One);

    if (gamePad.PacketNumber == lastPacketNumber)
    {
        return;
    }
    lastPacketNumber = gamePad.PacketNumber;

    if (FocusedSegmentIndex >= 0 &&
        gamePad.IsButtonDown(Buttons.A) &&
        lastGamePadState.IsButtonUp(Buttons.A))
```

```
    {
        SelectedIndex = FocusedSegmentIndex;
        HasSelected = true;
        IsDisplayed = false;
    }

    UpdateFocusedSegment(gamePad);
}
```

8. Add the logic to detect what, if any, item the player's left thumbstick is pointing toward:

```
private void UpdateFocusedSegment(GamePadState gamePad)
{
    direction.X = gamePad.ThumbSticks.Left.X;
    direction.Y = gamePad.ThumbSticks.Left.Y;
    var minimumDistance = .35;

    if (direction.Length() <= minimumDistance)
    {
        return;
    }

    var angle = (float)-Math.Atan2(direction.Y, direction.X) +
                (float)MathHelper.PiOver2;
    if (angle < 0)
    {
        angle += MathHelper.TwoPi;
    }

    var segmentIndex = (int)(angle /
                (MathHelper.TwoPi / segments.Count()));
    if (!string.IsNullOrWhiteSpace(segmentTexts[segmentIndex]))
    {
        FocusedSegmentIndex = segmentIndex;
    }
}
```

9. Begin the `Draw()` method by iterating through each of the wheel segments, determining the corresponding imagery and text:

```
public void Draw(SpriteBatch spriteBatch, Vector2 origin)
{
    if (!IsDisplayed)
    {
        return;
    }

    for (var segmentIndex = 0;
```

```
        segmentIndex < segments.Count();
        segmentIndex++)
    {
        var segment = segments[segmentIndex];
        var text = segmentTexts[segmentIndex];
```

10. Render the segment's image in a different color, depending on whether it has focus or not:

```
var segmentColor = Color.DarkRed;

if (segmentIndex == FocusedSegmentIndex)
{
    segmentColor = Color.Orange;
}

spriteBatch.Draw(
    segment,
    origin - segmentOrigin,
    segmentColor);
```

11. Complete the loop and the method by rendering each segment's text, changing the color, and adding a drop shadow depending on if it's the focused segment:

```
        var textOrigin = segmentTextOrigins[segmentIndex];
        var textOffset = textOffsets[segmentIndex];

        var textColor = Color.Gray;

        if (segmentIndex == FocusedSegmentIndex)
        {
            textColor = Color.White;

            spriteBatch.DrawString(
                font, text,
                origin +
                    textOrigin +
                    textOffset +
                    textShadowOffset,
                Color.Black);
        }

        spriteBatch.DrawString(
            font, text,
            origin +
                textOrigin +
                textOffset,
            textColor);
    }
}
```

12. In your game's `LoadContent()` method, create a new instance of the wheel, loading it with the segment imagery, font, and text positions before requesting it be displayed in the middle, at the bottom of the screen:

```
Wheel wheel;
Vector2 wheelOrigin;

protected override void LoadContent()
{
    spriteBatch = new SpriteBatch(GraphicsDevice);
    wheel = new Wheel(
        new List<Texture2D>() {
            Content.Load<Texture2D>("Wheel0"),
            Content.Load<Texture2D>("Wheel1"),
            Content.Load<Texture2D>("Wheel2"),
            Content.Load<Texture2D>("Wheel3"),
            Content.Load<Texture2D>("Wheel4"),
            Content.Load<Texture2D>("Wheel5") },
        Content.Load<SpriteFont>("WheelText"),
        new List<Vector2>() {
            new Vector2(80,-110),
            new Vector2(140,-40),
            new Vector2(110,40),
            new Vector2(-110,40),
            new Vector2(-140,-40),
            new Vector2(-80,-110) });
    wheelOrigin = new Vector2(
            GraphicsDevice.Viewport.Width / 2,
            GraphicsDevice.Viewport.Height - 100);
    wheel.Display(
        new List<string>() {
            "I love you",
            "Huh?",
            "I hate you",
            "Only on Tuesdays",
            "",
            "Try the fish" });
}
```

13. Update the state of the wheel regularly:

```
protected override void Update(GameTime gameTime)
{
    wheel.Update(gameTime);

    base.Update(gameTime);
}
```

14. Render the wheel to the screen as part of your game's normal draw sequence:

```
protected override void Draw(GameTime gameTime)
{
    GraphicsDevice.Clear(Color.DarkSlateGray);

    spriteBatch.Begin();
    wheel.Draw(spriteBatch, wheelOrigin);
    spriteBatch.End();

    base.Draw(gameTime);
}
```

Upon executing the code, you should find yourself with a brand new dialogue wheel as seen here:

How it works...

One of the key aspects of this example is in the `UpdateFocusedSegment()` method, where the X and Y ranges from the gamepad's left thumbstick are translated into a single number that goes from zero when the thumbstick is directed straight up, and proceeds through to two Pi as it's directed in a clockwise circle, back around the top again.

Once this single number representation of the thumbstick angle is achieved, it's just a case of dividing up the possible range into the number of segments, and calculating which segment's range the number currently resides in.

There's more...

You may have noticed that we only perform these calculations if the thumbstick's "distance" from the center is greater than a predefined threshold. This is for the player's comfort, and means that a segment won't gain focus until the player actively pushes the thumbstick in a particular direction. Without it, the wheel starts to feel very "twitchy" to the player, and it's all too easy to accidently select the wrong segment.

Dragging, dropping, and sliding

If you're writing a game for a platform that has either touch or mouse support, then offering the ability for players to drag, drop, and slide elements around the screen can be a surprisingly compelling motivation to play in and of itself.

Getting ready

This recipe requires a selection of 100 by 100 pixel images to form both the background areas and the foreground draggable items. In my example, I created a blank, white texture named "block" for the background and a series of simple, white-lettered textures for the draggable item textures, as shown in the following illustration:

How to do it...

To start dragging and dropping items in your own games:

1. Begin by adding a new class to hold the state of what has been dropped onto the board and where:

    ```
    class Map
    {
        private Dictionary<Point, Icon> iconByPosition =
                    new Dictionary<Point, Icon>();

        public bool TryGetIcon(Point position, out Icon icon)
        {
            return iconByPosition.TryGetValue(position, out icon);
        }

        public Icon this[Point position]
    ```

```
    {
        get
        {
            return iconByPosition[position];
        }
        set
        {
            iconByPosition[position] = value;
        }
    }

    public void Remove(Point position)
    {
        iconByPosition.Remove(position);
    }
}
```

2. Create a new class to hold the design surface logic:

```
class Designer
{
```

3. Add an instance-level variable to hold what mode the design surface is currently in:

```
DesignerMode mode;
```

4. Insert variables to hold the state of the palette:

```
int paletteHeight;
int paletteMinimumVerticalOffset;
float paletteVerticalOffset;
float paletteVerticalStartOffset;
float snapBackSpeed = 2400;
Vector2 paletteOffset;
```

5. Add variables for the state of the player's cursor:

```
Point pointerPosition;
bool pointerPressed;
bool lastPointerPressed;
Point pointerPressStartPosition;
```

6. Continue by adding variables for dragging items from the palette over to the board:

```
int selectedPaletteIndex;
Vector2 selectedPaletteOrigin;
Vector2 selectedPaletteDropPosition;
bool selectedPaletteDropPositionValid;
```

7. Add variables for the position of the board:

```
Vector2 boardStartOffset;
Vector2 boardOffset;
```

8. Append variables to hold the details of the display:

```
SpriteBatch spriteBatch;
Rectangle displayArea;

List<Vector2> paletteItemOffsets;
List<Icon> paletteItemIcons;
Point iconSize;
int paletteRight;
Map map;

Texture2D blockTexture;
Dictionary<Icon, Texture2D> textureByIcon;
```

9. Add a constructor to load the palette and the board map:

```
public Designer(
    GraphicsDevice GraphicsDevice,
    ContentManager Content,
    Rectangle displayArea,
    Map map)
{
    spriteBatch = new SpriteBatch(GraphicsDevice);
    this.displayArea = displayArea;
    this.map = map;

    blockTexture = Content.Load<Texture2D>(@"block");
    textureByIcon = new Dictionary<Icon, Texture2D>();
    textureByIcon.Add(Icon.A, Content.Load<Texture2D>(@"A"));
    textureByIcon.Add(Icon.B, Content.Load<Texture2D>(@"B"));
    textureByIcon.Add(Icon.C, Content.Load<Texture2D>(@"C"));
    textureByIcon.Add(Icon.D, Content.Load<Texture2D>(@"D"));
    textureByIcon.Add(Icon.E, Content.Load<Texture2D>(@"E"));
    textureByIcon.Add(Icon.F, Content.Load<Texture2D>(@"F"));
    textureByIcon.Add(Icon.G, Content.Load<Texture2D>(@"G"));
    textureByIcon.Add(Icon.H, Content.Load<Texture2D>(@"H"));

    iconSize = new Point(blockTexture.Width, blockTexture.Height);
    paletteRight = iconSize.X;

    paletteItemIcons = new List<Icon>() {
        Icon.A,
        Icon.B,
        Icon.C,
        Icon.D,
```

```
                Icon.E,
                Icon.F,
                Icon.G,
                Icon.H,
        };

        paletteItemOffsets = new List<Vector2>();
        for (var iconOffsetIndex = 0;
            iconOffsetIndex < paletteItemIcons.Count;
            iconOffsetIndex++)
        {
            paletteItemOffsets.Add(new Vector2(
                0,
                iconOffsetIndex * iconSize.Y));
        }

        paletteHeight = iconSize.Y * paletteItemIcons.Count;
        paletteMinimumVerticalOffset =
            displayArea.Height - paletteHeight;
    }
```

10. Create an `Update()` method that determines the player's cursor state, and then reacts depending on what state the designer is in:

```
public void Update(GameTime gameTime)
{
    var mouse = Mouse.GetState();
    pointerPosition.X = mouse.X;
    pointerPosition.Y = mouse.Y;
    pointerPressed = (mouse.LeftButton ==
        ButtonState.Pressed);

    switch (mode)
    {
        case DesignerMode.Waiting:
            UpdateWhileWaiting(gameTime);
            break;
        case DesignerMode.PaletteSliding:
            UpdateWhilePaletteSliding();
            break;
        case DesignerMode.DraggingFromPalette:
            UpdateWhileDraggingFromPalette();
            break;
        case DesignerMode.BoardSliding:
            UpdateWhileBoardSliding();
            break;
    }
```

```
        paletteOffset.Y = paletteVerticalOffset;
        lastPointerPressed = pointerPressed;
    }
```

11. Add a method to detect the beginning of any new action by the player:

```
private void UpdateWhileWaiting(GameTime gameTime)
{
    if (pointerPressed &&
        !lastPointerPressed)
    {
        pointerPressStartPosition = pointerPosition;
    }

    SnapPaletteBack(gameTime);

    DeterminePaletteDragAction();
    DetermineBoardDragAction();
}
```

12. Create a method to "snap" the palette back if it's been dragged beyond the edges of the screen:

```
private void SnapPaletteBack(GameTime gameTime)
{
    if (paletteVerticalOffset > 0)
    {
        paletteVerticalOffset -= snapBackSpeed *
            (float)gameTime.ElapsedGameTime.TotalSeconds;
        if (paletteVerticalOffset < 0)
        {
            paletteVerticalOffset = 0;
        }
    }

    if (paletteVerticalOffset < paletteMinimumVerticalOffset)
    {
        paletteVerticalOffset += snapBackSpeed *
            (float)gameTime.ElapsedGameTime.TotalSeconds;
        if (paletteVerticalOffset >
                paletteMinimumVerticalOffset)
        {
            paletteVerticalOffset =
                paletteMinimumVerticalOffset;
        }
    }
}
```

13. Add a method to determine whether the player is sliding the palette in a vertical direction, or beginning to drag a palette item in a horizontal direction toward the board:

```
private void DeterminePaletteDragAction()
{
    if (mode != DesignerMode.Waiting ||
        !pointerPressed ||
        pointerPressStartPosition.X > paletteRight ||
        pointerPosition.DistanceSquaredTo(
            pointerPressStartPosition) < 400)
    {
        return;
    }

    var direction = Vector2.Dot(
                        Vector2.Normalize(
                         pointerPressStartPosition.ToVector2() -
                          pointerPosition.ToVector2()),
                        Vector2.UnitY);

    if (Math.Abs(direction) > .7)
    {
        mode = DesignerMode.PaletteSliding;
        paletteVerticalStartOffset = paletteVerticalOffset;
    }
    else
    {
        mode = DesignerMode.DraggingFromPalette;
        selectedPaletteIndex = (int)(
            (pointerPressStartPosition.Y -
                paletteVerticalOffset) /
            iconSize.Y);
        selectedPaletteOrigin = new Vector2(
            -pointerPressStartPosition.X,
            -pointerPressStartPosition.Y +
            (selectedPaletteIndex * iconSize.Y) +
                paletteVerticalOffset);
        selectedPaletteDropPosition = new Vector2(
                -iconSize.X, 0);
    }
}
```

14. Create a method to determine if the player is beginning to drag the board:

```
private void DetermineBoardDragAction()
{
    if (mode != DesignerMode.Waiting ||
        !pointerPressed ||
            pointerPressStartPosition.X < paletteRight ||
            pointerPosition.DistanceSquaredTo(pointerPressStartPos
ition) < 5)
        {
            return;
        }

    mode = DesignerMode.BoardSliding;
}
```

15. Add a method to continue sliding the palette for as long as the player is holding down the mouse button:

```
private void UpdateWhilePaletteSliding()
{
    if (!pointerPressed)
    {
        mode = DesignerMode.Waiting;
    }

    paletteVerticalOffset = (pointerPosition.Y -
                            pointerPressStartPosition.Y) +
                        paletteVerticalStartOffset;
}
```

16. Insert a method to continue sliding the board around for as long as the player is holding down the mouse button:

```
private void UpdateWhileBoardSliding()
{
    if (!pointerPressed)
    {
        boardStartOffset = boardOffset;
        mode = DesignerMode.Waiting;
        return;
    }
    boardOffset.X = pointerPosition.X +
        boardStartOffset.X -
        pointerPressStartPosition.X;
    boardOffset.Y = pointerPosition.Y +
        boardStartOffset.Y -
```

```
                    pointerPressStartPosition.Y;
    }
```

17. Add a method to handle the dragging of a palette item over the board and releasing it:

```
private void UpdateWhileDraggingFromPalette()
{
    selectedPaletteDropPosition = new Vector2(
        (iconSize.X *
            (int)((pointerPosition.X - boardOffset.X) /
            iconSize.X)) + boardOffset.X,
        (iconSize.Y *
            (int)((pointerPosition.Y - boardOffset.Y) /
            iconSize.Y)) + boardOffset.Y);
    selectedPaletteDropPositionValid =
        selectedPaletteDropPosition.X >
            (paletteRight / 2) &&
        displayArea.Contains(
(int)(selectedPaletteDropPosition.X - boardOffset.X),
(int)(selectedPaletteDropPosition.Y - boardOffset.Y));

    if (!pointerPressed)
    {
        mode = DesignerMode.Waiting;

        if (selectedPaletteDropPositionValid)
        {
            var mapPosition = new Point(
                (int)(selectedPaletteDropPosition.X -
                        boardOffset.X) / iconSize.X,
                (int)(selectedPaletteDropPosition.Y -
                        boardOffset.Y) / iconSize.Y);
            map[mapPosition] =
                paletteItemIcons[selectedPaletteIndex];
        }
    }
}
```

18. Create a method to render the designer surface to the screen:

```
public void Draw()
{
    spriteBatch.Begin();

    DrawBoard();
    DrawDropTarget();
    DrawPalette();
```

```
        DrawDragFromPalette();

        spriteBatch.End();
    }
```

19. Add a method to render the board to the screen:

```
private void DrawBoard()
{
    Point mapPosition;
    Vector2 displayPosition;

    for (var y = 0; y < 6; y++)
    {
        mapPosition.Y = y;
        for (var x = 0; x < 6; x++)
        {
            mapPosition.X = x;
            displayPosition.X =
                    (x * iconSize.X) +
                    boardOffset.X;
            displayPosition.Y =
                    (y * iconSize.Y) +
                    boardOffset.Y;

            spriteBatch.Draw(blockTexture,
                            displayPosition,
                            Color.DarkGreen);

            Icon icon;
            if (map.TryGetIcon(mapPosition, out icon))
            {
                Draw(
                    spriteBatch,
                    icon,
                    IconDrawMode.Board,
                    displayPosition);

            }
        }
    }
}
```

20. Create a method to indicate where on the screen the palette item would "drop", if it were released:

```
private void DrawDropTarget()
{
    if (mode == DesignerMode.DraggingFromPalette &&
```

```
                    selectedPaletteDropPositionValid)
        {
            Draw(spriteBatch,
                paletteItemIcons[selectedPaletteIndex],
                IconDrawMode.DropTarget,
                selectedPaletteDropPosition);
        }
    }
```

21. Add a method to render the item being dragged:

```
private void DrawDragFromPalette()
{
    if (mode == DesignerMode.DraggingFromPalette)
    {
        Draw(spriteBatch,
            paletteItemIcons[selectedPaletteIndex],
            IconDrawMode.Dragging,
            pointerPosition.ToVector2() +
                selectedPaletteOrigin);
    }
}
```

22. Create a method to render the palette:

```
private void DrawPalette()
{
    var paletteComponentIndex = 0;
    foreach (var paletteItemIcon in paletteItemIcons)
    {
        Draw(spriteBatch,
            paletteItemIcons[paletteComponentIndex],
            IconDrawMode.Palette,
            paletteItemOffsets[paletteComponentIndex] +
            paletteOffset);
        paletteComponentIndex++;
    }
}
```

23. Add a method to render an item in context, be it in the palette, being dragged, or on the board:

```
private void Draw(
    SpriteBatch spriteBatch,
    Icon icon,
    IconDrawMode mode,
```

```
        Vector2 position)
    {
        DrawIconBackground(spriteBatch, mode, position);
        DrawIconForeground(spriteBatch, icon, mode, position);
    }
```

24. Create a method to render an item's background if it's being displayed in the palette or on the board:

```
private void DrawIconBackground(SpriteBatch spriteBatch,
IconDrawMode mode, Vector2 position)
{
    switch (mode)
    {
        case IconDrawMode.Board:
            spriteBatch.Draw(blockTexture,
                position,
                Color.DarkGreen);
            break;
        case IconDrawMode.Palette:
            spriteBatch.Draw(blockTexture,
                position,
                Color.Navy);
            break;
    }
}
```

25. Complete the class by adding a method to draw an item's foreground:

```
private void DrawIconForeground(
    SpriteBatch spriteBatch,
    Icon icon,
    IconDrawMode mode,
    Vector2 position)
    {
        var color = Color.White;
        switch (mode)
        {
            case IconDrawMode.Palette:
            case IconDrawMode.Dragging:
                color = Color.LightBlue;
                break;
            case IconDrawMode.DropTarget:
                color = Color.Green;
                break;
            case IconDrawMode.Board:
```

```
                color = Color.White;
                break;
        }

        Texture2D foregroundTexture;
        if (textureByIcon.TryGetValue(
                icon,
                out foregroundTexture))
        {
            spriteBatch.Draw(
                foregroundTexture, position, color);
        }
    }
}
```

26. In your game's constructor, set the mouse to be visible:

```
IsMouseVisible = true;
```

27. Add the creation of the designer surface and map to your game's
    `LoadContent()` method:

```
Designer designer;
Map map;

protected override void LoadContent()
{
    spriteBatch = new SpriteBatch(GraphicsDevice);
    map = new Map();
    designer = new Designer(
        GraphicsDevice, Content,
        GraphicsDevice.Viewport.Bounds,
        map);
}
```

28. Ensure that the designer is updated regularly:

```
protected override void Update(GameTime gameTime)
{
    designer.Update(gameTime);

    base.Update(gameTime);
}
```

29. Render the designer to the screen as part of your game's regular draw cycle:

```
protected override void Draw(GameTime gameTime)
{
```

```
GraphicsDevice.Clear(Color.CornflowerBlue);

designer.Draw();

base.Draw(gameTime);
}
```

Upon running the example, you should find yourself with the ability to drag and drop like so:

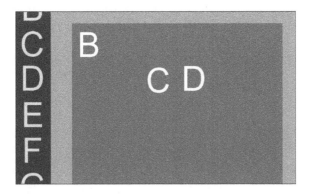

How it works...

The key to this recipe is breaking the problem down into a set of smaller distinct ones.

We set up the notion of modes and have the design surface in only one mode at a particular time. That way we can divide the challenge of determining the player's intent down into smaller, more manageable chunks.

Out of the challenges, the most notable one is probably the determination of what a player is attempting to achieve when he or she is dragging the cursor while over the palette region.

Treating the "drag" as if it were a vector allows us to perform a dot product calculation on it with an "up" vector, which tells us how close our "drag" vector is to being parallel or perpendicular to the "up" vector.

If it's close to zero, that means it's close to being parallel, and thus, the player is dragging in mostly a vertical direction. On the other hand, if it's close to one, then it's closer to being perpendicular to our "up" vector, and thus, the player is dragging in mostly a horizontal fashion.

For this example, I picked the threshold value of 0.7 as being the indicator of dragging horizontally, based purely on my own experimentation, and how natural it felt using the interface. You may find that different thresholds are required depending on the situation.

The rest of the example is really just an exercise in trying to keep things working as a player might expect. For example, the palette can be slid beyond the bounds of the screen, but it springs back into position upon release. In this manner, it retains its functionality but gains a comforting elasticity.

There's more...

If you're after other ways to determine the angle between two points, then the *Creating dialog wheels recipe* in this chapter offers another example that may help.

9
Networking

In this chapter we will cover:

- ▶ Connecting across a LAN
- ▶ Connecting across the Web
- ▶ Synchronizing client states

Introduction

It's pretty rare to find a game these days that doesn't include some sort of network-based functionality, be it anything from a simple online scoreboard through to complex, real time, team-based play. This chapter is all about understanding some of the key techniques used in creating network enabled games.

The first two recipes are for when you either want or need to supply the low-level networking yourself. The last recipe is all about how to share states between clients once they're talking to each other.

Connecting across a LAN

If you're interested in writing games that can operate across a LAN, then there's a very good chance that you'll be interested in some sort of broadcast messaging service to initially allow clients to discover each other, and possibly for fast peer-to-peer game play.

This example demonstrates how to send and receive broadcast messages between both clients on local, as well as remote, machines.

Getting ready

This example requires a `SpriteFont` file with the asset name of **Text** to be present in your solution. As it's purely for debugging purposes, any typeface and size will do.

How to do it...

To start broadcasting across the network yourself:

1. Add a class named `BroadcastClient` to the solution:

    ```
    class BroadcastClient
    {
    ```

2. Insert the instance-level variables to hold the state of the broadcast networking client:

    ```
    const int udpRangeStart = 15123;
    const int localMaximumPortCount = 16;
    UdpClient udpClient;
    IPEndPoint udpReceiveEndPoint;
    List<IPEndPoint> udpSendEndPoints;

    public int LocalPort;
    public bool IsListening = false;
    public Queue<Message> MessagesReceived = new Queue<Message>();
    ```

3. Add a constructor to set up the prerequisites for sending and receiving broadcast messages:

    ```
    public BroadcastClient()
    {
        BeginListening();
        SetupSendPorts();
    }
    ```

4. Add a method to iterate through a range of ports, selecting the first available port in the range as the port to listen on:

    ```
    private void BeginListening()
    {
        var portTestCount = 0;
        var udpPortFound = false;
        do
        {
            try
            {
                LocalPort = udpRangeStart + portTestCount;
    ```

```
                udpReceiveEndPoint = new IPEndPoint(
                                        IPAddress.Any, LocalPort);
                udpClient = new UdpClient(udpReceiveEndPoint);
                udpPortFound = true;
            }
            catch (SocketException)
            {
                portTestCount++;
            }

        } while (!udpPortFound &&
                portTestCount < localMaximumPortCount);

        if (udpPortFound)
        {
            udpClient.BeginReceive(UdpMessageReceived, udpClient);
            IsListening = true;
        }
    }
```

5. Insert the method that will be called upon receiving any broadcast messages:

```
private void UdpMessageReceived(IAsyncResult asyncResult)
{
    var receivedBytes = udpClient.EndReceive(
                            asyncResult,
                            ref udpReceiveEndPoint);
    udpClient.BeginReceive(UdpMessageReceived, udpClient);
    if (udpReceiveEndPoint.Port != LocalPort)
    {
        MessagesReceived.Enqueue(
            new Message()
            {
                Address = udpReceiveEndPoint.Address,
                Port = udpReceiveEndPoint.Port,
                Bytes = receivedBytes
            });
    }
}
```

6. Create a method to set up the end points in advance for the various broadcast ports:

```
private void SetupSendPorts()
{
    udpSendEndPoints = new List<IPEndPoint>();
    for (var sendPortOffset = 0;
```

```
            sendPortOffset < localMaximumPortCount;
            sendPortOffset++)
    {
        udpSendEndPoints.Add(
            new IPEndPoint(
                IPAddress.Broadcast,
                udpRangeStart + sendPortOffset));
    }
}
```

7. Complete the class by adding a method to broadcast data and the corresponding placeholder method to perform any post-broadcasting activities:

```
public void Send(byte[] data)
{
    foreach (var endpoint in udpSendEndPoints)
    {
        udpClient.BeginSend(
            data,
            data.Length,
            endpoint,
            UdpMessageSent,
            udpClient);
    }
}

private void UdpMessageSent(IAsyncResult asyncResult)
{
}
```

8. Add a new class to hold the details of a broadcast message:

```
class Message
{
    public IPAddress Address;
    public int Port;
    public byte[] Bytes;
}
```

9. In your game's startup, create a new broadcast client along with a counter for the number of peers and a font to display it with. Once this is done, send a message to let other clients know of your game's presence:

```
SpriteFont font;
BroadcastClient broadcastClient;
int peerCount;

protected override void LoadContent()
```

```
{
    spriteBatch = new SpriteBatch(GraphicsDevice);
    font = Content.Load<SpriteFont>("text");
    peerCount = 0;
    broadcastClient = new BroadcastClient();
    if (broadcastClient.IsListening)
    {
        broadcastClient.Send(new byte[] { 1, 2, 3 });
    }
}
```

10. During your game's update cycle, process any incoming messages as an indication of a new peer:

```
protected override void Update(GameTime gameTime)
{
    if (broadcastClient.IsListening &&
        broadcastClient.MessagesReceived.Count > 0)
    {
        var message = broadcastClient.MessagesReceived.Dequeue();
        peerCount += 1;
    }
    base.Update(gameTime);
}
```

Complete the example by rendering the number of peers to the screen:

```
protected override void Draw(GameTime gameTime)
{
    GraphicsDevice.Clear(Color.Black);

    spriteBatch.Begin();
    spriteBatch.DrawString(font, peerCount.ToString(), Vector2.
Zero, Color.White);
    spriteBatch.End();

    base.Draw(gameTime);
}
```

How it works...

The `UdpClient` that comes supplied with the .NET framework takes care of most of the hard work for us in terms of low-level network communications. This leaves us to contend with higher-level concerns, such as how to handle multiple instances of the game client running on a single machine.

As each UDP port can only have a connection with by one process at a time (at least if we want to keep things relatively obvious in nature for the benefit of demonstration), we create a broadcast listening port for each game client running on the local machine in the `BeginListening()` method.

To accommodate sending to multiple listening ports, we set up a range of broadcast address endpoints with one endpoint for each possible listening port in the `SetupSendPorts()` method.

When we wish to send a message, we simply cycle through each one of the send endpoints, directing the `UdpClient` to send a broadcast message to all machines on that specific port.

Receiving messages is equally easy with the setup of the `UdpMessageReceived()` method. This moves any incoming messages that haven't been sent by this game instance into a queue for later processing once the game next hits its update cycle.

The messages are stored temporarily in a queue to take into account that messages could be received at any time and, given the chance, we'd prefer to not have something time–critical, such as our draw cycle, interrupted by any message processing.

Delayed processing via a queue also lets us sidestep a number of issues raised by the fact that the various callback methods utilized by the `UdpClient`, such as `UdpMessageReceived()`, could be called on a different thread to our game loop.

There's more...

You may have noticed a distinct lack of strings being passed around as messages in this example. This was intentional, despite the relative ease of the `System.Encoding.ASCII` conversion methods available in the framework, as the immutable nature of strings in .NET means it's all too easy to start producing fodder for the garbage collector with a heavily utilized functionality such as networking.

I would recommend keeping any string transmission to an absolute minimum for the best possible chance of avoiding costly garbage collection cycles.

See also

▸ *Connecting across the web* recipe in this chapter.

Connecting across the Web

Competing against friends and family at home can be a lot of fun, but being able to broaden one's gaming horizons to the wider world can bring a whole other level of possibilities.

In addition to demonstrating how to get started with writing HTTP-enabled clients, we'll also have a peek at one possible approach for constructing a web service for use within Microsoft's IIS web server platform.

Getting ready

This example requires that the ASP.NET components of Visual Studio be installed, and that a single SpriteFont file with the asset name of Info is used.

How to do it...

Dive into the world of web communications by:

1. Creating a new **ASP.NET Empty Solution** with the project name of **Server.Iis** and the solution name of **WebDemo**.

2. Alter the **Web.config** file of the newly created project so all web traffic will be directed towards a single handler class:

```xml
<?xml version="1.0"?>
<configuration>
  <system.web>
    <compilation debug="true" targetFramework="4.0" />
    <sessionState mode="Off" />
    <httpHandlers>
      <clear/>
      <add path="*" verb="*"
          type="Server.Web.Handler, Server.Web" />
    </httpHandlers>
  </system.web>
</configuration>
```

3. Add a new **Class Library** project to the solution named **Server.Web**.

4. Create a new reference to the **System.Web** assembly in the **Server.Web** project.

5. Add a new reference to the **Server.Web** assembly in the **Server.Iis** project.

6. Within the **Web** tab of the **Properties** window for the **Server.Iis** project, enable the **Use Visual Studio Development Server** option and set its **Specific port** option to **18000**.

7. Add a new XNA **Windows Game** project to the solution named **Client.Windows**.

8. Right-click on the newly created game project within the solution explorer, and select **Set as StartUp Project**.

9. Add a new SpriteFont file to the XNA game content project with the asset name of **Info**.

10. Add a new class to the **Server.Web** project to serve some demo data:

```csharp
public class Handler : IHttpHandler
{
    public bool IsReusable
    {
        get { return true; }
    }

    public void ProcessRequest(HttpContext context)
    {
        var path = context.Request.Path.ToLower();
        switch (path)
        {
            case "/time":
                var currentUtcTime =
                    DateTime.Now.ToUniversalTime();
                context.Response.Write(
                    currentUtcTime.ToString("HHmmss"));
                break;
            case "/yogurt":
                context.Response.Write("Banana");
                break;
            default:
                context.Response.Write("Hello World");
                break;
        }
    }
}
```

11. Add a new class to the **Client.Windows** project to handle the implementation details of HTTP networking:

```csharp
class ServerProxy
{
```

12. Insert the instance-level variables into the class to hold the networking state:

```csharp
string serverName;
WebClient client;

Uri timeUri;
public bool IsUpdatingTime;
public int Hour;
public int Minute;
```

```
public int Second;

Uri yogurtUri;
public bool IsUpdatingYogurt;
public StringBuilder Yougurt;

public bool IsInError;
```

13. Add a constructor to initialize the underlying `WebClient` instance along with details of the two types of service calls it will be making:

```
public ServerProxy(string serverName)
{
    this.serverName = serverName;
    client = new WebClient();
    client.OpenReadCompleted += new OpenReadCompletedEventHandler(
OpenReadCompleted);

    timeUri = new Uri(serverName + "/time");
    yogurtUri = new Uri(serverName + "/yogurt");
    Yougurt = new StringBuilder();
}
```

14. Create a new method for the game to indicate that it would like updated time details from the server:

```
public void BeginUpdatingTime()
{
    if (IsBusy ||
        IsUpdatingTime)
    {
        throw new Exception("Proxy is Busy");
    }
    IsUpdatingTime = true;
    IsInError = false;
    client.OpenReadAsync(timeUri, "gettime");
}
```

15. Add a new method to allow the game to indicate that it would like the latest yogurt details from the server:

```
public void BeginUpdatingYogurt()
{
    if (IsBusy ||
        IsUpdatingTime)
    {
        throw new Exception("Proxy is Busy");
    }
```

```
        IsUpdatingYogurt = true;
        IsInError = false;
        client.OpenReadAsync(yogurtUri, "getyogurt");
    }
```

16. Provide a property to relay to the outside world whether the proxy is currently engaged in retrieving other information:

```
public bool IsBusy
{
    get
    {
        return client.IsBusy;
    }
}
```

17. Add a method to process any data returned from the server:

```
void OpenReadCompleted(object sender, OpenReadCompletedEventArgs e)
{
    if (e.Error != null)
    {
        IsInError = true;
        return;
    }

    switch ((string)e.UserState)
    {
        case "gettime":
            ReadTime(e);
            break;
        case "getyogurt":
            ReadYogurt(e);
            break;
    }
}
```

18. Insert a new method to translate the returning data from the server into text:

```
private void ReadYogurt(OpenReadCompletedEventArgs e)
{
    Yougurt.Clear();
    var data = 0;
    var singleByte = new byte[1];
    while ((data = e.Result.ReadByte()) > -1)
    {
```

```
            singleByte[0] = (byte)data;
            Yougurt.Append( Encoding.ASCII.GetChars(singleByte));
        }
        e.Result.Close();
        IsUpdatingYogurt = false;
    }
```

19. Add a new method to translate the returning data into a set of time-related variables:

```
private void ReadTime(OpenReadCompletedEventArgs e)
{

    var data = 0;
    var byteIndex = 0;
    while ((data = e.Result.ReadByte()) > -1)
    {
        switch (byteIndex)
        {
            case 0:
                Hour = 10 * ToInt(data);
                break;
            case 1:
                Hour += ToInt(data);
                break;
            case 2:
                Minute = 10 * ToInt(data);
                break;
            case 3:
                Minute += ToInt(data);
                break;
            case 4:
                Second = 10 * ToInt(data);
                break;
            case 5:
                Second += ToInt(data);
                break;
        }
        byteIndex++;
    }
    e.Result.Close();

    IsUpdatingTime = false;
}
```

20. Complete the class by adding a helper method to translate individual bytes back into digits:

```
private static int ToInt(int data)
{
    var character = (char)data;
    return int.Parse(character.ToString());
}
```

21. Within the content loading of the game class, set up an instance of the proxy along with the items needed for display:

```
ServerProxy proxy;
SpriteFont font;
StringBuilder timeText;
bool isYogurtPending;
StringBuilder yogurtText;

protected override void LoadContent()
{
    spriteBatch = new SpriteBatch(GraphicsDevice);

    proxy = new ServerProxy("http://localhost:18000");
    timeText = new StringBuilder();
    yogurtText = new StringBuilder();
    font = Content.Load<SpriteFont>("info");
    isYogurtPending = true;
}
```

22. Add calls to retrieve the various pieces of information from the server:

```
protected override void Update(GameTime gameTime)
{
    UpdateYogurtDisplay();
    UpdateTimeDisplay();


    base.Update(gameTime);
}
```

23. Create a method to manage the retrieval and updating of the server-supplied time details:

```
private void UpdateTimeDisplay()
{
    if (!proxy.IsBusy &&
        !proxy.IsUpdatingTime)
    {
```

```
            timeText.Clear();
            timeText.Append("The server time is ");
            timeText.Append(proxy.Hour);
            timeText.Append(":");
            timeText.Append(proxy.Minute);
            timeText.Append(":");
            timeText.Append(proxy.Second);
            proxy.BeginUpdatingTime();
        }
    }
```

24. Add a method to manage the yogurt-based data retrieval and display:

```
    private void UpdateYogurtDisplay()
    {
        if (isYogurtPending)
        {
            if (!proxy.IsUpdatingYogurt &&
                proxy.Yougurt.Length > 0)
            {
                yogurtText.Clear();
                yogurtText.Append("Yogurt is ");
                yogurtText.Append(proxy.Yougurt);
                isYogurtPending = false;
            }
            if (!proxy.IsBusy &&
                !proxy.IsUpdatingYogurt)
            {
                if (yogurtText.Length == 0)
                {
                    yogurtText.Clear();
                    yogurtText.Append("Yogurt is pending");
                }
                proxy.BeginUpdatingYogurt();
            }

        }
    }
```

25. Render the details to the screen:

```
    protected override void Draw(GameTime gameTime)
    {
        GraphicsDevice.Clear(Color.CornflowerBlue);

        spriteBatch.Begin();
```

```
spriteBatch.DrawString(
    font, timeText, Vector2.Zero, Color.White);
spriteBatch.DrawString(
    font, yogurtText, new Vector2(0, 100), Color.White);
spriteBatch.End();

base.Draw(gameTime);
}
```

How it works...

On the server side, even just keeping to the only options supplied to us via the ASP.NET framework, there are lots of ways we could have created a website. This particular option seemed to offer the best possible chance or performance through its limited number of moving parts, and the smallest number of lines of code to get it working.

We create a single `HttpHandler` to handle all of the incoming requests and feed all of them into a single switch statement based off the requested path and provide a different streamed response accordingly.

As this service is being built specifically for a game, it forgoes all the niceties of HTML or JSON formatted content for a custom binary format that can be consumed in a processor and memory-efficient manner in our game client.

The bulk of the complexity on the client is surrounding the possibly multithreaded nature of any callbacks from the `WebClient` to process response data from the server.

We try to minimize the chance of multithreading hijinks happening by using flags to indicate to the wider game when it's safe to ask for and retrieve the latest data from the server.

There's more...

Real world concerns, such as proxies, caching, and holding state via cookies, have been intentionally excluded from this example as each one of them could possibly fill a book on their own.

However, that doesn't mean that they're hard to utilize, at least on the server side of the ASP.NET framework, as there's plenty of helper methods and properties contained within the framework to make your life as easy as possible.

If you're writing games for a device such as a Windows Phone, then the pressures on memory, disk, and CPU utilization can be even more intense. With this in mind, I would recommend keeping any communication (and associated responsibilities such as security) as simple as possible.

See also

▸ *Connecting across the LAN* recipe in this chapter

▸ The official ASP.NET site at `http://asp.net`

Synchronizing client states

After you've got game clients talking to each other comes the challenge of working out what they should actually say, and that can be a more difficult problem than what one might initially suspect.

Presented in this example are the beginnings of a multiplayer-networked version of Pong, or more specifically, a simulation of two clients and a server instance of a game of Pong.

With this simulation, you'll hopefully get a chance to experiment with and discover some useful strategies on how to architect holding and transferring state between networked clients.

Getting ready

This example relies upon a single texture file named `block`, from which it stretches into various sizes to form the onscreen elements. Any texture will do but I would recommend a small, completely white texture as a starting point.

How to do it...

To see a working example of synchronization:

1. Begin a new class to simulate the gameplay with the various bits of state pertinent to the game:

```
class Simulation
{
    public double PlayerOneBatWidth;
    public double PlayerOneBatHeight;
    public double PlayerOneBatX;
    public double PlayerOneBatY;
    public double PlayerOneBatVelocityY;
    public double PlayerTwoBatWidth;
    public double PlayerTwoBatHeight;
    public double PlayerTwoBatX;
    public double PlayerTwoBatY;
    public double PlayerTwoBatVelocityY;
    public double BallWidth;
```

```
        public double BallHeight;
        public double BallX;
        public double BallY;
        public double BallVelocityX;
        public double BallVelocityY;

        public bool PlayerOneUpKeyIsDown;
        public bool PlayerOneDownKeyIsDown;
        public bool PlayerTwoUpKeyIsDown;
        public bool PlayerTwoDownKeyIsDown;
```

2. Add a constructor to start the simulation in a known state:

```
public Simulation()
{
        PlayerOneBatWidth = 0.01f;
        PlayerOneBatHeight = 0.21f;
        PlayerOneBatX = 0.125f;
        PlayerOneBatY = 0.5f;
        PlayerOneBatVelocityY = 0d;

        PlayerTwoBatWidth = 0.01f;
        PlayerTwoBatHeight = 0.21f;
        PlayerTwoBatX = 1f - 0.125f;
        PlayerTwoBatY = 0.5f;
        PlayerTwoBatVelocityY = 0d;

        BallWidth = 0.05f;
        BallHeight = 0.05f;

        BallVelocityX = -0.15f;
        BallVelocityY = -0.1f;

        BallX = 0.5f;
        BallY = 0.5f;
}
```

3. Insert the beginning of a method to simulate a defined period of gameplay:

```
public void Update(double elapsedGameTimeSeconds)
{
```

4. Continue the method with the game logic that allows player one's bat to not go any further than the top of the playing field:

```
PlayerOneBatVelocityY = 0;
var minimumPlayerOneBatY = PlayerOneBatY -
        (PlayerOneBatHeight / 2);
if (PlayerOneUpKeyIsDown &&
    minimumPlayerOneBatY > 0)
```

```
{
    PlayerOneBatVelocityY -= 1;
}
```

5. Add similar logic to prevent player one's bat from going past the bottom of the field:

```
var maximumPlayerOneBatY = PlayerOneBatY +
        (PlayerOneBatHeight / 2);
if (PlayerOneDownKeyIsDown &&
    maximumPlayerOneBatY < 1)
{
    PlayerOneBatVelocityY += 1;
}
```

6. Constrain player two's bat in a similar fashion to player one's:

```
PlayerTwoBatVelocityY = 0;
var minimumPlayerTwoBatY = PlayerTwoBatY -
        (PlayerTwoBatHeight / 2);
if (PlayerTwoUpKeyIsDown &&
    minimumPlayerTwoBatY > 0)
{
    PlayerTwoBatVelocityY -= 1;
}
var maximumPlayerTwoBatY = PlayerTwoBatY +
        (PlayerTwoBatHeight / 2);
if (PlayerTwoDownKeyIsDown &&
    maximumPlayerTwoBatY < 1)
{
    PlayerTwoBatVelocityY += 1;
}
```

7. Instantiate the local copies of the gameplay states that will be used during the simulation run:

```
var nextPlayerOneBatY = PlayerOneBatY;
var nextPlayerOneBatVelocityY = PlayerOneBatVelocityY;
var nextPlayerTwoBatY = PlayerTwoBatY;
var nextPlayerTwoBatVelocityY = PlayerTwoBatVelocityY;

var nextBallX = BallX;
var nextBallY = BallY;

var nextBallVelocityX = BallVelocityX;
var nextBallVelocityY = BallVelocityY;

var timeRemaining = elapsedGameTimeSeconds;
```

8. Calculate bat and ball movement in second intervals, flipping the velocity if the ball hits a surface:

```
while (timeRemaining > 0)
{
    var stepSize = 1d;
    if (timeRemaining < 1d)
    {
        stepSize = timeRemaining;
    }
    timeRemaining -= stepSize;

    nextPlayerOneBatY += nextPlayerOneBatVelocityY * stepSize;
    nextPlayerTwoBatY += nextPlayerTwoBatVelocityY * stepSize;
    nextBallX += nextBallVelocityX * stepSize;
    nextBallY += nextBallVelocityY * stepSize;

    if (BallDoesCollideVertically(
            nextPlayerOneBatY,
            nextPlayerTwoBatY,
            nextBallX,
            nextBallY))
    {
        nextBallVelocityY *= -1;
        nextBallY += nextBallVelocityY * stepSize * 2;
    }

    if (BallDoesCollideHorizontally(
            nextPlayerOneBatY,
            nextPlayerTwoBatY,
            nextBallX,
            nextBallY))
    {
        nextBallVelocityX *= -1;
        nextBallX += nextBallVelocityX * stepSize * 2;
    }

}
```

9. Complete the method by updating the game state with the results of the simulation run:

```
PlayerOneBatY = nextPlayerOneBatY;
PlayerOneBatVelocityY = nextPlayerOneBatVelocityY;
PlayerTwoBatY = nextPlayerTwoBatY;
PlayerTwoBatVelocityY = nextPlayerTwoBatVelocityY;

BallX = nextBallX;
BallY = nextBallY;
```

```
    BallVelocityX = nextBallVelocityX;
    BallVelocityY = nextBallVelocityY;

}
```

10. Create a method to determine when the ball has collided with a vertical surface, be it the field walls or one of the players' bats:

```
private bool BallDoesCollideVertically(
    double nextPlayerOneBatY,
    double nextPlayerTwoBatY,
    double nextBallX,
    double nextBallY)
{
    var minimumBallY = nextBallY - (BallHeight / 2d);
    if (minimumBallY < 0)
    {
        return true;
    }

    var maximumBallY = nextBallY + (BallHeight / 2d);
    if (maximumBallY > 1)
    {
        return true;
    }

    if (DoesCollideWithBatVertically(
        PlayerOneBatWidth,
        PlayerOneBatHeight,
        PlayerOneBatX,
        nextPlayerOneBatY,
        BallWidth,
        BallHeight,
        nextBallX,
        nextBallY))
    {
        return true;
    }

    if (DoesCollideWithBatVertically(
        PlayerTwoBatWidth,
        PlayerTwoBatHeight,
        PlayerTwoBatX,
        nextPlayerOneBatY,
        BallWidth,
        BallHeight,
        nextBallX,
        nextBallY))
```

```
        {
            return true;
        }

        return false;
    }
```

11. Add a method to determine if a ball has collided with a bat:

```
private static bool DoesCollideWithBatVertically(
    double batWidth,
    double batHeight,
    double batX,
    double batY,
    double ballWidth,
    double ballHeight,
    double ballX,
    double ballY)
{
    var minimumBallX = ballX - (ballWidth / 2d);
    var maximumBallX = ballX + (ballWidth / 2d);

    var minimumBatX = batX - (batWidth / 2d);
    var maximumBatX = batX + (batWidth / 2d);

    if (minimumBallX < maximumBatX &&
        maximumBallX > minimumBatX)
    {
        var minimumBallY = ballY - (ballHeight / 2d);
        var maximumBallY = ballY + (ballHeight / 2d);

        var minimumBatY = batY - (batHeight / 2d);
        var maximumBatY = batY + (batHeight / 2d);

        if (minimumBallY < minimumBatY &&
            maximumBallY > minimumBatY)
        {
            return true;
        }

        if (minimumBallY < maximumBatY &&
            maximumBallY > maximumBatY)
        {
            return true;
        }
    }

    return false;
}
```

12. Create a method to determine if a ball has collided with either a horizontal wall or one of the players' bats:

```
private bool BallDoesCollideHorizontally(
    double nextPlayerOneBatY,
    double nextPlayerTwoBatY,
    double nextBallX,
    double nextBallY)
{
    var minimumBallX = nextBallX - (BallWidth / 2d);
    if (minimumBallX < 0)
    {
        return true;
    }

    var maximumBallX = nextBallX + (BallWidth / 2d);
    if (maximumBallX > 1)
    {
        return true;
    }

    if (DoesCollideWithBatHorizontally(
        PlayerOneBatWidth,
        PlayerOneBatHeight,
        PlayerOneBatX,
        nextPlayerOneBatY,
        BallWidth,
        BallHeight,
        nextBallX,
        nextBallY))
    {
        return true;
    }

    if (DoesCollideWithBatHorizontally(
        PlayerTwoBatWidth,
        PlayerTwoBatHeight,
        PlayerTwoBatX,
        nextPlayerOneBatY,
        BallWidth,
        BallHeight,
        nextBallX,
        nextBallY))
    {
        return true;
    }
```

```
        return false;
    }
```

13. Add a method to determine if the ball has collided with one of the horizontal surfaces of the players' bats:

```
private static bool DoesCollideWithBatHorizontally(
    double batWidth,
    double batHeight,
    double batX,
    double batY,
    double ballWidth,
    double ballHeight,
    double ballX,
    double ballY)
{
    var minimumBallX = ballX - (ballWidth / 2d);
    var maximumBallX = ballX + (ballWidth / 2d);

    var minimumBatX = batX - (batWidth / 2d);
    var maximumBatX = batX + (batWidth / 2d);

    if (minimumBallX < maximumBatX &&
        maximumBallX > minimumBatX)
    {
        var minimumBallY = ballY - (ballHeight / 2d);
        var maximumBallY = ballY + (ballHeight / 2d);

        var minimumBatY = batY - (batHeight / 2d);
        var maximumBatY = batY + (batHeight / 2d);

        if (minimumBallY > minimumBatY &&
            maximumBallY < maximumBatY)
        {
            return true;
        }
    }

    return false;
}
```

14. Complete the class by adding a method to transfer the entire simulation state over to another simulation container:

```
public void TransferTo(Simulation other)
{
    other.PlayerOneBatWidth = PlayerOneBatWidth;
    other.PlayerOneBatHeight = PlayerOneBatHeight;
    other.PlayerOneBatX = PlayerOneBatX;
    other.PlayerOneBatY = PlayerOneBatY;
```

```
        other.PlayerOneBatVelocityY = PlayerOneBatVelocityY;
        other.PlayerTwoBatWidth = PlayerTwoBatWidth;
        other.PlayerTwoBatHeight = PlayerTwoBatHeight;
        other.PlayerTwoBatX = PlayerTwoBatX;
        other.PlayerTwoBatY = PlayerTwoBatY;
        other.PlayerTwoBatVelocityY = PlayerTwoBatVelocityY;
        other.BallWidth = BallWidth;
        other.BallHeight = BallHeight;
        other.BallX = BallX;
        other.BallY = BallY;
        other.BallVelocityX = BallVelocityX;
        other.BallVelocityY = BallVelocityY;

        other.PlayerOneUpKeyIsDown = PlayerOneUpKeyIsDown;
        other.PlayerOneDownKeyIsDown = PlayerOneDownKeyIsDown;
        other.PlayerTwoUpKeyIsDown = PlayerTwoUpKeyIsDown;
        other.PlayerTwoDownKeyIsDown = PlayerTwoDownKeyIsDown;
    }
```

15. Begin a new class to manage a simulation along with the data that goes into and out of it by creating some instance-level variables used to communicate with other game elements:

```
class Engine
{
    public double PlayerOneBatDisplayWidth;
    public double PlayerOneBatDisplayHeight;
    public double PlayerOneBatDisplayX;
    public double PlayerOneBatDisplayY;
    public double PlayerTwoBatDisplayWidth;
    public double PlayerTwoBatDisplayHeight;
    public double PlayerTwoBatDisplayX;
    public double PlayerTwoBatDisplayY;
    public double BallDisplayWidth;
    public double BallDisplayHeight;
    public double BallDisplayX;
    public double BallDisplayY;
    public List<InputAction> PendingExternalPlayerOneActions;
    public List<InputAction> PendingExternalPlayerTwoActions;
```

16. Add in the private instance variable used to hold the state of the simulation:

```
Queue<InputAction> pendingLocalActions;
Queue<InputAction> pendingPlayerOneActions;
Queue<InputAction> pendingPlayerTwoActions;

Simulation lastKnownSimulation;
```

```
    private double lastKnownTotalGameTime;

    Simulation extrapolationSimulation;
    private double extrapolationTotalGameTime;

    public readonly EngineType Type;
```

17. Create a constructor to instantiate the fresh instances of the internal state:

```
public Engine(EngineType type)
{
    Type = type;

    lastKnownSimulation = new Simulation();
    extrapolationSimulation = new Simulation();

    pendingLocalActions = new Queue<InputAction>();
    pendingPlayerOneActions = new Queue<InputAction>();
    pendingPlayerTwoActions = new Queue<InputAction>();

    PendingExternalPlayerOneActions = new List<InputAction>();
    PendingExternalPlayerTwoActions = new List<InputAction>();

}
```

18. Add a method to record a newly detected action by player one into various queues and lists for later processing:

```
public void LogPlayerOneAction(
    InputAction inputAction,
    bool isLocal)
{
    if (isLocal &&
        Type == EngineType.PlayerOne)
    {
        pendingLocalActions.Enqueue(inputAction);
    }

    pendingPlayerOneActions.Enqueue(inputAction);

    if (Type == EngineType.PlayerOne ||
        Type == EngineType.Passive)
    {
        PendingExternalPlayerOneActions.Add(inputAction);
    }
}
```

19. Create a corresponding method to record any new actions detected by player two for later processing:

```
public void LogPlayerTwoAction(
    InputAction inputAction,
    bool isLocal)
```

```
    {
        if (isLocal &&
            Type == EngineType.PlayerTwo)
        {

            pendingLocalActions.Enqueue(inputAction);
        }

        pendingPlayerTwoActions.Enqueue(inputAction);

        if (Type == EngineType.PlayerTwo ||
            Type == EngineType.Passive)
        {

            PendingExternalPlayerTwoActions.Add(inputAction);

        }
    }
```

20. Add a method to update the internal simulations along with the data used to display them on screen:

```
public void Update()
{
    UpdateLastKnownSimultation();
    UpdateExtrapolationSimulation();
    if (Type == EngineType.Passive)
    {

        UpdateDisplay(lastKnownSimulation);

    }
    else
    {

        UpdateDisplay(extrapolationSimulation);

    }
}
```

21. Create a method to update the internal simulations only when data has been found for both players for a given time period:

```
private void UpdateLastKnownSimultation()
{
    var lastKnownSimulationUpdated = false;
    while (pendingPlayerOneActions.Count >= 2 &&
        pendingPlayerTwoActions.Count >= 2)
    {
        var nextPlayerOneAction =
                pendingPlayerOneActions.Peek();
        var nextPlayerTwoAction =
                pendingPlayerTwoActions.Peek();

        if (nextPlayerOneAction.Timestamp <
```

```
                    nextPlayerTwoAction.Timestamp)
        {
            var action = pendingPlayerOneActions.Dequeue();
            lastKnownSimulation.Update(
                action.Timestamp -
                    lastKnownTotalGameTime);
            ApplyAction(action, lastKnownSimulation, true);
            lastKnownTotalGameTime = action.Timestamp;
            lastKnownSimulationUpdated = true;
        }
        else
        {
            var action = pendingPlayerTwoActions.Dequeue();
            lastKnownSimulation.Update(
                action.Timestamp -
                    lastKnownTotalGameTime);
            ApplyAction(action, lastKnownSimulation, false);
            lastKnownTotalGameTime = action.Timestamp;
            lastKnownSimulationUpdated = true;
        }
    }
    if (lastKnownSimulationUpdated)
    {
        lastKnownSimulation.TransferTo(
            extrapolationSimulation);
    }
}
```

22. Add a method to update the internal simulation specifically dedicated to when only local player update data is available for processing:

```
private void UpdateExtrapolationSimulation()
{
    foreach (var pendingAction in pendingLocalActions)
    {
        extrapolationSimulation.Update(
            pendingAction.Timestamp -
                extrapolationTotalGameTime);
        ApplyAction(pendingAction,
            extrapolationSimulation,
            Type == EngineType.PlayerOne);
        extrapolationTotalGameTime = pendingAction.Timestamp;
    }
    pendingLocalActions.Clear();
}
```

23. Create a method to populate an internal simulation with a given player's recorded actions:

```
private void ApplyAction(InputAction action, Simulation
simulation, bool isPlayerOne)
{
    if (isPlayerOne)
    {
        simulation.PlayerOneUpKeyIsDown =
            ((action.Type & InputActionType.Up) ==
                InputActionType.Up);
        simulation.PlayerOneDownKeyIsDown =
            ((action.Type & InputActionType.Down) ==
                InputActionType.Down);

    }
    else
    {
        simulation.PlayerTwoUpKeyIsDown =
            ((action.Type & InputActionType.Up) ==
                InputActionType.Up);
        simulation.PlayerTwoDownKeyIsDown =
            ((action.Type & InputActionType.Down) ==
                InputActionType.Down);

    }
}
```

24. Complete the class with a new method to update the external display-specific variables with the latest data:

```
private void UpdateDisplay(Simulation simulation)
{
    PlayerOneBatDisplayWidth = simulation.PlayerOneBatWidth;
    PlayerOneBatDisplayHeight = simulation.PlayerOneBatHeight;
    PlayerOneBatDisplayX = simulation.PlayerOneBatX;
    PlayerOneBatDisplayY = simulation.PlayerOneBatY;

    PlayerTwoBatDisplayWidth = simulation.PlayerTwoBatWidth;
    PlayerTwoBatDisplayHeight = simulation.PlayerTwoBatHeight;
    PlayerTwoBatDisplayX = simulation.PlayerTwoBatX;
    PlayerTwoBatDisplayY = simulation.PlayerTwoBatY;

    BallDisplayWidth = simulation.BallWidth;
    BallDisplayHeight = simulation.BallHeight;
    BallDisplayX = simulation.BallX;
    BallDisplayY = simulation.BallY;
}
```

25. Add a new enum file to indicate what sort of role the engine will be playing in terms of data processing:

```
enum EngineType
{
    Passive,
    PlayerOne,
    PlayerTwo,
}
```

26. Create a new class to hold a player's action:

```
class InputAction
{
    public InputActionType Type;
    public double Timestamp;
}
```

27. Add a new enum file to indicate what type of input an action might be:

```
[Flags]
enum InputActionType
{
    None = 0,
    Up = 1,
    Down = 2
}
```

28. Begin a new class to render the playing field of a given engine to the screen by adding the logic to render two bats and a ball:

```
class Display
{
    static Point rectangleLocation;
    static Rectangle rectangle;

    public static void Draw(
        SpriteBatch spriteBatch,
        Engine engine,
        Rectangle displayArea,
        Texture2D block)
    {
        spriteBatch.Draw(block, displayArea, Color.Black);

        DrawRectangle(spriteBatch,
            displayArea,
            block,
            engine.PlayerOneBatDisplayWidth,
            engine.PlayerOneBatDisplayHeight,
```

```
            engine.PlayerOneBatDisplayX,
            engine.PlayerOneBatDisplayY);
        DrawRectangle(spriteBatch,
            displayArea,
            block,
            engine.PlayerTwoBatDisplayWidth,
            engine.PlayerTwoBatDisplayHeight,
            engine.PlayerTwoBatDisplayX,
            engine.PlayerTwoBatDisplayY);
        DrawRectangle(spriteBatch,
            displayArea,
            block,
            engine.BallDisplayWidth,
            engine.BallDisplayHeight,
            engine.BallDisplayX,
            engine.BallDisplayY);
    }
```

29. Complete the class with the addition of a method to render a rectangle to the screen:

```
    private static void DrawRectangle(
        SpriteBatch spriteBatch,
        Rectangle displayArea,
        Texture2D block,
        double width, double height,
        double x, double y)
    {

        var screenSpaceWidth = displayArea.Width * width;
        var screenSpaceHeight = displayArea.Height * height;
        rectangle.Width = (int)(screenSpaceWidth);
        rectangle.Height = (int)(screenSpaceHeight);

        var screenSpaceX = displayArea.Width * x;
        var screenSpaceY = displayArea.Height * y;
        rectangleLocation.X = displayArea.Left +
            (int)(screenSpaceX - (screenSpaceWidth / 2d));
        rectangleLocation.Y = displayArea.Top +
            (int)(screenSpaceY - (screenSpaceHeight / 2d));
        rectangle.Location = rectangleLocation;

        spriteBatch.Draw(block, rectangle, Color.White);
    }
}
```

30. In your game class' loading of content, ensure that a simulated server and two clients are created along with their respective onscreen display measurements:

```
Engine serverEngine;
Engine playerOneEngine;
Engine playerTwoEngine;
Rectangle serverDisplayArea;
Rectangle playerOneDisplayArea;
Rectangle playerTwoDisplayArea;
bool simulateNetwork = true;
Random random;

protected override void LoadContent()
{
    spriteBatch = new SpriteBatch(GraphicsDevice);
    random = new Random();

    block = Content.Load<Texture2D>("block");

    serverEngine = new Engine(EngineType.Passive);
    serverDisplayArea = new Rectangle(250, 25, 300, 200);

    playerOneEngine = new Engine(EngineType.PlayerOne);
    playerOneDisplayArea = new Rectangle(25, 250, 300, 200);

    playerTwoEngine = new Engine(EngineType.PlayerTwo);
    playerTwoDisplayArea = new Rectangle(475, 250, 300, 200);
}
```

31. Upon each update cycle, simulate the processing that occurs on the server and the two clients, along with the sometimes quite fickle virtual networking that occurs between them:

```
protected override void Update(GameTime gameTime)
{
    var keyboard = Keyboard.GetState();

    UpdateServerEngineLocally(gameTime);
    UpdatePlayerOneEngineLocally(gameTime, keyboard);
    UpdatePlayerTwoEngineLocally(gameTime, keyboard);

    if (!simulateNetwork || random.NextDouble() > 0.9d)
    {
        TransferFromPlayerOneToServer();
    }
    if (!simulateNetwork || random.NextDouble() > 0.9d)
    {
        TransferFromPlayerTwoToServer();
    }
    if (!simulateNetwork || random.NextDouble() > 0.9d)
```

```
    {
        TransferFromServerToPlayerTwo();
    }
    if (!simulateNetwork || random.NextDouble() > 0.9d)
    {
        TransferFromServerToPlayerOne();
    }
    base.Update(gameTime);
}
```

32. Add the methods that transfer data between the various simulated machines:

```
private void TransferFromPlayerTwoToServer()
{
    foreach (var action in
        playerTwoEngine.PendingExternalPlayerTwoActions)
    {
        serverEngine.LogPlayerTwoAction(action, false);
    }
    playerTwoEngine.PendingExternalPlayerTwoActions.Clear();
}
private void TransferFromPlayerOneToServer()
{
    foreach (var action in
        playerOneEngine.PendingExternalPlayerOneActions)
    {
        serverEngine.LogPlayerOneAction(action, false);
    }
    playerOneEngine.PendingExternalPlayerOneActions.Clear();
}
private void TransferFromServerToPlayerTwo()
{
    foreach (var action in
        serverEngine.PendingExternalPlayerOneActions)
    {
        playerTwoEngine.LogPlayerOneAction(action, false);
    }
    serverEngine.PendingExternalPlayerOneActions.Clear();
}
private void TransferFromServerToPlayerOne()
{
    foreach (var action in
        serverEngine.PendingExternalPlayerTwoActions)
    {
```

```
            playerOneEngine.LogPlayerTwoAction(action, false);
        }
        serverEngine.PendingExternalPlayerTwoActions.Clear();
    }
```

33. Create a method to procure input for player one's machine and initiate the appropriate simulation:

```
private void UpdatePlayerOneEngineLocally(
    GameTime gameTime,
    KeyboardState keyboard)
{
    var playerOneActionType = InputActionType.None;

    if (keyboard.IsKeyDown(Keys.Q))
    {
        playerOneActionType = playerOneActionType |
            InputActionType.Up;
    }
    if (keyboard.IsKeyDown(Keys.A))
    {
        playerOneActionType = playerOneActionType |
            InputActionType.Down;
    }
    var playerOneAction = new InputAction()
    {
        Type = playerOneActionType,
        Timestamp =  gameTime.TotalGameTime.TotalSeconds
    };
    playerOneEngine.LogPlayerOneAction(playerOneAction, true);
    playerOneEngine.Update();
}
```

34. Add a corresponding method to handle the input and simulation of player two's machine:

```
private void UpdatePlayerTwoEngineLocally(
    GameTime gameTime,
    KeyboardState keyboard)
{
    var playerTwoActionType = InputActionType.None;

    if (keyboard.IsKeyDown(Keys.P))
    {
        playerTwoActionType = playerTwoActionType |
            InputActionType.Up;
    }
```

```
    if (keyboard.IsKeyDown(Keys.L))
    {
        playerTwoActionType = playerTwoActionType |
            InputActionType.Down;
    }
    var playerTwoAction = new InputAction()
    {
        Type = playerTwoActionType,
        Timestamp = gameTime.TotalGameTime.TotalSeconds
    };
    playerTwoEngine.LogPlayerTwoAction(playerTwoAction, true);
    playerTwoEngine.Update();
}
```

35. Create a method to coordinate the simulation of the server machine:

```
private void UpdateServerEngineLocally(GameTime gameTime)
{
    serverEngine.Update();
}
```

36. Complete the example by rendering the three machines to the screen:

```
protected override void Draw(GameTime gameTime)
{
    GraphicsDevice.Clear(Color.CornflowerBlue);

    spriteBatch.Begin();

    Display.Draw(spriteBatch,
        serverEngine, serverDisplayArea,
        block);
    Display.Draw(spriteBatch,
        playerOneEngine, playerOneDisplayArea,
        block);
    Display.Draw(spriteBatch,
        playerTwoEngine, playerTwoDisplayArea,
        block);

    spriteBatch.End();

    base.Draw(gameTime);
}
```

Upon running the code, you should be presented with a screen similar to the following:

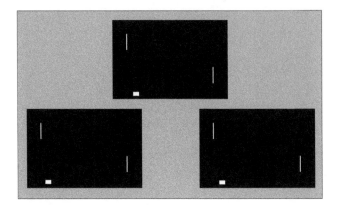

How it works...

We simulate three networked machines in this example, one server and two clients, as seen here:

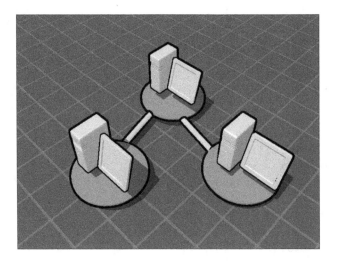

Between each of the machines we send regular updates on the player's input.

We don't transfer other information, such as bat and ball positions, as we have a single, predetermined "source of truth" for such things in the form of the server simulation. Doing so would just increase our networking data burden for little benefit and place us at a much greater risk of cheating or hacking issues later.

Each player's machine records the local player's input, keeping one copy for local processing and sending another copy to the server for redistribution.

The server receives input from each player's machine and rebroadcasts it to the alternate player machine.

Within each machine there are two simulations being run.

The first is a primary simulation, the **last known** simulation, used to recreate the virtual playing field as accurately as possible, so the player can play the game.

The second simulation, the **extrapolation** simulation, is used to account for the fact that there's usually a notable delay between a user performing an action on one machine, and it arriving for processing at another machine.

On the player's machine, the extrapolation simulation is the one updated most regularly and with the most immediacy. As such, it's the one that gets displayed to the player.

When new data is received from another machine, the last known simulation comes to the fore, providing a point in time to merge the local player input data with the external player input data in a chronologically correct fashion.

Once the last known simulation is up-to-date, the state is copied across to the extrapolation simulation so the onscreen action can continue seamlessly until the next batch of external data is received.

There's more...

If you run the example, there's a good chance you'll notice that any movements from a remote player on a given machine appear rather jerky. This is due to the time it takes to communicate the state from one machine to another. It is a problem faced by pretty much any software, be it business application or game, that needs to communicate over a distance.

The most common way that games hide this ever-present issue from players is by extrapolation, also known as guessing, what the other player would do next.

For example, if the remote player seems to be moving in a particular direction for the last few updates, maybe it's reasonable to guess that they'll continue moving in that direction a little longer.

Having a separate extrapolation simulation allows us to enact these guesses, display them on screen to hide the fact that we're temporarily without the latest data from the other player(s), and hopefully smoothly transition back to the real data once it's been received.

If your guesses are good, then the player will never notice, and happily assume that the network is blazingly fast.

If your guesses are not so good, or continue on for too long, then the snap back to the real data when it arrives could be a little jarring, as anyone who has experienced characters suddenly popping or snapping between locations in a fast-paced network game could testify to.

Index

triangle
  dynamic vertex buffers 104
  GeometricBuffer class, working 103
  modeling 95-103
  vertex array type 104
Triangle class 106
triangle modeling 94

U

UdpMessageReceived() method 308
UpdateFocusedSegment() method 288
**Update() method 39, 51, 60, 133, 183, 240,
    256, 262**

V

vehicles, creating
  reflective materials, rendering 263
  simple car physics, applying 243
  simple plane controls, implementing 257
**VertexPositionNormalTextureGeometricBuffer-
    Factory class 100**
ViewPort class 24

W

water
  creating, within HiDef profile 127-134
  deep water 139
  fresnel effect 136, 137
  reflection 135
  refraction 136
  shallow water 139
  specular highlighting 138
  surface distortion 137
  tinting 136
web connections
  about 309
  using 309-316
  working 316

Z

zoom mechanism 70

Thank you for buying
Microsoft XNA 4.0 Game
Development Cookbook

About Packt Publishing

Packt, pronounced 'packed', published its first book "*Mastering phpMyAdmin for Effective MySQL Management*" in April 2004 and subsequently continued to specialize in publishing highly focused books on specific technologies and solutions.

Our books and publications share the experiences of your fellow IT professionals in adapting and customizing today's systems, applications, and frameworks. Our solution based books give you the knowledge and power to customize the software and technologies you're using to get the job done. Packt books are more specific and less general than the IT books you have seen in the past. Our unique business model allows us to bring you more focused information, giving you more of what you need to know, and less of what you don't.

Packt is a modern, yet unique publishing company, which focuses on producing quality, cutting-edge books for communities of developers, administrators, and newbies alike. For more information, please visit our website: www.packtpub.com.

Writing for Packt

We welcome all inquiries from people who are interested in authoring. Book proposals should be sent to author@packtpub.com. If your book idea is still at an early stage and you would like to discuss it first before writing a formal book proposal, contact us; one of our commissioning editors will get in touch with you.

We're not just looking for published authors; if you have strong technical skills but no writing experience, our experienced editors can help you develop a writing career, or simply get some additional reward for your expertise.

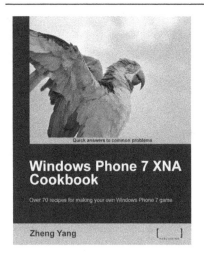

XNA 4.0 Game Development by Example: Beginner's Guide – Visual Basic Edition

ISBN: 978-1-84969-240-3   Paperback: 424 pages

Create your own exciting games with Visual Basic and Microsoft XNA 4.0

1. Visual Basic edition of Kurt Jaegers' XNA 4.0 Game Development by Example. The first book to target Visual Basic developers who want to develop games with the XNA framework

2. Dive headfirst into game creation with Visual Basic and the XNA Framework

3. Focuses entirely on developing games with the free version of XNA

3D Graphics with XNA Game Studio 4.0

ISBN: 978-1-84969-004-1   Paperback: 292 pages

Create attractive 3D graphics and visuals in your XNA games

1. Improve the appearance of your games by implementing the same techniques used by professionals in the game industry

2. Learn the fundamentals of 3D graphics, including common 3D math and the graphics pipeline

3. Create an extensible system to draw 3D models and other effects, and learn the skills to create your own effects and animate them

Please check **www.PacktPub.com** for information on our titles

www.ingramcontent.com/pod-product-compliance
Lightning Source LLC
LaVergne TN
LVHW062304060326
832902LV00013B/2039